HEINEMANN
GNVQ

This book is to be returned on or before
the last date stamped below.

Hala Seliet

NORTHUMBERLAND COLLEGE
OF ARTS & TECHNOLOGY

LIBRARY

CLASS No.   ACCESSION No.

D0231492

HEINEMANN GNVQ

FOUNDATION

Business

Hala Seliet

NORTHUMBERLAND COLL. LIBRARY OF ARTS & TECHNOLOGY

Edexcel
Success through qualifications

Heinemann Educational Publishers,
Halley Court, Jordan Hill, Oxford OX2 8EJ
A division of Reed Educational & Professional Publishing Ltd

Heinemann is a registered trademark of Reed Educational & Professional Publishing Limited

OXFORD MELBOURNE AUCKLAND JOHANNESBURG BLANTYRE GABORONE
IBADAN PORTSMOUTH NH (USA) CHICAGO

© Hala Seliet 2000

First published 2000
2004 2003 2002 2001 2000
10 9 8 7 6 5 4 3 2 1

A catalogue record for this book is available from the British Library on request.

ISBN 0 435 45297 5

All rights reserved.

Apart from any fair dealing for the purposes of research or private study, or criticism or
review as permitted under the terms of the UK Copyright, Designs and Patents Act, 1988,
this publication may not be reproduced, stored or transmitted, in any form or by any means,
without the prior permission in writing of the publishers, or in the case of reprographic
reproduction only in accordance with the terms of the licences issued by the Copyright
Licensing Agency in the UK, or in accordance with the terms of licenses issued by the
appropriate Reproduction Rights Organization outside the UK. Enquiries concerning
reproduction outside the terms stated here should be sent to the publishers at the United
Kingdom address printed on this page.

Typeset by TechType, Abingdon, Oxfordshire

Printed and bound in Great Britain by The Bath Press Ltd, Bath

Tel: 01865 888058 www.heinemann.co.uk

Contents

Introduction   vii

UNIT 1 HOW A BUSINESS WORKS   1

Chapter 1   An introduction to business   2

Chapter 2   How businesses are divided into functional areas   7

Chapter 3   Customer service   41

Chapter 4   Business communications   46

Unit 1   *Test your knowledge*   *54*

Unit 1   *Assessment*   *56*

UNIT 2 INVESTIGATING BUSINESSES   57

Chapter 5   The ownership of businesses   58

Chapter 6   Business activities   74

Chapter 7   The location of businesses   82

Chapter 8   How competitors affect business activities   86

Chapter 9   Businesses and their stakeholders   90

Unit 2   *Test your knowledge*   *98*

Unit 2   *Assessment*   *100*

UNIT 3 FINANCE IN BUSINESS   101

Chapter 10   Investigating costs and revenue, profit and loss   102

Chapter 11   Investigating financial documents for buying and selling   112

Unit 3   *Test your knowledge*   *146*

BLANK DOCUMENTS FOR PHOTOCOPYING   149

UNIT 4 PERSONAL FINANCE 156

UNIT 5 LOOKING AFTER CUSTOMERS 176

UNIT 6 PEOPLE IN BUSINESS 187

UNIT 7 THE ENVIRONMENT AND THE CUSTOMER 204

UNIT 8 PREPARING FOR EMPLOYMENT 215

UNIT 9 HEALTH AND SAFETY 226

UNIT 10 WORKING AS PART OF A TEAM 234

INDEX 241

Acknowledgements

The author and publishers would like to thank the following individuals and organisations for permission to reproduce photographs and other copyright material:

p. 3 The Body Shop; p. 8, 20, 24, 27, 30, 42, 46, 50, 79, 91, 109, 141, 142 Photodisc; p. 14, 94 McDonald's; p. 31, 77 Sally & Richard Greenhill; p. 43 Focus Do It All; p. 45 Customer Services Department, Heinemann; p. 47 Alliance & Leicester; p. 62 River Island; p. 63 Joseph Dobson & Sons Ltd; p. 64 Halifax PLC; p. 67 Co-Operative Wholesale Society (CWS); p. 71, 76 Corbis; p. 74, 87 Boots PLC; p. 75 Northern Foods PLC; p. 83 Meadowhall, Sheffield; p. 102 Tony Stone.

Every effort has been made to contact the copyright holders of material published in this book. We would be glad to hear from unacknowledged sources at the first opportunity.

Hala Seliet
August 2000

Introduction

How to use this book

This book has been written as a brand new text for students who are working to the 2000 national standards for Foundation GNVQ in Business. It covers the three compulsory units for the award.

These units are:

1   How a business works
2   Investigating business
3   Finance in business
4   Personal finance
5   Looking after customers
6   People in business
7   The environment and the consumer
8   Preparing for employment
9   Health and safety
10 Working as part of a team.

Within each unit, the text is organised under chapters and headings which closely match the headings in the GNVQ units, making it easy for you to find your way around the unit.

By working through the units, you will find all the knowledge and ideas you need to prepare your assessment.

Assessment

Assessment in the new GNVQ is carried out on the whole unit, rather than by many smaller pieces of work. The methods of assessment are:

- one major assignment, for example, carrying out an investigation into the features of two different kinds of businesses
- an external test, set and marked by the awarding body, for example, Edexcel.

At the end of units 1 and 2, you will find a unit assessment section which provides you with practice for both forms of assignment. At the end of each compulsory unit in the book, you will find a short unit test. This can be used to check your knowledge of the unit and also to prepare for the external test. Your tutor will give you materials to help you pass the optional unit assessments from the tutor pack.

Special features of the book

Throughout the text there are a number of features which are designed to encourage discussion and group work, and to help you relate the theory to real work in business.

Activity: Activities that encourage you to apply the theory to a practical situation

Did you know?: Interesting facts and snippets of information about business.

Case studies: Examples of real (or simulated) situations in business. Questions on the case studies will enable you to explore the key issues and deepen your understanding of the subject.

Key Terms: Throughout the text, you will find sections containing definitions of important or new terms that you have come across in that chapter. These are a useful reference source, and they will help you reinforce what you have learnt.

Other features included at the end of the book are: **Blank documents for photocopying** – in Unit 3, there are lots of opportunities for you to practise filling in the financial documents that are used in business, and your tutor will photocopy the blank forms for you to use; and a useful **Index**.

Related titles for Foundation GNVQ in Business:

Student book without Edexcel options (043545305 X)

Tutor Resource Pack (0435452983)

viii

How a business works

In this unit you will look at a business to find out how it operates. You will find out about:

- what your chosen business does

- how businesses are structured

- how businesses are divided into functional areas

- how businesses look after customers

- how businesses communicate with customers and employees.

During your study of the unit, you will need to collect information about a business of your choice so that you can produce an illustrated case study. This must demonstrate that you understand why the business operates, how it is organised and the type of functional areas within it (one of which must be explained in detail). You also need to demonstrate your understanding of what customer service is, along with a clear knowledge of communication methods within your chosen business.

Chapter I An introduction to business

What businesses do

All businesses have a main activity which involves producing goods, providing a service, or both. You will need to find out the main activity of a business and understand what it is aiming to do.

ACTIVITY

1 What is the main activity of a hairdressing salon?
2 What is the main activity of a supermarket?
3 What is the main activity of your favourite clothes shop?

How businesses are structured

The structure of a business means the way in which activities are arranged by putting people who do similar work together, so they can communicate effectively and the work can be divided between them efficiently.

Organisation charts

The structure of a business can be illustrated in an organisation chart. Page 4 shows an organisation chart for a manufacturing business. An organisation chart usually shows the job titles of employees and their relationships with each other. Sometimes the job-holder's name is shown. An organisation chart can benefit a business in a number of ways by showing:

1 different functional areas
2 job titles and job roles
3 how many staff are under a particular manager's control
4 lines of decision-making and levels of responsibility
5 potential communication problems
6 opportunities for promotion
7 new employees where they fit into the overall organisation.

Major roles in an organisation are usually those of directors, managers, supervisors and team members. The organisation chart on page 4 illustrates this:

CASE STUDY – Boots' business objectives

The Boots Company operates in the retailing, manufacturing and marketing of health and personal care products throughout the world.

Boots' main aim is to make a good profit. It will do this by investing in the business and making sure that people who have invested in the company (shareholders) get a fair reward. However, the company also wants to make sure it has a good business reputation as a well-managed, ethical and socially responsible company.

With your tutor, read the case study carefully and answer the following questions:

1 What is Boots' main aim?
2 Why does Boots look after shareholders' interests?
3 What other aims does the business have?
4 What does "socially responsible company" mean?

CASE STUDY – The Body Shop
and environmental commitment

In 1976, Anita Roddick opened the first Body Shop in Brighton. It sold 25 skin and hair care products. Body Shop International PLC now has over 1500 shops in 47 countries selling over 400 different products. However, Body Shop does not just make and sell toiletries and cosmetics. The organisation campaigns on issues relating to human rights, and animal and environmental protection. This has included campaigning for women's rights and against nuclear testing.

The Body Shop's main business aim is to make social and environmental changes happen. Businesses need to make a profit to survive. The emphasis at Body Shop is on profit with a social responsibility, i.e. "profit with principle". As a public limited company, the legal owners of The Body Shop are shareholders. Although shareholders may recognise the value of campaigning on social and environmental issues, the share price remains important.

Read the above case study carefully and answer the following questions:

1   What is The Body Shop's main business objective?
2   Who are the owners of The Body Shop?
3   What is the shareholders' main objective?
4   How do you think The Body Shop management tries to satisfy their shareholders?

Chairperson

He or she will chair the board meetings and have significant influence in the appointment of the managing director.

Board of directors

Members of the board of directors are the representatives of the shareholders (the owners). Their role is to deal with major policy matters such as decisions on capital investment. The directors have a responsibility to act in the interests of the company. They are also normally shareholders in the company.

Managing Director

As the name suggests, he or she is an executive director who takes the leading role in the day-to-day running of the company. He or she will be supported by a number of specialist managers.

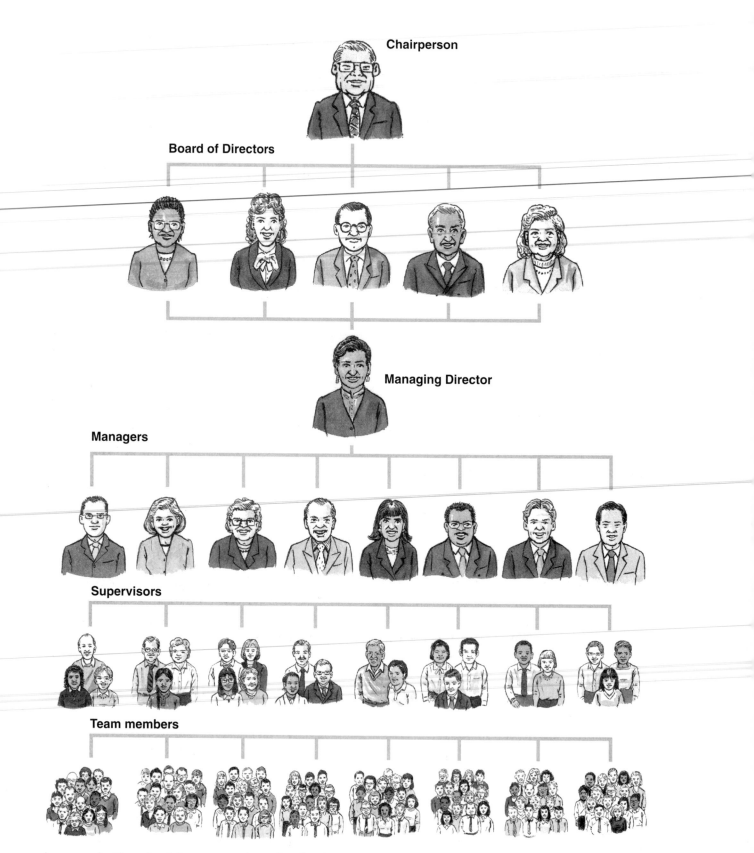

Chairperson

Board of Directors

Managing Director

Managers

Supervisors

Team members

An organisation chart for a manufacturing business

Managers

Senior managers may be heads of department. They may be assisted by middle or junior managers who each run their own section or unit. Some managers look after people, others look after tasks. Managers in a business are responsible for five main areas of activity:

1 decision making
2 problem solving
3 planning and setting long-term objectives
4 ensuring targets are achieved
5 organising the working environment.

Supervisors

Supervisors are responsible to the junior or middle management, and responsible for the team members. Their main tasks are to supervise the team work and make sure that daily targets are met and problems solved. A supervisor is a leader who is responsible for probably five or six people, sometimes in an individual department or section.

Production operatives

Production operatives work on the day-to-day jobs that make the business run, e.g. they will be shop assistants, operate machines in a factory, or be clerks. Their tasks involve the intake of materials, processing, production, transport and distribution of products and, often, the use of machinery or equipment to manufacture them.

Team members/Support staff

These are people who support the internal workings of the organisation and perform support tasks for managers. When you start work, your first role might be that of team member, i.e. a clerk in the wages section or an administrative assistant in a solicitor's office. The main duties of team members are to:

* carry out the duties as specified on the job description, as required by the manager or supervisor

* obey reasonable instructions (remember your legal obligations)

* co-operate with other team members.

ACTIVITIES

Draw an organisational chart for your school or college. The chart should show who makes the decisions in your school or college, and who carries out the instructions. Find a tutor in your school or college who has been working there for more than seven years and show him or her the current chart of your school or college.

1 Ask him or her if this chart is any different from the school or college chart seven years ago.
2 Find out who left the school or college and who joined it.
3 Find out if any new posts have been created during the past seven years.
4 Find out if there are any jobs that no longer exist.
5 Find out which tutor(s) is/are still working in the school or college.
6 Find out which tutor(s) is/are new in your school or college.

Discuss, in your groups, the following statement:

> "Organisation charts quickly become out of date".

Do you agree or disagree?

CASE STUDY –
Ali, Crombie and Patel Partnership

Ali, Crombie and Patel Partnership is a dental surgery that is owned by three people who met as students at the London Dental Institute. The dental surgery employs two dental nurses, a hygienist, a receptionist, and a cleaner. The three dentists are joint managers of the business as well as its owners.

Draw an organisation or business chart for the above dental surgery – who do you think will be at the top of this chart? Who will be at the bottom of the chart?

Key Terms

Board of directors Those persons employed by the shareholders of a company. Their task is to look after the interests of the shareholders.

Chairperson The person elected by the shareholders to oversee the decisions made by the Board of Directors and ensure the company achieves its aims.

Managing Director The person appointed by the Board of Directors to be responsible for the management team that runs the company on a day-to-day basis.

Organisation chart A chart that illustrates the job titles of employees and their relationships with each other in a business.

Shareholders These are the people who have invested money in the business and take a share in the profits. They elect the Board of Directors.

Chapter 2 How businesses are divided into functional areas

Even for small businesses with only one or two employees, different tasks must be carried out. For example, in a corner shop, the owner must divide his or her time between different tasks such as:

- serving customers
- purchasing goods
- pricing the goods
- promoting the shop (advertising)
- receiving customers' payments
- cleaning the shop
- displaying products on the shelves.

Task

What tasks will an ice cream seller do, in addition to selling ice cream?

Why different functions?

Most businesses are made up of different departments, each with their own specialised function. All these functions work together to help the business perform efficiently and achieve its objectives. The different departments usually include human resources, finance, administration, production, marketing and customer services. In this chapter you will learn about how each of these different departments is run, and you will also find out how they work together. There is a separate chapter on the customer services department (see Chapter 3).

The Human Resources function

The human resources (or personnel) department within a business is responsible for making sure that employees can work

Light Delight Ltd

To show you what people in each of the functional areas do in their jobs, this unit includes 'personal profiles' which focus on different people and their jobs. You will see that all of these people work for a made-up business called Light Delight Ltd, an ice cream manufacturing company. For example, on page 30, there is a section about Mike Johnson, the Marketing Manager for Light Delight Ltd. These profiles will help you understand what daily activities might be carried out by someone who works in each of the functional areas: human resources, finance, administration, production, marketing and sales, and customer service. You will come across the Light Delight business again in Unit 3, when you learn about financial documents.

effectively and safely. They cover the following areas:

- recruitment, retention and dismissal
- health and safety
- training, development and promotion
- maintaining staff records
- employee organisations and unions.

Recruitment, retention and dismissal

Recruitment

It is important for any business to recruit the right people. If the right people are recruited, they are likely to stay with the company. If the wrong people are recruited, they will either leave (and the company will have to go through the expensive recruitment process again) or they will stay, but do their job badly.

Any system of recruitment should have three main features:

1 be effective in choosing the right candidate
2 cheap to operate
3 fair to all candidates.

Businesses should recruit the best workforce for the job regardless of their colour, religion, disability or ethnic origin. The law requires that all companies must state in their job advertisements that they are equal opportunity employers.

The first stage of the recruitment process is to decide upon the job that needs to be done and the type of person you are looking for to do it.

Jack Evans, Human Resources (Personnel) Manager

Jack is the Human Resources Manager at Light Delight Ltd. He is 35 years old and joined the company three years ago. After leaving school at the age of 16, Jack did a BTEC National in Business and Finance and later did an HNC including personnel management.

People are the most important resources in ensuring the successful running of a company. Jack believes that the main task of a Human Resources Manager is to help the business gain the maximum benefit from its people.

He is very keen to create a friendly and motivating business working environment. As Human Resources Manager he will play a central role in looking after the company's workforce.

Jack's main responsibilities are:

- **To look** after the welfare of the staff.
- **To select** and recruit the best workforce to work for the company.
- **To provide** adequate and effective training programmes for staff.

- **To ensure** a safe and healthy environment and to make sure that all employees understand the health and safety issues.
- **To provide** expertise and support in motivating the workforce.
- **To deal** with conflict between the management team and the workforce.
- **To take** disciplinary action if employees don't meet the required standards of conduct, attendance, time keeping and job performance.

Jack expects staff to stay in the business for an average of 2 to 3 years. He gets concerned if a member of staff leaves the business after only a few months. He believes that the recruitment, selection and training of staff is very expensive and losing them quickly means that money has been wasted.

Jack has a weekly meeting with his assistant to discuss any recent human resources, health and safety and training and development issues.

He also has a monthly meeting with the Board of Directors to report on any changes in personnel.

Job description

The job description will include an outline of the tasks that are to be carried out and the responsibilities of the person doing the job, for example:

'Come and work for the UK's premier bus company'

'Our PCV drivers receive competitive rates of pay plus benefits'

PremierBus Cardiff

PCV DRIVER

Main purpose of the job

To sell a service in the form of a bus journey to customers, satisfying their needs and encouraging them to travel again.

Main Duties

- *Greeting customers and ensuring customer satisfaction through answering customer queries, providing information on services, routes, and fares.*

- *Operating a service for customers on designated routes to a designated timetable, ensuring the safety and comfort of passengers at all times.*

- *Taking fares and issuing tickets, using computerised equipment, and checking concessionary fare tickets, multi-journey cards etc.*

- *Balancing and accounting for cash receipts taken during the course of duties, paying in cash to cash-counting machines in accordance with company procedures.*

- *Operating radio equipment in line with operational requirements.*

- *Conducting, within their expertise and training, vehicle checks and reporting any faults.*

- *Collecting information (ie witness statements) and submitting written reports regarding accidents, incidents etc, as necessary to minimise potential claims against the Company.*

Job description for PCV driver

ACTIVITIES

Read the job description for a PCV Driver at PremierBus Cardiff on page 9 and answer the following questions:

1 What do you think is the most important duty for a bus driver among those listed above? Explain your answer.

2 PremierBus is very keen to provide a high quality customer service. Find, from the job description, what supports this statement.

3 FirstBus is committed to Health and Safety issues. Find, from the job description, what supports this statement.

Person specification

Once a job description has been produced, it is possible to describe the kind of person you would want to fill that job. This involves drawing up a person specification.

ACTIVITIES

Read the person specification (left) for PCV Drivers and answer the following questions:

1 What does the person specification describe?

2 Which of the skills (in the person specification) is necessary for a bus driver to carry out each of the following duties:

a Greeting customers and ensuring customer satisfaction through answering customer queries, providing information on services, routes, and fares.

b Operating a service for customers on designated routes to a designated timetable, ensuring the safety and comfort of passengers at all times.

c Taking fares and issuing tickets, using computerised equipment, and checking

---

PremierBus Cardiff

PCV DRIVER, AGE 21-60 YEARS

1 *Must be able to write legibly.*

2 *Must be able to read.*

3 *Must be able to follow verbal and written instructions.*

4 *Must be able and willing to use the telephone/radio in communication with the company.*

5 *Must be able to communicate clearly, concisely and courteously with the public, including irate and anxious passengers.*

6 *Must demonstrate some understanding of, and agreement with, the principles of Equal Opportunity.*

7 *Must be able and willing to work alone for long periods without close supervision.*

8 *Must be able to identify enquiries which can be dealt with by themselves and those which require referral.*

9 *Must be able to deal effectively with frequent interruptions and resume the task in hand without loss of efficiency.*

10 *Must be able to demonstrate a positive approach to change.*

Person specification for PCV driver job

concessionary fare tickets, multi-journey cards etc.

d Collecting information (i.e. witness statements) and submitting written reports regarding accidents, incidents etc, as necessary to minimise potential claims against the Company.

Having drawn up a job description and person specification, the human resources department advertise the job. Organisations can recruit internally or externally, i.e. they can choose people from inside the organisation or widen the field to outsiders.

Internal recruitment

This means recruiting someone who already works within the company. Methods of internal recruitment include staff notice boards and staff magazines. Recruiting from within the organisation has a number of advantages and disadvantages.

ACTIVITY

Match the following sentences under the two headings – **Advantages** and **Disadvantages** of internal recruitment:

- Appointing from within the organisation may cause jealousy and resentment among other staff, who may feel they have been "passed over" for promotion.
- There is less risk involved, because the employer already knows the person who will be filling the vacancy.
- There is no "buzz" that follows when a new person joins the organisation.
- It's cheaper because it saves the costs of advertising.
- It saves the cost of training a new employee to introduce him or her to the job.

- No new ideas are brought into the business from outside.
- The opportunity for promotion in the organisation encourages people to work hard.

External recruitment

Sometimes the management will decide to appoint someone from outside. Having decided on how widely to advertise, the company must choose the method it will use. In making this decision, the firm will have to balance the cost of advertising against the need to attract a high quality of applicants. Many employers advertise vacancies in:

- local schools and colleges
- local newspapers
- national newspapers
- job centres
- internet.

Interviews

After the human resources department has advertised the job, they will usually deal with the letters of application that the business hopes to receive from people who are interested in the job. The human resources department will often sort through the applications before passing them on to whichever manager is advertising for a new employee. The manager will look through the applications and will make a list of those people who look most suitable. The human resources department will contact these people to arrange a time when they can be interviewed. Someone from the human resources department will often help the manager to conduct the interviews. After all of the candidates have been interviewed, the manager and/or human resources department will select who they think is the best person for the job. If this person decides to take the job, it will then be up to the human

NORTHUMBERLAND COLL
LIBRARY
OF ARTS & TECHNOLOGY

11

resources department to sort out the details of when he or she will start the job etc.

BUS DRIVERS *required*

PremierBus Cardiff, a subsidiary of PremierBus Group PLC, is seeking to recruit high quality staff who are:

- *smart in appearance*
- *can work flexible hours*
- *have an outgoing and friendly manner*
- *enjoy driving.*

So, if you currently hold a PCV licence, or have a clean driving licence and would like to train as a bus driver, then we want to hear from you. Call in at our Macaulay Street Travel Shop for an application form.

All application forms must be returned by Tuesday 22 December. We offer secure employment with all the expected benefits from the UK's largest bus company.

*Free travel pass *Free uniforms

Advertising for a job vacancy at PremierBus PLC in *The Examiner* local newspaper

ACTIVITY

Read the advertisement (left) and answer the following questions:

1 What information about the job is included in the advertisement?
2 What benefits do bus drivers get from joining the company?
3 What sort of person is required for the bus driver job? Why do you think this is the case?
4 How could people who are interested apply for this job?
5 Why do you think this advertisement appeared in the local newspaper for the Cardiff area?

Staff welfare (perks and benefits)

Nowadays businesses are keen to look after the welfare of their staff in order to increase productivity. These additional services, such

---

CASE STUDY — Perks at PremierBus Company

PremierBus is the largest bus service company in the UK, and employees are entitled to the following perks:

- a contributory pension scheme
- free uniform for staff who deal directly with customers or those whose work requires protective clothing
- free travel for the employees and his or her immediate family
- holiday pay and sickness benefit
- opportunities for career development
- employee's share scheme.

1 Why does PremierBus Company provide the above perks to employees?
2 What is the effect of the above perks on employees' motivation and attitude to work?
3 In your view, what is the most important perk which employees will benefit from?
4 Discuss in your group the following statement:

"Happy employees make happy customers".

as staff discount, the provision of a social club and private medical insurance, are called benefits or "perks".

End of employment

Employers seek to end the employment of workers for two basic reasons:

1 redundancy – where workers are not needed in the business any more (surplus to requirements)

2 dismissal for misconduct, incapacity or incompetence.

However, a major constraint on employers is the rights of employees under various Employment Protection Acts.

Redundancy

It is the situation that results when an employee's contract of employment is ended because that job no longer exists either because the company is closing down, new technology has taken over, or costs need to be cut.

Dismissal

Over the years, the rules for dismissing employees have become quite complex. The heart of the matter lies in the difference between what the courts regard to be "fair" and "unfair" dismissal.

Fair dismissal can take place when an employee can be shown to be guilty of:

a wilful destruction of company property

b sexual or racial harassment

c continuous bad timekeeping

d a negative attitude at work

e inability to do the job

f sleeping on the job.

Health and safety

Working conditions can have a direct effect on the health and safety of the people in the workplace. One of the main functions of the human resources department is to provide the best possible working conditions for employees, and to ensure that they work in a healthy and safe environment.

Nowadays, increasing attention is paid to certain safety hazards that have previously been ignored. "Sick building syndrome" is a term used to describe buildings that are thought to cause illness amongst staff. Possible causes could be:

* poor air conditioning

* poor ventilation

* dust from carpets and furnishings

* ineffective lighting.

There is also concern that staff who operate computer equipment for long periods of time may suffer from eye strain, tiredness or stress. Another, increasing, threat to staff, particularly those who deal with the general public or work in areas which are open to general public, is violence. Many employers now make sure that the work environment is made as safe as possible by:

* improving communications systems (installing panic buttons)

* installing glass screens in reception areas

* reorganising work schedules so that no one has to be alone in a high risk area.

Did you know?

Under the Employer's Liability (Compulsory Insurance) Act 1982 every employer carrying on a business in the UK must be insured against any injury to an employee during the course of his or her employment.

Health and Safety at Work Act, 1974 (HASAWA)

The health and safety of employees is a major aspect of working conditions. The duty of employers to provide safe working conditions is often backed up by statutory (legal) requirements. The Health and Safety Act sets out the duties of both the employer and the employee relating to health and safety (*contd. on page 15*):

CASE STUDY – Health and safety at McDonald's

All McDonald's restaurants comply with the Building and Health and Safety regulations. A safety management and training system ensures that employees at all levels have all necessary knowledge of the policies and procedures to protect the safety of customers, fellow employees and themselves. McDonald's commitment to safety is ongoing, with a system designed to allow continuous improvement. The company views compliance with legislation as a minimum requirement, and aims for the highest standards of health and safety. The company has a National Safety Manager and seven Regional Hygiene and Safety Advisors.

Health and Safety training for all staff is a priority. All food preparation and service staff, and all dining area staff, receive safety training before they start work for McDonald's, with ongoing training throughout their employment. All management staff complete additional safety training, with a dedicated health and safety training course. Managers also receive training to become qualified first aiders. There will always be at least one qualified first aider in duty at any time. A more advanced safety course is provided for the Restaurant Manager and Regional Training Officers.

Source: Educational Package (McDonald's)

Read the above case study carefully and answer the following questions:

1 Why do you think Health and Safety is important for McDonald's customers?

2 Why do staff at McDonald's receive Health and Safety training? How will the business benefit from this training?

3 Why do you think Assistant Managers and Regional Training officers at McDonald's receive more Health and Safety training than Restaurant Managers?

4 Dining Area staff receive specific Health and Safety training. Why do you think this is the case?

The employers' main duty or responsibility is to provide a safe workplace, including arrangements for hazards such as fire, and the maintenance and safety of machinery and equipment.

Employees have the duty to take reasonable care for the safety of themselves and other working colleagues at all times, and to co-operate with the employer on all matters of safety.

ACTIVITY

Find out about the Health and Safety regulations in your school or college. Ask your tutor about regulations for fire practice and emergency situations.

Employers' obligations for Health and Safety

Every employer should produce a written statement of the organisation's Health and Safety policy together with details of the arrangements for carrying out that policy. A health and safety policy should include details of:

- how accidents should be reported
- those who are trained in first aid
- those who are safety representatives (and the duties they must undertake)
- the person responsible overall for the Health and Safety policy
- safe working practices.

Safe working practices can be divided into:

- good housekeeping
- the provision of suitable equipment and training in the use of it
- the provision of suitable furniture and proper care and use of it

- suitable accommodation
- reduction in noise
- safe working habits
- provision of information.

Employees' obligations to health and safety

Although your employer cannot delegate his or her responsibility for health, safety and welfare, you must remember that under the Health and Safety at Work Act you also have an obligation to make sure that you:

- take care of your health and safety
- take reasonable care of the health and safety of other people who may be injured by your careless actions
- co-operate with your employer or any other person carrying out the duties under the Act.

Training

Training is all activities involved in teaching someone the skills, attitude and knowledge required for a job. It involves guiding or teaching people to do something by providing them with a planned programme of exercises and activities. Training should involve workers before they actually start the job, during the first few weeks of employment (induction) and throughout their careers.

Benefits of training

Training develops the skills and knowledge of employees to help them to do their jobs better, and prepares them for more demanding jobs in the future. It should be a rewarding process. If employees can do their jobs well, they will feel confident in their abilities and enjoy their work more. This leads to greater job satisfaction.

Training benefits those being trained and the organisations for whom they work. Training can therefore be one of the most effective ways for a business to add value.

Benefits to individuals include:

- greater skills
- more knowledge
- more confidence
- better career prospects
- better opportunities for promotion.

Benefits to the business include:

- more motivated and productive employees
- better quality work
- more job satisfaction
- greater ability to use the latest technology
- easier to achieve business objectives.

Staff development and promotion

Staff development is slightly different from training. It is concerned with identifying the abilities of employees and providing them with training opportunities that will prepare them for promotion, e.g. staff development programmes in River Island and Marks & Spencer.

Staff appraisal interviews

Training is not the only way of improving the performance of staff. Some organisations use a system of appraisal for staff development. This means that the employee's standards of work are discussed and assessed by the employee and his or her manager. It is usual for the manager to write a report of the discussion. Sometimes the report is read by the employee, who

checks that it is an accurate record of what was discussed.

An appraisal system helps to identify a person's areas of strength and weaknesses at work. If weaknesses are identified, appropriate training can be offered to help the worker improve in his or her job. This benefits the firm, by increasing labour productivity and efficiency, and the employee, by providing him or her with opportunities for promotion. In some large organisations the appraisal report will be taken into account when considering employees for promotion or salary increases.

Some businesses are also quite keen to have constant contact with employees by holding staff interviews. For example the management in River Island finds out staff views and training needs in appraisal interviews every year. The interviews offer an ideal opportunity to discuss any problem staff might have. If members of staff are unhappy they will not perform to the best of their abilities.

Other forms of staff development

There are other ways which large businesses use to develop staff skills, and experience which offer them wider opportunities for career progress and promotion. For example:

Job rotation: changing jobs at regular intervals. This makes the job less boring and provides staff with new experience in different areas of the business. For example, bank staff are usually rotated between different departments such as saving or current accounts.

Job enrichment: gives greater responsibilities to the person who is doing the job to provide him or her with a sense of achievement. For example, a car designer could be given the opportunity to create new ideas and design.

Job enlargement: makes the job as big as possible by adding more tasks and responsibilities, but without sense of achievement e.g. bus driver giving him more responsibilities to maintain and clean the bus.

Working hours

Flex-Time System: flexible working time (FWT) is increasingly used in the modern workplace. At 'peak' times all members of staff will be at work. Outside these 'core' hours, there is more flexibility and staff have a certain amount of choice about when they work, provided they work a minimum number of hours.

 **ACTIVITY**

Find a member of your family, a relative or a friend who benefits from the flexible time system. Ask them about the advantages and drawback of this system.

Shift work: in many industries it is important to have machinery working all the time in order to make the most efficient and profitable use of resources. This is true of industries such as textiles, chemicals, steel coal mining, food processing and many others.

Staff records

The human resources department will keep a record of every employee, past and present. This is usually kept on a computer database. The record will include details of the employee's name and address, date of birth, current job title and salary, starting and leaving date, qualifications and experience and payroll number. There is usually a place for the personnel section to record additional training courses and qualifications that are obtained.

Employees' organisations

One of the main functions of the human resources department is to resolve conflicts between management and staff in order to create stability and ensure the smooth running of the business.

These days employees take a more active role in a business. Management is generally keen to inform, consult or involve employees in decision making through different channels of communication.

In a small business, each employee is probably able to negotiate with management on his or her own behalf. In medium and large businesses, however, it is not possible for each employee to deal directly with management. Therefore, the employees usually elect a body, such as a staff association or works council, to represent them. A staff association provides a meeting ground for employees and employer. Sometimes it is also involved in management decision making. In industries with a recognised trade union, it is often the trade union which negotiates with the employer on behalf of the employee.

Trade unions

A trade union is an organisation that represents employees at work. The Employment Act gives employees the right to either join or not join a trade union. Whether or not an employer must recognise a trade union is being debated at the moment. The law will be changed in the near future.

Trade unions mainly exist in large businesses where communication between management and employees is more remote. The trade union's main role is to negotiate with management, on behalf of employees, to improve working conditions and wages.

Key Terms

Dismissal The ending, by an employer, of the contract of employment with an employee because he or she has broken the contract.

External recruitment When an employee is appointed from outside the organisation.

Health and Safety at Work Act (1974) An act that ensures employees have a degree of protection against having an accident or contracting a disease at their place of work.

Induction Training given to a new employee starting a job so that he or she can get used to the place and the people who work there.

Internal recruitment Recruiting the workforce from within the organisation.

Interview The most common method of selection. This is a face-to-face meeting between the candidate and the employer to find out whether the applicant will be suitable for the job, and vice versa.

Job description A detailed written account agreed between employers and employees of the duties and the responsibilities that make up a particular job.

Motivation The reason, or incentive, for doing something. It is especially important when assessing the reasons why people work.

Perk (fringe benefits) Payment in kind over and above the wage or salary, such as extra holiday, staff discount, or a company car.

Person specification A description of the detailed features of the person required to do a job, e.g. experience, qualifications, attitude etc.

Personnel (Human Resources) department The department within a firm that is responsible for the relationship between the employer and employee and for the employee's general welfare.

Recruitment The process of obtaining a supply of new workers to enter an organisation that is usually the responsibility of a human resources department in larger organisations.

Redundancy The situation that results when an employee's contract of employment is ended because that job no longer exists or is no longer needed, i.e. a factory might close down which would make all the workforce redundant.

Trade union An organisation that represents employees at work.

Training The process of improving and extending a person's skills or knowledge.

Unemployment Having no work.

Unfair dismissal The ending of a person's employment by an employer without good reason, for example, a result of discriminating against someone because of their race or sex.

Working conditions A general term used to describe the physical conditions under which a job takes place, e.g. heat, light, noise etc.

ACTIVITY

Try out this role play in pairs. Imagine you and your partner are working in a large supermarket. You are working as a shelf stacker or checkout assistant, and you are also the trade union representative. Your partner represents the management of the supermarket.

There are some issues of concern:

a mending a broken door that is creating a nasty draught

b providing a more comfortable chair which does not hurt your back

c providing a cleaner staff toilet which does not smell.

You and your partner are going to negotiate the above issues. Remember that you are representing the staff in the supermarket. The staff are fed up with the above situations and have approached you to negotiate on their behalf. Your partner has to remember that he or she represents the management. Issues such as cost and staff attitude concern them most.

The Finance function

The Finance Department deals with all the financial matters in the business. The modern finance department has an extensive data processing system backed up by computers.

The main functions of the finance department are:

- obtaining financial information from different departments
- recording financial information (this is commonly known as book-keeping)
- working out payment of staff wages/salaries

- providing information about the amount of money (capital) needed to run the business efficiently
- analysing and interpreting financial information
- providing information about the business's performance to teams and shareholders.

The activities within the finance department include:

- raising invoices and obtaining payment for goods or services supplied to customers
- making sure that invoices from suppliers match the goods or services that are supplied to the organisation
- dealing with payments to suppliers.
- paying staff
- dealing with debts
- analysing the financial performance
- providing financial information on business performance to managers and shareholders
- arranging loans and additional finance for the business.

Preparing accounts

One of the main functions of a finance department is to record and keep financial records (accounts) so that the firm can keep track of how much money has come in and how much money has gone out. This allows costs to be measured against revenue (income) so that it is possible to calculate levels of profits or losses made. The Finance Department also has to supply accounts to the Inland Revenue for tax purposes, and keep accurate records of all VAT (Value Added Tax) for Customs and Excise. Another job of the Finance Department is to produce the annual report if the company is a public limited company

(PLC). You will learn about public limited companies in Unit 2 (see page 62).

ACTIVITY

Finish off the following sentences:

1   If a business's revenues are more than its costs it will make a ....
2   If a business's costs are more than its revenue it will make a ....
3   A business has to pay .... to the Inland Revenue if it makes ....

Management accounting

One of the main functions of the Finance Department is not only to obtain financial information, but also to analyse this information. This analysis is important because it helps managers to make the right decisions about the running of the business and find out how well the business is doing. and helps them to make decisions about the business. For example, the Finance Department keeps accurate records of all payments so it will be able to help the marketing department decide on prices.

Ismat Niaz, Finance Manager

Ismat has been working at Light Delight Ltd for three years. When she left school she got a job as a trainee accountant in a property development company. After she qualified, she worked in various accountancy firms and later had a few years out of employment when her children were young. She joined Light Delight as Assistant Finance Manager and was promoted to Finance Manager 18 months ago.

Ismat's main responsibilities are:

• To decide on the business credit policy.

• To ensure the effectiveness of the payroll system.

• To make sure that outstanding bills are paid and money has been collected.

• To make sure that the business's financial books are balanced and kept in order.

• To decide on the best method of obtaining finance for the business.

• To ensure that the company's activities are profitable.

Ismat recently expressed concern that too many customers were allowed too high a level of credit.

She meets regularly with the credit controller to discuss the existing credit policy.

Ismat also looks after the book-keeping, and is responsible for staff wages. She has to check the time sheets for staff, to make out wages and has to make the deductions and complete the return for tax and insurance. A daybook is kept which returns the financial transactions which have taken place, and Ismat checks that there is a correct balance. A record also has to be kept for the VAT.

The Finance Department will be able to help managers decide which are the profitable lines of the business (and which might be expanded) and which might be making a loss (so management can improve matters). Sometimes a business may have a 'cash flow' problem. (The business needs to buy a lot of raw materials or goods for resale – and pay for these – before it receives money from its customers.) The Finance Department will know if there is likely to be a problem and will arrange a loan with the bank.

Obtaining capital and resources

One of the aims of many organisations is to grow. In order to grow the business will need money to invest in new equipment, more raw materials, developing new products, larger buildings. All this costs money (and it could be several years before the business starts to make extra profits). Therefore the business will need to borrow money to expand. Limited companies (see page 61) may sell more shares. All businesses will go to banks for loans. It is the Finance Department that arranges the sale of more shares or makes arrangements with the bank.

Paying wages and salaries

The Finance Department is responsible for the payment of wages and salaries. If employees are paid weekly, this is normally called a wage and if employees are paid monthly, this is normally called a salary. Wages and salaries are the returns (payment) for people who work (labour). Whether payment is made by cash, cheque or credit transfer to the bank account, the employee receives a pay advice. This is usually a slip of paper that is filled in by the wages section in the Finance Department and often done by computer. Employees can see how much their gross pay is and what deductions there are.

There are two different types of deductions:

1 compulsory deductions such as income tax and National Insurance

2 voluntary deductions such as union membership fees, contributions to company social club, private pension schemes, private medical schemes (e.g. BUPA) payments.

What employees actually receive is called net pay. This is the amount of money left after all deductions have been made.

Key Terms

Accounts The financial records of a business that are used by managers, owners, employees, creditors and others to show how well the business is doing.

Finance department Deals with all the financial matters in the business.

Gross pay Is the total amount earned by the employee before any deductions have been made.

Income tax Money deducted from each wage/salary payment through the PAYE (Pay As You Earn) system.

National Insurance Is a weekly or monthly contribution to the state welfare scheme (e.g. health services) taken from each payment of wages/salaries. Both employers and employees make a contribution to this scheme.

Net pay The amount of money an employee receives after deductions have been made for income tax, national insurance and any voluntary contribution.

Pay The reward for labour providing its service, usually comprising either a weekly wage or a monthly salary.

Payment system A method of organising the payment of employees, i.e. time rate, piece rate and bonus.

Salary A type of payment to an employee where a certain sum is negotiated on an annual basis and is paid monthly. Salaries are common for payment of workers in professional, managerial and scientific employment.

Tax The compulsory contribution of money to the government. It is a major source of income to the government.

Wage The basic reward paid for the provision of labour as a factor of production. A wage is usually paid on an hourly or weekly basis.

The Administration function

This function deals with the internal housekeeping of the organisation. Administration, secretarial and clerical costs can account for a high percentage of business costs, so it is essential that this part of an organisation is run efficiently.

The main role of the administration function is to provide office services for all other departments in the business, for example:

- collecting and distributing mail
- dealing with and responding to enquiries
- organising meetings
- filing and keeping records
- cleaning and maintaining the workplace
- security.

Other functions include:

- data and word processing
- photocopying
- dealing with e-mails
- switchboard and reception.

Collecting and distributing mail

The administration department deals with the collection and the distribution of incoming mail.

Large organisations will have a specialised mail room that receives all the incoming mail. Small organisations will receive their mail from the postman and it may be opened by the owner or the manager or his or her secretary.

Mail must be opened quickly, sorted accurately and distributed promptly, so that managers and staff can organise their work priorities for the day, know what needs "chasing up" and act on the most up-to-date information available.

Sorting the mail

When mail has been sorted the office clerk must read what is written on the envelope and react accordingly.

Marked	Action
Mail marked urgent	Open immediately
Mail marked personal or private and confidential	Never open
Recorded Delivery	Sign for the delivery and keep record in the Mail Register
Mail wrongly delivered	Re-post unopened
1st and 2nd class mail	Open 1st class first: it is more likely to have urgent information

ACTIVITY: SORTING MAIL

Mail is often placed in mail baskets for distribution or collection. Rearrange the following mail in the right order by starting with the most important one and ending with the least important.

Circulars and magazines, 1st class mail, urgent letters, 2nd class mail, private and confidential or personal letters, wrongly delivered letters.

Dealing with and responding to enquiries

A business's success is determined, to a great extent, by the way it deals with stakeholders' enquiries and how the business communicates generally with its stakeholders. Stakeholders are people who have an interest in a business's activities, and they include customers, suppliers, employees, management and shareholders. The administration department in a business is often the first point of contact when stakeholders telephone. They may be able to deal with stakeholders' enquiries, including customer enquiries, themselves or they will direct the caller to the person or department in the organisation who can deal with the query. In this way, the administration department fulfils an important customer service function. A business will be able to deal with those people's enquiries by establishing an effective communication system. For example, a large proportion of business today is conducted on the telephone. Unfortunately, receiving and making telephone calls is probably one of the most dreaded jobs for the inexperienced office worker. Fears, for example might include giving the wrong information or getting a message muddled.

ACTIVITY

1 What other fears might face a telephonist who deals with customer or supplier enquiries?
2 Make a list of the personal skills that are needed by an office worker or an employee dealing with enquiries. (Activity contd. over page.)

Renata Ottolini, Office Manager

Renata was appointed to work as Assistant Administration Manager at Light Delight Ice Cream Ltd.

"Some people don't appreciate how the administration function is a very important function in the business – it co-ordinates the functions of the other department", Renata says.

She explains how her job is very demanding. For example she has to monitor the collection and distribution of mail each day, the setting up of computers for staff use, electronic mail, cleaning and maintenance etc.

Renata has an administration assistant, Emma Baker, who has been working at Light Delight for 2 years.

Emma Jebson, Administration Assistant

Emma's main job roles are:

- **To ensure** that all mail and correspondence is opened daily.
- **To file** and keep records.
- **To ensure** that all the mail marked urgent or private or confidential or personal is sorted out as soon as possible and distributed to staff.
- **To ensure** that the mail is delivered to the right people.
- **To ensure** that the place is clean and well maintained.

She is also required to carry out some routine tasks, e.g. photocopying, filing, answering telephone calls and ordering stationery.

Activity contd.

3 Compare the above list with your partner's list and write all the personal skills that you have thought of in a separate list.

4 Discuss your and your partner's list with other members of the group.

5 Imagine you are an angry customer of one of the banks who rang to complain about a mistake in his/her bank statement. You play the role of the customer and your partner the role of the telephonist who deals with enquiry.

Organising meetings

When organising meetings, always remember to:

- identify the purpose of the meeting
- make the necessary arrangements, e.g. when and where
- contact, in good time, all people who should attend the meeting
- make the necessary arrangements for refreshments

- make the arrangements for car park facilities
- make the arrangements for any necessary equipment, e.g. overhead projectors.

The agenda for the meeting is the list of items to be dealt with, for example:

- apologies for absence
- minutes of last meeting
- reports
- any other business (AOB)
- date for next meeting.

Writing the minutes

Sometimes the manager asks one of the administrative clerks to attend the meeting to take minutes (the record of what was said). These are typed up afterwards and circulated to all the people who attended.

Filing and keeping records

In any business there is a need to file and keep records about suppliers, customers and other stakeholders. An effective filing system helps the business to operate efficiently for the following reasons:

- up-to-date information can be found immediately
- queries can be answered immediately
- time and effort can be saved in finding the relevant and required information.

What is a good filing system?

A filing system must be easy to understand and use for everyone requiring access to it. Where a number of departments require access to the same information, a centralised filing system is often set up for the whole company. However, most departments also

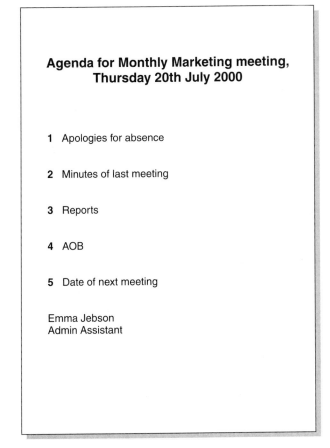

Agenda for Monthly Marketing meeting, Thursday 20th July 2000

1 Apologies for absence

2 Minutes of last meeting

3 Reports

4 AOB

5 Date of next meeting

Emma Jebson
Admin Assistant

Agenda

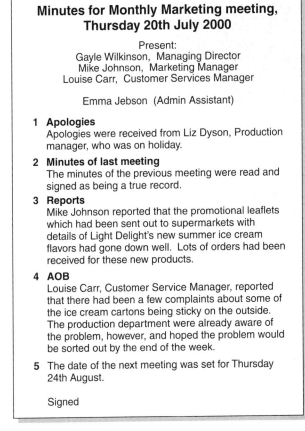

Minutes for Monthly Marketing meeting, Thursday 20th July 2000

Present:
Gayle Wilkinson, Managing Director
Mike Johnson, Marketing Manager
Louise Carr, Customer Services Manager

Emma Jebson (Admin Assistant)

1 **Apologies**
Apologies were received from Liz Dyson, Production manager, who was on holiday.

2 **Minutes of last meeting**
The minutes of the previous meeting were read and signed as being a true record.

3 **Reports**
Mike Johnson reported that the promotional leaflets which had been sent out to supermarkets with details of Light Delight's new summer ice cream flavors had gone down well. Lots of orders had been received for these new products.

4 **AOB**
Louise Carr, Customer Service Manager, reported that there had been a few complaints about some of the ice cream cartons being sticky on the outside. The production department were already aware of the problem, however, and hoped the problem would be sorted out by the end of the week.

5 The date of the next meeting was set for Thursday 24th August.

Signed

Minutes

file relevant information within their own sections. To make these systems easy to understand and use, it is helpful to display a set of instructions on the current filing system that everybody in the administration department can follow.

Filing confidential information

A locked drawer with limited access to keys should be provided in which to file all confidential documents. Confidential documents that are not required any more should be destroyed.

Most businesses use computers to record and keep information. Information is kept in database programs. The names of files are kept in a directory that contains information on the size of every file and dates when they were created. Confidential files can be password protected.

Cleaning and maintaining the workplace

According to the Health and Safety at Work Act (1974), all employers and employees are responsible for the health and safety of the workplace. Employers must make sure that the place is clean and well maintained for employees to work effectively. Hazardous situations usually result from poor maintenance and a dirty or unclean workplace. For example, wet floors or poorly lit areas can cause accidents such as falls or slips. Faulty machines can cause electric shocks and accidents.

The administration staff in large businesses are involved in organising cleaning and keeping the workplace tidy and well maintained. They must be aware of what makes for organising a safe workplace.

Security

Some of the administration staff in large organisations work in a security department. Their job is to make sure the workplace is secure and no strangers are on the premises of whom they are not aware. They check buildings after staff leave and make sure all doors are locked and security cameras are in operation.

They also deal with visitors who come to visit the business. Many large businesses have a gatehouse where security staff check visitors as they enter the premises and issue a special visitor's badge. Visitors' badges may be colour-coded to show which areas the visitor has access to and which he or she has not. The visitor will also be asked to "sign in" using the Visitor's Book. He or she will write down his or her name, the organisation he or she belongs to, the date, and his or her car registration number. The gatehouse will also check out visitors as they leave and take back their badges.

Reception

Some of the administration staff in medium to large businesses work on the reception. Most large offices employ receptionists to act as the first point of contact when someone enters the building. Because the people who work on reception are the first people you will meet when you go into a business, it is very important that they are polite, well presented and helpful. If they give a good impression, this reflects on the business. A receptionist is very often also the first person you will speak to if you telephone the company, and it is his or her job to deal with your enquiry or put you through to another person in the business who can help you. In this way, receptionists provide an important customer service function. Receptionists therefore need to have a good understanding of the business, the people who work for it and its customers.

ACTIVITY

1 Find out from the reception or office staff in your school or college what security procedure the school or college follows when someone visits.

2 Find out why visitors are asked to write down their car registration number in the Visitor's Book.

The Production function

Production is at the heart of any organisation. In a manufacturing company it turns raw materials (sheet metal, cocoa beans) into finished products (washing machines, bars of chocolate). The type of production will depend on the end product – the production or building of an ocean liner will be very different from the production of chocolate mini-eggs.

In the service sector, production is the process by which a service is provided to a customer.

Liz Dyson, Production Manager

Liz's role at Light Delight Ltd started even before the company was set up. She set up the business and was very keen that it should succeed.

Liz's main responsibilities are:

- **To plan** the best way to make ice-cream.
- **To introduce** new ideas to improve the product.
- **To purchase** the necessary raw materials at the lowest price and highest quality.
- **To make sure** that the quality of ice-cream is of the highest standard.
- **To ensure** that the machines are in good working order.
- **To decide** on the best and safest method of production.
- **To plan** with the Managing Director when equipment should be replaced.
- **To check** regularly that the production team is adequately trained, especially when new production processes are introduced.

- **To check** that her team is working to Health and Safety regulations and ensure her team is supervised at all times.
- **To ensure** that all equipment and tools are well looked after and stored away safely.

Every day Liz checks that everyone in her team has arrived on time. She checks the weekly rota of duties to see that everything is covered. She has to notify the human resources/personnel department of the absence of any member of the team.

At midnight she makes a tour of the production department to check that everything is operating smoothly.

During lunch time she has an informal discussion with her Production Assistant Managers to make sure that everything is in order.

Liz is required to present a progress report at the weekly meeting with the Managing Director.

She is also required to prepare a more detailed report for the monthly Board of Director's meeting.

(Often in the service sector it is called "Operations".) For example, a company which sells insurance will have different types of policy, and a theme park will develop new attractions and rides.

Planning is a very important part of Production:

- What raw materials will be needed? How many?

CASE STUDY — Production at Light Delight Ltd

Mr Grey has just bought a "family block" of ice cream. As he leaves the local shop his daughter asks him where the ice cream comes from. He answered 'cows'. Darren the shop keeper knows that before he sells the ice cream he has to order it from the factory. The factory is called Light Delight Ice Cream. Irene works at the factory in the administration department. She takes orders over the phone or by letters or e-mails and passes them to Emma who types them into the firm's computer. Carol also makes out the bill/invoice for Darren's shop.

In order to make the ice cream Asha the Production Assistant Manager for Purchasing has to order the raw materials, such as milk powder, sugar or fruit. She uses the computer to check what raw materials are not available in stock and therefore need to be ordered (stock control), and how much ice cream needs to be made that day.

There was a time when it took three or more people to mix and freeze the ice cream. These days, with the development in new technology, it can be done with computer-controlled machines. The frozen ice cream is forced along pipes (at the beginning of the production lineunder high pressure until it comes out of a tap at the other end of the production line where Liz sits, waiting to collect the ice cream in plastic containers. Then she passes these to Ahmed who seals them with lids so that

Gemma can take them into a cold store to be frozen solid. Then Mary and Carl will transfer them on to shelves in the refrigerated warehouse.

Terry and David, the warehouse foremen, control the despatch of stock. To help the lorry drivers they have to arrange all the boxes of ice cream in the correct order for loading and delivery. They also help the driver to load up the refrigerated lorries.

Only then can the ice cream be delivered to shops or supermarkets.

Read the above case study carefully and use examples to answer the following questions:

1 What are the natural resources, e.g. raw materials, that are needed to make ice cream?
2 What are the human resources that are needed to make ice cream?
3 What are the man-made resources, e.g. machinery and equipment, needed to make ice cream?
4 Explain the effect of the use of computers on the production process in the Light Delight ice cream factory.
5 When do you think the role of the purchase function takes place in the above factory?
6 Visit your local supermarket and choose an ice cream container. Find out the ingredients which are used to produce it

- What will need to be stored?
- What machines will be needed?
- Who will operate the machines?
- Do these people need to be hired? Will they need training?
- How long will it take to produce the item?
- Will it need to be stored?

For service industries similar planning must take place. In eductaion, the government needs to plan how many school places to provide, what subjects will be taught, the number of teachers who need to be trained, the computers and books that need to be bought – all within a budget.

Key Terms

Administration department The department which deals with all the administration activities in a business, for example, filing records and organising meetings.

Agenda A list of items to be discussed in a meeting, e.g., plans for a new factory, employing more people, reporting accidents, etc.

Consumer A person who buys goods and services for his or her own use or consumption.

Employees People who are employed by the owners or managers of a business. They get paid a wage or salary for working in the business.

Goods A general term used to represent the wide variety of items that are produced as a result of economic activity.

Human resources People (labour) that work in the business, e.g. managers, supervisors, cashiers, etc.

Natural resources Raw materials which come from the land and are used to make final products, e.g., wool is used to make jumpers and coats, and wheat grain is used to make flour and bread.

Production The process by which an organisation transforms raw materials, using financial and human resources into an end product that is consumed by someone else, for example, bread.

Purchasing An important function in organisations dealing with the purchase of the materials necessary to allow the goods or services of that organisation to be produced.

Service sector Sometimes called the tertiary sector, this includes all services such as banking, insurance, education, policing etc.

Stakeholders Anyone who has an interest in a business's activities and who can therefore influence business decisions. Stakeholders include a business's customers, suppliers, employees, management and shareholders.

Stock control The process of trying to establish the best level of stocks to hold.

The Marketing and Sales function

Marketing is responsible for finding out and satisfying customer needs and wants. Good marketing can be the key to the success of a business

Customers will buy a product only if it will help them:

- to do something that they cannot do now
- to do something better than they can do it now
- to do something more quickly than they can do it now
- to do something more easily than they can do it now
- to do something more cost effectively (more cheaply) than they can do it now
- to get more satisfaction than they are getting now
- to get something different from what they are getting now.

However, a company or a business will make a profit only if customers buy their good or service at a price that will give them a profit after all production costs have been taken into consideration.

Mike Johnson, Marketing Manager at Light Delight

Mike was appointed as Marketing Manager at Light Delight six years ago. He had previously been working as a sales representative for a large chilled foods manufacturer.

However, when Mike and his wife were divorced and he had to look after their children by himself, he wanted a job which would not involve travelling around the country, so he could be at home when he needed to be. Mike has two assistant managers, Jenny and Raheem, who work under his supervision and are responsible to him.

Mike's main responsibilities are:

- **To formulate**, recommend and implement the company's marketing strategy.

- **To decide** on the best pricing strategy to increase sales and attract more customers.

- **To monitor and implement** the development of a new product.

- **To monitor and analyse** sales figures with his team.

- **To decide** on the best promotion method to promote the ice-cream.

His responsibilities also include doing everything he can to ensure that the company retains 'delighted customers with a delightful ice-cream'.

Mike works very closely with his sales team and encourages their sales efforts. His experience in sales make him good at motivating the sales staff. He meets every week with his Assistant Manager for Sales to make sure that sale targets are met and customers needs and wants are met.

How does marketing do this?

By researching about the market and customers:

1 **Product:** Do customers even know they want this product yet? Will they want an expensive top-of-the-range version or a cheap and cheerful version? Will they want exotic packaging or a plain bag?

2 **Price:** the price must be one that customers see as good value and one that provides good profit for the business. The price should also reflect the image of the product.

3 **Place:** how and where a business makes the product and makes it available to customers. It should make it easy for customers to buy and obtain the product. For example, if you were selling a new sports drink would you make it available in sports centres or supermarkets? When do customers want to buy sports drinks?

4 **Promotion:** only when a business has got the product, price and place right should they promote the product and persuade customers to buy it.

ACTIVITY

Complete the following statement.

The main function of the marketing department in an organisation is to make sure that the right .... is produced at the right .... in the right .... using the right ....

Market research

Business organisations need to have information that will enable them to make decisions about:

- what products to produce
- whom to produce the products for
- when to produce the products
- how many products to produce
- how to produce the products
- how to make the products look attractive.

Market research is a good way of obtaining information about potential and existing customers' needs and wants. In this section you are going to learn about:

- the meaning of market research
- the stages of market research
- the methods of market research.

What is the meaning of "market research"?

A market researcher carrying out a survey

Market research is finding out information about customer needs and wants, before and after the development of new products, to make sure that these needs and wants are met and customers are satisfied.

What stages are involved in market research?

1   **Asking the right questions:** Put simply, a business must ask the right questions to get useful answers that can help them during product development.

2   **Finding out who and where the customers are:** Businesses must clearly identify the potential customers at whom the product will be targeted. For example, if a business decides to develop a new and expensive perfume, it must first identify the customers at whom the product will be aimed.

In this case, the target market would be women who enjoy trying new fragrances and have enough money to be able to afford the perfume.

The methods of market research

Once a business decides who its target customers are, the next stage of the market research is to choose the methods of research to ascertain how to reach the target market.

Two methods are usually adopted:

1   **Field research:** This method of research is used to collect information or data directly from the market. This data is called **primary data.**

Primary data is information not already in published form and which must, therefore, be obtained by the business. Examples of field research methods are questionnaires, interviews, observing customers on the shop floor, tests in the market before the launch of a new product, and analysing sales records.

2   **Desk research:** This method of research is used to collect **secondary data.**

Secondary data is information collected for specific purposes such as government statistics, trade publications, and published academic research. You do not need to go out into the field to collect it. It has already been collected for other purposes and is recorded.

ACTIVITY: THE ADVANTAGES AND DISADVANTAGES OF RESEARCH METHODS

Each research method has advantages and disadvantages. Draw a table with three headings – **Research method, Advantages, Disadvantages.** Write the heading **Advantages** in black and the heading **Disadvantages** in red. Find out the advantages and disadvantages of the following research methods:

- questionnaires
- interviews
- observing customers' attitudes and behaviour on the shop floor
- testing the market before the launch of a new product
- analysing sales records.

Consider the following points:
- time required to collect the information
- effort required to collect the information
- cost of collecting the information
- accuracy of the information collected
- ease of access
- number of people who are approached.

1   Fill in the table using the above criteria.
2   From the information in the table, write down the advantages and disadvantages of field research and desk research.

ACTIVITY: MARKET RESEARCH

In this activity you are going to learn how to carry out market research.

The list below is for the top ten cereals from the British Market Research Bureau's 1991 Target Group Index (the survey was carried out among 25,600 adults between April 1990 and March 1991). It is a detailed study of regular purchases, shopping habits and lifestyle. It is not a market research study.

Type of cereal	Percentage of buyers
Kellogg's Corn Flakes	43.1%
Weetabix	41.8%
Kellogg's Rice Krispies	28.5%
Kellogg's Frosties	20.3%
Shredded Wheat	17.0%
Kellogg's Crunchy Nut Flakes	16.1%
Kellogg's Bran Flakes	15.4%
Kellogg's All-Bran	12.0%
Sugar Puffs	11.8%
Alpen	10.6%

1   From this list find out:
   a   the number of cereal products which are made by Kellogg's
   b   the number of cereal products which are supermarket own brands
   c   the number of cereal products which are sugar-coated
   d   which cereal products are associated with healthier eating
   e   the brand of cereal that is most popular
   f   the brand of cereal that is least popular.
2   Using your IT skills, present the above table as a bar chart.
3   Ask all members of the group which cereals they eat for breakfast. Make a list of the group's top ten breakfast cereals.
4   Present the findings of the group survey in a similar table to the one above.
5   Using your IT skills, present the group survey table as bar charts.
6   Compare the students' top ten with the list above for the top ten cereals:
   a   Are there any products which are on the group's list?
   b   Which products are not in the national top ten?
   c   Is it possible to draw any conclusion?

Promotion

Promotion means informing the customers about the product and persuading them to buy it. All businesses are regularly involved in promotional activities to make sure that customers do not forget their products (the goods they produce or the services they supply).

In general terms, there are three main aims of promotion:

1   to inform customers about a new product
2   to persuade customers to buy the product
3   to promote the product.

The aim and type of promotion will affect the range and style of the promotional materials. As an example, a university may produce quite formal brochures and booklets with photographs of the campus, facilities and students' accommodation. A promotional leaflet from McDonald's is likely to be far more informal with a different style of wording and less formal illustrations.

A promotional flyer for a new sandwich shop

ACTIVITY

In your groups, list five different methods which businesses use to persuade customers to buy their products.

Each member of the group has to think of a recent example of a business that tries to persuade customers to buy its products.

Why use promotional materials?

All businesses use promotional materials to achieve the following objectives:

1 To create demand by:

- persuading customers that they will benefit from buying the product or service

- giving information about new or improved products or services

- giving information about special offers

- keeping the name of the business and/or the product at the forefront of the customer's mind.

2 To increase demand by:

- persuading existing customers to buy more of the product

- attracting more potential customers to the product.

3 To create sales by:

- informing people about where and how they can obtain the product or service

- building up customer loyalty to a brand or business

- persuading consumers that this particular product or service is better than those offered by competitors

- creating consumer awareness of a range of products.

ACTIVITY

Discuss in your groups how your local supermarket tries to build customer loyalty.

Ask yourselves the following questions:

a Does it have a petrol station?
b Does it offer a loyalty card for shoppers?
c Is there any other service which you can obtain from your local supermarket, for example, restaurant, or chemist?

4   To influence customer perceptions by:

- improving general awareness of the business and its policies
- creating a favourable image in the mind of the public.

The image created may simply be to convince consumers that the business has good customer relations, is environmentally friendly and provides quality products. The hope is that the public will think highly of this company and therefore buy its goods.

A business will achieve the objectives of creating demand and increasing sales only if the promotional materials themselves:

a   attract the attention of consumers

b   gain their interest by, for example, including special offers or eye-catching pictures

c   create a desire to own the product or to buy the service

d   explain to the consumers how they can take action, for example, where goods are on sale, what they must do next.

Forms of promotion

Promotion takes two forms:

1   advertising
2   sales promotion.

1   Advertising

Advertising is the presenting of a product to the public to encourage sales – it can have spectacular results.

For example, in 1996, jeans manufacturers such as Levi's suddenly switched to using female models in their television adverts. Sales of jeans shot through the roof.

ACTIVITY

Look through three or four magazines and newspapers. Select ten advertisements that attract your attention and make you interested.

Analyse what it was that caught your eye and made you interested. What features of the advertisement do you think have been deliberately included to create desire.

Look around the area where you live and find examples of three posters that attract your attention. Look for those with a strong, clever, interesting, eye-catching or witty headline, message or design. Describe the position of each of these posters, i.e. near a supermarket, a bank or an airport. Give examples of the types of goods advertised.

Media is the method used to communicate with the public. Types of advertising media include newspapers, television, commercial radio, direct mail, cinema and posters.

2   Sales promotion

Sales promotion is often thought of as being the same as advertising. However, although the objectives of promotion and advertising are the same (to persuade the consumer to buy), there are differences in the way they are practised. Sales promotion often takes the form of an incentive, e.g. a free sample or a special offer.

There are many methods of sales promotion such as:

Logos These are symbols used by companies so that its adverts and products are instantly recognisable. Both logos and trademarks are protected by law once they have been registered by a company. No one else can use or reproduce them without the company's permission.

Slogans These are often employed because they are memorable. "Put a tiger in your tank" was a famous Esso slogan for many years. The benefit of a short, punchy slogan is that it is easily remembered and becomes associated with the product (or company).

Another way of making adverts memorable is to make them **humorous.** Two of the most famous and successful campaigns have been the PG Tips and Heineken adverts.

ACTIVITIES

I   Find out the logo for each of the following:
   a   Virgin Trains
   b   Barclays Bank
   c   Toyota Cars
   d   British Telecom
   e   Kentucky Fried Chicken.
2   Collect a minimum of six adverts from newspapers or magazines that you think use either a good slogan, humour or some other device that attracts you.
3   Which companies use the following slogans?
   "Everything we do is driven by you."
   "It's the real thing."
   "Helps you work, rest and play."
   "The ultimate driving machine."

For each one, note down the features you like.

Branding
A company uses packaging and labels or trademarks to separate its product from those of its rivals. This is called "branding" and brand names are a common form of promotion. Branding does not stop with

just the name – it translates through to packaging design and colour.

ACTIVITY

I   Find a picture of a bar of chocolate and explain why it is attractive.
2   Visit a local supermarket and select three products where colour has been used effectively for the packaging or container.
3   Write a summary of each one. State the product and its purpose. Why do you think the colours used were chosen?

Personal appearances
Celebrities often appear on "television programmes" (e.g. 'TFI Friday') to promote a new product. Authors and sports people sometimes make personal appearances at bookshops to sign copies of their novels to promote sales.

Exhibitions and demonstrations
Many products are displayed at exhibitions open to the general public. A product may sometimes be tested by the public in a supermarket. In large department stores, aftershave and perfumes are available for testing.

Sampling
One method of promoting a new product is to provide free samples of it to households. The company hopes that once consumers have tried a small sachet sample of the product, they will go and buy the larger size bottle or packet at the shop.

Special offers
Some businesses give their customers special offers to promote and increase sales, i.e. buy one get one free, or selling a bigger pack of a product at the same price as the smaller one.

ACTIVITY

Visit one or two of the big retailers in your local area. Find out examples of special offers on some products (goods or services).

Pricing promotions

The idea behind a pricing promotion is to try to persuade consumers that they are getting value for money. A seasonal sale, to clear out stock from the previous season to make room for the new season's collection, is an example of a pricing promotion, e.g. summer sale or Christmas sale.

Direct mail

The use of computers to maintain consumer records has enabled more and more companies to use mailing methods to promote their products.

GROUP ACTIVITY

In your groups, think of three businesses that sell their products by direct mail. What do you think are the advantages of this method?

Sponsorship

This is frequently done to promote the name of the company rather than a particular product. For example, Sainsbury's and Tesco sponsor Art School kits, events and computer equipment.

GROUP ACTIVITY

In your group, think of an event either in your school or college or in your local area that was sponsored by big business, for example, collecting coupons from large supermarkets for school computers. Think about the benefits of this sponsorships for both businesses and your local community.

The sales function

The sales function is the responsibility of the sales department in a large organisation or business. However, in small businesses, the sales function is usually a part of the marketing function.

The main responsibilities of the sales department are to identify potential customers and encourage them to buy, and to deal directly with customers and provide

(contd. on page 39)

Key Terms

Advertising The process of informing a customer about a product or service, and persuading that customer to buy it.

Advertising media The channels through which businesses and other organisations communicate with their customers, for example, newspapers, TV, billboards etc.

Brand A trade name or trademark created for a product in order to persuade the customer that this product is different from that of competitors, e.g. Coca-Cola.

Competition The idea that in a market one producer should always be rivalled by another producer to ensure that prices are kept low and the customer is not exploited.

Consumer A person who buys goods and services for his or her own use or consumption.

Customer A person who buys a product either for his or her own use or for someone else. For example, if your friend buys you a CD for your birthday, he is the customer and you are the consumer. All businesses work very hard to please customers and satisfy their needs.

Demand The desire or need of a consumer backed up by the ability to pay over a period of time.

Desk research It is a research method to collect secondary data, e.g. company's old records.

Field research It is a research method to collect primary data, e.g. interviews and questionnaires

Logo A symbol or picture, often based on a brand name or trademark, which is used by a company to help consumers identify and remember their products.

Marketing Finding out about customer demand, and the satisfaction of that demand by the development, distribution and exchange of goods and services.

Market research The finding out of information about customers' needs and wants to help with the making of marketing decisions.

Price The market value of goods and services that are bought by consumers and firms.

Primary data Information not already in published material and which must, therefore, be obtained by the researcher. Primary data is obtained from the field research.

Promotion The various ways by which an organisation attempts to persuade consumers to purchase its product, e.g. advertising and special offers. It is one of the four elements of the marketing mix.

Secondary data Information collected for a specific purpose such as government statistics, trade publications and published academic research. You do not need to go out into the field to collect it, e.g. data from books or magazines.

Survey A piece of research carried out to establish the opinions and attitudes of individuals to an existing or new product.

Trademark A particular logo that a business uses to distinguish its product from another one. Examples are Nike and Coca-Cola.

customer support. In this way, they are fulfilling an important customer service function.

The Customer Service function

All of the functional areas work towards providing the customer service function. It is essential that a business looks after its customers if it wants to remain in business. Although all of the functional areas are concerned with customer service, most companies also have a special department which looks after the customers after they have bought something from the company. The customer services department provides an after sales service and deals with customer enquiries. Information about the customer service function and customer services department can be found in chapter 3.

How departments within an organisation work together

All the functions within a company are interdependent. For example, it is pointless having a very efficient finance/accounting function if the firm's marketing function is extremely inefficient. Similarly, a business may have an excellent marketing department but sell few products because of a low standard of quality.

To be successful, a business also needs a motivated workforce that is willing to work hard. Therefore, it is very important that the human resources department liaises with other departments to ensure that employees are happy and motivated.

ACTIVITY: WHICH DIRECTOR TO LIAISE WITH

In this activity you are going to learn how different functional directors need to liaise with other functional directors.

Fill in the gaps in the following sentences by using one of the following directors:

Marketing; Sales; Human Resources; Production; Finance; Administration.

1   The Sales Director works closely with the .... Director to ensure that the sales plan is implemented and monitored.

2   The Marketing Director liaises with the .... Director to identify the skills and experience of his team members.

3   The Marketing Director liaises with the .... Director to manage and check quality, at the design and development stage and regularly throughout production.

4   The Production Director should liaise with the ...., and .... Directors to determine a selling price for a new product.

5   The Human Resources Director liaises with the ...., ..., ..., and .... Directors to ensure that all company members are motivated and adequately trained for the job they are expected to do.

6   The Production Director liaises with the .... and .... Directors on working out the cost and the design of the product.

7   The Production Director liaises with the .... to ensure that the production team complies with the health and safety regulations.

8   The .... department works closely with the production, finance, marketing, sales and human resources departments to ensure the accessibility of communication and the flow of information between them.

ACTIVITIES: FUNCTIONS IN A BUSINESS

The aims of this activity are:

To understand more about the functions within a business.

To apply and relate these functions to different departments in the business.

To understand how these functions are linked and related to the stakeholders (people who influence business decisions).

1 Work out which department (Production, Marketing, Finance, Human resources, Customer Service, Administration) would carry out the following functions.
   a Training of human resources
   b Advertising
   c Marketing
   d Recruitment
   e Holidays
   f Job advertisements
   g Sending application forms
   h Writing job specifications
   i Purchasing raw materials
   j The delivery of goods to customers in time
   k Typing pool and data processing
   l Quality control
   m Dealing with faulty goods
   n Payment of wages
   o Organising the flow of money in and out of the business
   p Make customers aware of new products
   q Dealing with customers' complaints

2 You have learned before that there are different groups of people (stakeholders) who influence business decisions, e.g. customers, shareholders, employees and trade unions.

Revise what you have learnt in Chapter 2 and try to answer the following questions:
   a Which department deals directly with customers?
   b Which department/departments deals indirectly with customers?
   c Which department deals with suppliers of raw materials?
   d Which department deals directly with employees in the business?
   e Which department/departments might deal directly with the local community?
   f Which department might deal with the financial affairs of the shareholders?

3 Which department/departments will be interested in recording and keeping the following information?
   a Information about the employee pay roll.
   b Information about a new advertising campaign.
   c Information about a new design for a product.
   d Information about how employees are paid.
   e Information about a new service to customers.
   f Information about the cost of new machinery.

4 "Effective administration function results in a good customer service."

In your groups discuss the above statement. Explain how an effective process of keeping and recording customer information could improve customer service.

Chapter 3 Customer service

Customer service means that the company is concerned with keeping the customer happy and satisfied. It is the job of all of the functional areas (departments) described in chapter 2 to make sure the company's customers are satisfied. For example, the Production Department must produce goods which are not faulty, and the Marketing Department needs to give customers the correct information. If the Marketing Department put the wrong prices in a catalogue, for instance, customers would get upset. All of the functional areas in a business work together to provide good customer service, because without customers there would not be a business. Most companies also have a department dedicated especially to customer service, which provides an after-sales service once a customer has bought a product from the company. The term customer service is used here to describe the way in which all functions of a business work together to ensure good customer service. Once the company has sold a product to the customer, the customer services department must see that the consumer is content with the product.

A dissatisfied customer may be a future sale lost and bad publicity.

A customer service department should be aware that all customers have the following rights:

- to find out information about the product
- to choose a product
- to buy a product
- to get value for money.
- to be satisfied and well looked after once the product has been purchased.

What does good quality customer service mean?

You will usually be able to buy what you want in more than one shop, but the range of goods, and the help you can expect from the staff can make one shop much more attractive to you than the other. Retailers attract regular customers by offering a good service. This includes:

- a choice of goods
- quality
- competitive prices
- reliable guarantees and after-sales service
- helpful, polite and knowledgeable staff
- pleasant surroundings.

ACTIVITY

1 Think back to a time when you feel you received excellent customer service – it may have been in a shop, restaurant or library. Describe it briefly.
2 Think of the characteristics of the person who provided you with excellent service. Describe this person.

Louise Carr, Customer Service Manager, Light Delight

I joined the company as Customer Service Manager 3 years ago and I am responsible to Mike Johnson, the Marketing Manager. My job after college was as a receptionist in a hospital. I enjoy the contact with people that this gave me, and I decided to get a job in a customer service call centre for a large telecommunications company while studying for an NVQ3 in Customer Service. When I got my NVQ, I decided that I wanted more responsibility, and Customer Service Manager job at Light Selight seemed like an exciting challenge. It certainly has been a challenge so far! I start my day at 8am and I don't finish before 7pm. Although my job us very tiring, I enjoy talking to, and dealing with, customers. The majority of our customers are big food retailers and supermarkets. These days customers have many expectations of a product they buy. They expect value for money, so we must provide them with a good quality product at a reasonable price.

The first thing I do when I get to work is read my e-mails and check whether there are any customer complaints. I ensure that any complaints are dealt with immediately. Most customers' complaints are due to late delivery, especially in summer when the demand for ice-cream is high. When customers order goods and services, it is to satisfy their needs and wants now – we would quickly lose customers if we kept delivering orders late. That is why I have a regular meeting once a week with Liz Dyson, the Production Manager, to ensure that we have enough stock and raw materials to meet supermarket demand.

I also have regular daily meetings with our sales team to ensure that our customers are satisfied with our product. We know that the ice-cream market is very competitive and if we don't provide good customer service we would lose customers.

In addition, one of my main tasks is to make sure that the ice-cream is available to consumers in shops and make sure that there are enough products reaching the people who want them. Light Delight employs people to organise how often deliveries must be made to the right retailers at the right time.

The most important part of my job is monitor the way customers are treated when they telephone us or visit our factory.

We are responsible for any faults with the ice-cream we sell. The customer automatically has the right to have his or her money back if the goods are faulty. As long as the customer was not responsible for the damage then we must return the customer's money.

Last year, as part of our commitment to customer service, we extend the customers' right to a refund on purchased ice-cream even if the goods are not faulty. For example, if a regular customer, such as a big supermarket like Sava Stores, mistakenly orders the wrong ice-cream flavour, we would give a refund as long as the goods were returned to us on the same day without being damaged or melted. We always manage to sell it to another retailer.

CASE STUDY — Focus Do It All and Customer Service

Focus Do It All (FDIA) is one of the largest DIY retailers in the UK. Do It All belonged to the Boots group until August 1998 when it was sold.

FDIA offers an extensive and exclusive range of tools and materials, complemented by a very high level of customer service from experienced and knowledgeable staff. FDIA has always sought to differentiate itself from its competitors by:

1 offering stylish and innovative products

2 extending an established strength in home decoration

3 increasing the amount of own-label and exclusive lines in stock

4 introducing additional service policies that customers value, for example no-quibble exchange on returned products even if they have been used.

DIA was highly commended in the 1997 *Daily Telegraph/British Telecom Customer Service Award* and commended in the 1996 Awards in recognition of its commitment to customer service.

Questions

Read the case study carefully and carry out the following tasks:

1 FDIA is highly committed to offering the best customer service. Get evidence from the case study to support this statement.

2 Explain how good quality customer service helps FDIA to compete.

3 Visit the FDIA in your local area. Obtain as much information as you can about the customer service that the store offers.

4 Visit another retailer that offers the same products as FDIA. Try to obtain similar information about its customer service facility.

5 Write a report to compare the customer service in the local FDIA store and the customer service that is offered by the other retailer.

Reasons for good customer service

Businesses are constantly trying to improve customer service for the following reasons:

1 to attract more customers

2 to increase sales

3 to improve a business reputation

4 to be able to compete.

For example, at Halifax PLC, one of the biggest banks in the UK, two of the main factors that contribute to its business success are the Halifax commitment to high standards of service and the expertise of its staff. To maintain these standards and keep staff up to date with new products, the Halifax invests in training.

Example of customer service at Halifax PLC:

- well-trained staff who are always there to help and offer advice
- free mortgage and loans counselling in all Halifax branches
- Halifax Visa Card
- Maxim current account
- Little Extra Club with its colourful money box
- free children's magazines.

Quality customer service means the FIVE C'S:

- Courtesy
- Care
- Communication
- Co-operation
- Compliment.

Effects of bad customer service

Businesses realise that bad customer service means a dissatisfied customer and this could lead to:

- a future sale lost
- bad publicity
- bad business image and reputation.
- inability to cope with the competition.

ACTIVITY: EXAMPLES OF CUSTOMER SERVICE

Salespeople have to deal with a wide range of situations and customers during the course of

a typical day. Classify each of the following situations under the correct area of customer service. In your groups, put forward your ideas and discuss how you would cope with the following situations.

1   A woman insists on trying on an expensive evening dress that is obviously too small for her and there is a definite risk that the dress will split at the seams.

2   A customer returns an expensive squash racket with a broken head. The customer explains that it just snapped when he made contact with the ball. You notice that the top edge of the racket head is well marked. It was purchased about 2 months earlier.

3   You have already shown a customer a large number of suits and a growing number of other people in the shop look as though they need attention. Nobody else is free to help them.

4   You have just started to serve someone when another customer claims that they should have been served first.

5   While his mother is looking at some dresses a little boy eating ice cream is idly brushing his hand along a rack of blouses.

6   You have a group of three young people who hang around inside your newsagent's shop just reading the magazines and occasionally being very familiar with female customers.

Areas covered by customer service

Customer service describes and covers different areas of dealing with customers during and after the purchase of the product. These include:

- the way a customer is treated by sales staff on the telephone, in the shop and at the checkout

- the way queries and complaints are handled
- refunds and replacement of goods
- related services, for example, free delivery, free help-line for customers, extended warranties or guarantees
- providing information about the products, to enable customers to choose the right ones
- assisting customers to use the products
- assisting customers with special needs
- after-sales service. This relates to the help and assistance that is given to customers after the sale has been completed. Customer service does not end with the selling of the product. It is extended after sale to provide the best possible service for the customer.

Many businesses have a dedicated customer service department to assist customers

ACTIVITY

In your group, think of a business that concentrates on giving excellent customer service and often relies on word of mouth rather than advertising to boost the number of its customers.

Customer services and nature of business

The nature and the extent of customer service activities depends on:

1. the nature of business, e.g. retailer manufacturer or service provider

2. the scale of business

3. the type of business ownership, e.g. a sole trader, partnership or Ltd

4. the type of product, e.g. goods or services

5. the use of the product, e.g. for consumer use or for industrial use

6. the competition in the market.

ACTIVITY

Find out the similarities and the differences between customer service activities that should be offered by the following businesses:

1. a big clothes retailer
2. a car manufacturer
3. a food retailer
4. a bank or a building society
5. a water company.

Chapter 4 Business communications

Successful communication between people is a vital activity within an organisation. Good communication not only aids motivation but also improves overall efficiency. The main emphasis of this section will be on communication between the businesses and their stakeholders.

Workplace communication is the passing of information and instructions that help the organisation to operate efficiently.

1 It increases employees' involvement in decision making.

2 It increases employees' satisfaction if they have been involved in decision making.

3 It increases employees' motivation and they will be more committed to their work if the system of communication is efficient.

4 It increases business efficiency, as employees will be more motivated and satisfied.

5 It improves the Industrial relations between management and trade unions.

Types of communication

1 internal communication between colleagues within the same company

2 external communication with outsiders such as customers, shareholders, local community, government, and suppliers (stakeholders).

Methods of communication

There are a number of ways in which a message can be passed from one person to another. Some of these are oral methods and some are written. The best method will depend on the nature of the message.

I Oral communication:

This has the advantage of being quick and allowing immediate response. Problems may arise, however, because there is no written record of the message for referencing at a later date. Also, when the message has to pass down a long chain, there is the possibility of distortion.

Oral methods of communications include:

* meeting
* face-to-face communication
* telephone conversations.

A meeting is a form of oral communication that businesses use

2 Written communication:

This has the advantages that the message is permanent and can be referred to at any time. Information is also likely to be more accurate as greater care will be taken in presenting the information. Written methods are also more appropriate when a business wants a message to be received by a lot of people.

Written methods of communication include:

- letters
- handbooks and manuals produced for reference purpose and dealing with personnel matters or technical details
- employee newsletters to keep workers informed about company activities
- circulars can be used to inform workers or for special events, and to provide important information
- much internal written communication takes place by means of memoranda (memos). A memo is a form of letter which is only used internally and is not usually private (it could be read by anyone in the business)
- the annual report and accounts of a company is a financial report that is made available to shareholders as well as managers. In many cases the report, in the form of a specially produced summary, is made available to employees to keep them informed as to the company's financial position
- e-mails are a new and fast way of communication that can be used as both an internal and external method of communication
- advertisements.

CASE STUDY – Alliance & Leicester

On 21 April 1997, Alliance & Leicester changed from being a building society to being a public limited company, listed on the London Stock Exchange. Alliance & Leicester is a major financial services group dedicated to the provision of a range of personal financial products for customers. Its objective is to provide customers with a comprehensive range of mortgage and other financial and banking services that are high in quality and competitive in price.

Alliance & Leicester has more than five million customers living in the UK. The company uses a wide network of communication whenever and wherever it best suits the needs of customers. For example, Girobank, acquired by Alliance & Leicester in 1990, was the first telephone bank in the UK. More Alliance & Leicester customers are able to use a full 24-hour telephone and postal banking

facility than with any other bank or building society in the UK.

Within Alliance & Leicester, efficient communication provides employees with information that assists their work. Informing employees about developments within the business helps to involve them further and create an understanding of how these developments may affect their daily decisions.

There are two different types of communication at the company:

1 internal communication between management and staff

2 external communication between the company and outsider.

Internal communication at Alliance & Leicester

Communication is not only used by senior managers for giving instructions downwards, but also for passing on business strategy so that more people within the company understand how Alliance & Leicester is working towards its objectives. The communication process also works in the opposite way, from lower to higher levels. Good internal communication enables employees to discuss issues within the workplace.

Various communication methods are used by Alliance & Leicester to motivate employees and improve teamwork. Team meetings, for example, bring employees together to focus upon certain issues. Informing employees about what is happening within the company helps them feel involved and improves their communication.

There are three main methods used for internal communication in the company:

1 written communication

2 electronic communication

3 verbal communication.

Written communication

At Alliance & Leicester written communication is particularly useful when:

- the information needs to be received by many people in different places

- the information needs to be referred to over a period of time.

Written communication in the company includes:

1 *Spectrum*   This is a staff newspaper which is distributed to all staff.

2 Team brief   This is a monthly production that contains business news from the whole of Alliance & Leicester.

3 Staff suggestion scheme   This was created to encourage and reward staff for suggestions. It was also introduced to improve customer service.

4 *Bulletin*   Knowledge of product changes and promotional activity is particularly important for staff employed by Alliance & Leicester. The *Bulletin* is produced by the company's Marketing Department to update staff on promotional activity.

5 Office instructions   These are paper-based instructions, sent to individual branches, used for updating staff on new product, launches and changes in the business.

6 Office communication   These are for branches and usually transmit (send) general messages.

7 One-offs   From time to time, one-off communications are produced to update or to emphasise important procedures

Electronic communication

Over recent years there have been many different developments in electronic technology that have affected all staff at Alliance & Leicester in one way or another. Initially the company, like any other business, was dependent on the telephone for internal and external communication.

However, with the recent developments in new technology Alliance & Leicester has invested in new methods of electronic communication:

- e-mail.
- Internet
- fax system
- screen messaging service.

Verbal communication

Verbal communication in the company involves the transmission of information effectively by word of mouth. For many people at Alliance & Leicester, verbal communication tends to be face-to-face messages, personal discussion and the provision of instruction and guidance. However, it also includes staff training sessions, internal conferences, team meetings, videos and audio tapes.

External communication at Alliance & Leicester

The company has a public face or image. This conveys a message that affects everyone who works with the business organisation. These include customers, suppliers, competitors, the government, communities, and agencies.

Methods of external communication include:

1 written communication

2 verbal communication.

Written communication

Alliance & Leicester provides a range of information for different stakeholder groups. In addition to business letters sent to personal customers, written communications include press releases, advertisements, posters, and mail shots.

Verbal communication

This type of communication is particularly important for a range of issues affecting Alliance & Leicester stakeholders. These include Annual General Meetings, press conferences and 24-hour telephone and postal banking.

ACTIVITIES

With your tutor read the above case study carefully and carry out the following activities:

1 Make a list of the different methods of communication that you use to communicate with other students or tutors. For example, writing, asking your tutor questions, etc. Describe the nature and the purpose of each form of communication that you use.

2 Compare and contrast one form of electronic communication with the written communication it was designed to replace.

3 Find out the meaning of the following words:
   a e-mail
   b Internet
   c fax.

The management of Alliance & Leicester believes that a motivated workforce that feels part of the organisation is the key to achieving its business objectives. Explain how methods of internal communication help the management of Alliance & Leicester to achieve this.

Two-way communications with customers in Alliance & Leicester

As the industry becomes more competitive, using feedback from customers is becoming increasingly important for Alliance & Leicester. Opportunities for two-way communication exist through:

1 Group Customer Relations Customer complaints are a valuable source of information used to improve products and services wherever possible. Customer relations provide a listening ear for customers who are unable to resolve problems with branches. It communicates the feedback to senior management.

2 A Customer Care leaflet This freely available leaflet enables customers to communicate their comments and suggestions to the company.

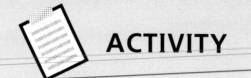

ACTIVITY

Explain how Alliance & Leicester has effective communication with customers.

....

Communication technology

Around 50% of Britain's workers are employed in offices. It has been calculated that if all the pieces of paper handled in the world's offices were laid end to end they would stretch from here to the sun! Methods of telecommunication include:

- fax (facsimile) machines
- pagers/bleepers
- mobile phones
- answering machines
- Internet
- teleworking.

ACTIVITIES

1 Fill in the gaps in the following statements. Use only one of two words, **written** or **verbal**.
   a Fax is an example of .... communication.
   b Pagers are examples of .... communication.
   c Mobile phones are examples of .... communication.
   d Answering machines are examples of .... communication.
   e The Internet is an example of .... communication.
   f Teleworking is an example of .... communication.

2 Fill in the gaps in the following statements. Use only one term/phrase, **allow(s)** or **do(es) not allow**.
   a Teleworking .... workers and employers to work from home.
   b Fax machines .... documents to be sent quickly from one place to another.

c Mobile phones .... workers to remain in contact with the office wherever they might be.

d Answer machines .... lots of important calls to be missed.

3 Discuss with your tutor whether the following statements are true or false.

a Teleworking reduces costs and reduces travel problems.

b Teleworking increases workers' social isolation.

c Fax machines waste time and delay communication.

d Fax machines increase the reliability and the use of traditional postal services.

e Mobile phones save time and effort.

f Mobile phones reduce the cost of communication.

g Answer machines increase employees' contact with their business.

h Answer machines increase the cost of communication.

Which media of communication?

A number of factors will determine the best choice of medium for any particular message.

A number of questions need to asked:

1 Is the message confidential?
2 Is speed important?
3 Who is to receive the message?
4 Is a permanent record required?
5 Is the message complicated or lengthy?
6 How much will it cost to send the message?

Directions of communication

In any hierarchical structure there are two different directions for formal communication:

1 **Vertical communication** This is the passing of instructions, messages or orders, from managers to employees through the levels of the hierarchy (from top to bottom), for example, between the marketing manager and the marketing team, or passing the information from employees to managers (from bottom to top).

2 **Horizontal communication** This is the type of communication that takes place between people at the same level within the organisation, for example, between the marketing manager and the production manager.

How to write a business letter

Business letters are a very important form of communication. It is essential to know how to communicate in the most effective way. If you are going to write a business

---

Writing a business letter – things to remember

1 Dear Sir or Madam at the beginning of the letter requires 'Yours faithfully' at the end.

2 Dear Mr, Miss, or Mrs at the beginning requires 'Yours sincerely' at the end.

3 The closing paragraph must be a complete sentence. This can be in a number of different forms, for example:

'I look forward to hearing from you' or,

'Please let me know if you require any further information.'

4 When you reply to someone, always start by saying 'Thank you for your letter of (date).'

---

letter, remember the tips in the box (below).

What is a business letter?

A business letter is different from an ordinary letter in the following ways.

- Business letters communicate information between businesses and others, e.g. customers and suppliers. It is important that these letters look good if a business is to give a good impression.
- A business letter is the most frequently used form of external communication for businesses.
- A business letter provides a written record that can be used to send almost any type of information.
- A business letter is usually on headed paper. Fully blocked layout is the most common form of display.

Format of a business letter

There is a basic format that most business letters tend to follow. Quite apart from the style or structure of the letter, the wording

Layout of a business letter

The Design Shop
22 Craft Centre
Deddingham
ML17 9AT

Mrs Smith
18 Meadow Way
Milton Keynes
ML2 1EJ

25 May 2000

Dear Mrs Smith

Order No. 19349 Chrome CD rack

Thanks for your recent order to purchase the above item. We do apologise, as the required item is currently out of stock. However, we promise to do our best to deliver your order in the next two weeks.

Thanks again for your interest in our products.

Yours sincerely,

M Wood

M. Wood

is important. The wording needs to be clear and precise if the message it contains is to be conveyed accurately.

ACTIVITIES

1 Design a suitable letter heading using desktop publishing software for use by:

Light Delight Ltd,
Unit 28, Penraven Industrial Estate,
Mean Wood Road,
Leeds,
LS7 2AP

2 Use your word processing skills to write a letter for the above company from the Production Manager to Speed Supply Ltd of 56 Marton Way, Middlesborough. The out the problems with a new freezer that the company bought 2 months ago. The freezer is still under the supplier's guarantee.

3 Write another letter to Lilter's Electrical Contractors, Grange Street, Leeds, pointing out that their invoice for £83.20 for a replacement light in the marketing department is £15.60 above their original estimate. Would they explain the reason for this?

Memos

Memos are used for internal correspondence/communication between people who work in the same business, usually between managers and employees. Memos are therefore generally less formal than letters in the following ways:

- the business or organisation name does not appear on the memo
- in memos there will be no salutation or complimentary closure such as 'Yours sincerely'
- the memo should be brief and as straightforward as possible
- memos are often distributed to a number of people in the business.

The main uses of memos are:

- the passing of information to people in the business
- requests for information
- confirmation of information, e.g. date of meeting.

ACTIVITY

What are the differences between a memo and a letter?
Fill in the gaps in the following statements using the word memo or letter:

1 A .... is usually shorter than a ....
2 A .... is more formal than a ....
3 A .... is normally initialled, but a .... is signed.
4 A .... is used for internal correspondence but a .... is used for external correspondence.
5 A .... is more confidential than a ....

Unit I Test your knowledge

This is a quick test to help you check how much you have understood.

In the following statements, there are some right and some wrong answers. Circle only the wrong answer/answers:

1   The following are elected management positions:

   a   Company secretary
   b   Board of directors
   c   Sales assistant
   d   Managing director

2   The department that has overall responsibility for staff training is:

   a   The Human Resources Department
   b   The Production Department
   c   The Finance Department
   d   The Marketing Department

3   The following business ownership has directors:

   a   Jones & Partners
   b   The Light Delight Ice Cream Ltd
   c   Marks and Spencer PLC

4   Advertising is one of the main functions of:

   a   The Human Resources Department
   b   The Marketing Department
   c   The Finance Department
   d   The Production Department

5   The purchasing function is sometimes incorporated in:

   a   The Marketing Department
   b   The Sales Department
   c   The Human Resources Department
   d   The Production Department

6   The following are the main functions of the Finance Department:

   a   Invoicing
   b   Payment of wages
   c   Balancing the books (accounts)
   d   Carrying out market research

7   The following member of Marks & Spencer PLC has overall responsibility for the running of the business:

   a   Chairman
   b   Managing director
   c   Sales manager
   d   Sales assistant

8   The following function(s) is/are under the direct control of the Production Department:

   a   Stock control
   b   Training of staff
   c   Advertising
   d   Quality control

9   The following products are examples of consumer durables:

   a   Ice cream
   b   TV
   c   Personal computer
   d   Dishwasher

10   The following people come at the top level of the hierarchy structure of a large company:

   a   Assistant sales manager
   b   Marketing director
   c   Shareholders
   d   Company secretary

11   A long chain of command in a large business leads to:

   a   Quicker communication
   b   Slow decision making
   c   Senior management being close to team workers in the hierarchy structure

12 The statement that includes the required details about a candidate is called:

    a Job description
    b Contract of employment
    c Job specification
    d CV

13 Induction is a type of training that is offered:

    a To any employee in the business
    b To old employees
    c To new employees
    d To senior management

14 The following are the functions of the Human Resources Department:

    a Dealing with resignations
    b Looking after staff welfare
    c Dismissing unsuitable workers
    d Payment of salaries

15 The following is an example of a written method of communication:

    a A letter
    b A memo
    c Telephone
    d Internet

16 The main objective of a business in the public sector is:

    a To make profit
    b To compete
    c To provide a service

17 The following media are examples of external methods of recruitment:

    a Word of mouth
    b Job centres
    c Staff notice board
    d Local newspaper

Unit I Assessment

Check with your tutor what you need to produce for your portfolio. If you do the assignment below, you will be on your way to completing the work you will need to do.

Choose a business either in your area or outside your area. Carry out the following tasks:

1 Draw the organisational chart for this business.

2 Explain the role of each of the following functional areas within the business: Marketing, Finance, Production and Human Resources. Choose one and describe its role in detail, using graphics, if you find this useful.

3 Investigate customer service in the business, and describe how it is carried out.

4 Give full descriptions of two different jobs involving customer service, for example, giving information, helping customers, after-sales service.

5 Evaluate the above two customer service jobs, and suggest how they could be improved.

6 Identify and give examples of types of communication used by the business.

7 Explain how these types of communication serve business activities.

8 Evaluate the above types of communication.

Investigating businesses

There are many different types of business organisation. This unit will help you to understand the activities that all businesses carry out and how you can identify the differences between them.

In this unit you are going to learn:

- what a business is

- what a business does

- where a business is.

To learn about businesses you have to cover the following topics:

- types of business ownership

- business activities

- people who influence businesses (stakeholders)

- size of business

- businesses location

- business and competition.

When studying businesses it can be useful to group together all businesses that share particular characteristics in order to gain an insight into the problems they face or the advantages they enjoy. Businesses can be classified using three main factors. These factors are:

1 ownership

2 activity

3 scale/size.

Chapter 5 The ownership of businesses

Britain is said to have a mixed economy because it consists of a private sector (privately owned businesses) and a public sector (owned by the government).

In the private sector, decisions about what to produce, how to produce it and where to produce it are made by private individuals. Virtually all businesses in the UK are now in the private sector.

In the public sector, decisions about what to produce, how to produce it and where to produce it are made by central government. The government owns the business.

Private sector ownership

Private sector (enterprise) refers to businesses that are owned by private individuals engaged in the production of goods or services. When you describe a business you must state its type of ownership. In the private sector there are several types of ownership:

- sole trader
- partnership
- private limited company
- public limited company.

There are also two special kinds of ownership in the private sector:

- co-operative
- franchise.

Sole traders

Sole traders are generally small and are often family-run businesses. There is only one owner. He or she has unlimited liability. This means that the owner or 'proprietor' is personally liable for the debts of the business under any circumstances. For example, if the business goes bankrupt, he or she might have to sell personal belongings, such as a car or a house, to pay the debts. There are no particular legal formalities involved in setting up the business apart from those which would apply to any business.

> **Facts to remember about sole traders:**
>
> 1 The business is in the private sector.
> 2 It is easy to set up.
> 3 There is only one owner.
> 4 Sole trader runs the business.
> 5 Sole trader has unlimited liability.
> 6 Sole trader has full responsibility of running the business.
> 7 Sole trader makes all the decisions.
> 8 Business affairs are private.
> 9 Death or illness of the sole trader could stop the running of the business.

Partnerships

In this type of business there is more than one owner. The control of the business is the responsibility of all the partners. Decisions taken by one partner are binding on the others. Partners have unlimited liability.

A partnership of accountants

Partnerships have a special legal status and are regulated by the Partnership Act of 1890 which allows up to a maximum of 20 partners. Special rules apply to large professional organisations of, for example, accountants and solicitors, where more partners are allowed.

Partnerships are a common type of business and widely used by firms of accountants, doctors, dentists, and other professionals. To avoid any disagreement between partners, it is advisable for a written agreement to be drawn up. This is called a Deed of Partnership.

Facts to remember about a partnership:

1 The business is in the private sector.
2 There can be between 2 and 20 owners.
3 The partners run the business.
4 The partners have unlimited liability.
5 The partners share the responsibility of running the business.
6 The partners share in the decisions.
7 Business affairs are private.
8 Death or illness of a partner does not affect the running of the business.
9 They need a deed of partnership to avoid any arguments.

CASE STUDY – Wild Rice

An idea for a new business can spring out of your daily life. You may notice a problem in getting something you need and then realise that here is a gap in the market that you could fill. That is the way it happened with Margaret.

Nature of business: Producing and supplying pre-packaged vegetarian meals for catering establishments
Location: Glasgow
Business structure: Sole trader (previously partnership)
Proprietor: Margaret Graham

Margaret is a vegetarian. The idea for the business really sprang from when she was going out for a pub lunch. It was very difficult in Glasgow to find vegetarian food in pubs. Margaret and her friend Linda considered various ideas for starting their own business, like a vegetarian restaurant or café. They decided it might be cheaper to set up a small kitchen and supply independent restaurants and pubs with ready-made vegetarian meals.

Market research

Margaret had studied Communications after school, aiming at a career in advertising. The course included market research, so when she and Linda decided to see if they were right about the demand for such meals, her knowledge came in very handy. Margaret and Linda took sample meals to various bars, restaurants, and health food shops, for sample tastings. They also interviewed 100 people for their comments. The feedback was favourable.

'The pub owners were very helpful. They saw that their customers liked our products and, when we told them our prices, they wanted to place orders,' Margaret said.

She continued, 'We went to the local Enterprise Development Unit for advice, and they suggested more market research to be absolutely certain that there was a market. We wrote to Marks and Spencer under the guise of students asking why M&S had started doing vegetarian food and did they see it as a growing field. We also wrote to bookshops and found out that the sale of vegetarian cook books was growing.'

Finance

With no capital of their own, Margaret and Linda had to look for grants. The advice agencies gave them a lot of guidance on this. Glasgow was a development area, so they got a regional development grant.

Also, being under the age of 25 worked in their favour. It enabled them to apply to the Prince's Scottish Youth Business Trust and receive another grant.

Location

Margaret and Linda looked at premises in the city but found nothing suitable that they could afford. Then they came across a huge disused bakery that had been converted into 60 small businesses by a community organisation. It was ideally situated for transport, being near the motorway and the tunnel into the city. It was also outside the city centre, so rates were quite low.

Product

Margaret said, 'Our recipes were adapted from things we made for family and friends. We had to go from making enough for 4 people to making 50 or 60 portions. That was quite difficult to begin with, getting the seasoning right, and the amount of spices and garlic.'

Margaret and Linda cook in bulk, then portion it into individual cardboard dishes. They are sealed in polythene by a machine, then they go into an outer cardboard sleeve printed with their own design. Finally, they are put into large boxes a dozen at a time.

They found that many customers wanted the meals frozen, so they bought a blast-freezer to do this. It also meant they did not have to cook every day.

Customers

Wild Rice has a network of pubs and restaurants in Glasgow and Edinburgh which are supplied either weekly or fortnightly. Orders are taken by telephone. The bulk of customers tend to be small independent grocers and health food shops.

Pricing

Margaret and Linda set prices by taking the costs of the raw materials, electricity, transport and other costs. They also looked at the prices of comparable offerings in the market place, and then discussed matters with business advisers. It was very difficult for them because they knew that if they did not make an income that covered their costs, they would not make any profit.

Margaret is thinking of raising prices slightly because she does not want people to think the products are not very good because they are cheap.

Competition

Wild Rice has competitors such as Birds Eye and Lean Cuisine. However, whereas many companies which sell vegetarian meals tend to just extract meat content from meals, and do not put portions back in, all Wild Rice products are wholefood. They are well balanced, all high in fibre, low in fat, and all the healthy things they should be.

Although it is difficult to compete on advertising with big firms, Margaret and Linda tried to piggy-back on their efforts.

For example, if they saw Lean Cuisine advertising a lot, they would hand out leaflets to their customers.

Business ownership

Margaret and Linda had a partnership agreement drawn up when they started. As it happened they were very close and the partnership was very good. 'As regards dividing up the work, I seemed to be better at the production side of things. Linda was very good on the book-keeping and chasing up payment of accounts,' Margaret said.

Unfortunately, Linda left the business after three years. She had a lot of personal problems. The relationship with her boyfriend broke up and she felt that a lot of it was due to the pressure of being self-employed. 'We got the partnership dissolved (ended) and that was fine. It was very much like a divorce but we were quite happy.'

At first, it was financially and physically difficult for Margaret. She could not prepare the same amount of food that two people could. However, her family was very supportive and she employed a woman who does deliveries and collections three days a week.

Now Margaret is a sole trader and is very happy. In the future, she would like to extend the business further south, down into England. She does not really want to turn the business into a big organisation or huge industry. In fact, she likes the idea that it is small.

ACTIVITY

Read the above case study carefully and answer the following questions:

1 Where did Margaret get her business idea from?
2 Which methods of market research did Margaret use?
3 How did Margaret and Linda manage to obtain money to finance the business?
4 What were the main factors which Margaret and Linda considered in choosing the business location?
5 Explain how the choice of the business premises contributed to the success of the business?
6 Who are Wild Rice's main competitors?
7 How does Wild Rice respond to the competition?
8 Who are Wild Rice's potential customers?
9 What were the main advantages for Margaret of being in a partnership with Linda?
10 What are Wild Rice's main objectives?
11 What are Wild Rice's main business activities?
12 Why do you think Wild Rice is a successful business?
13 Get in touch with the Economic Development Department at your local council. Find out how your local council supports small business in your local area.
14 Margaret is thinking of raising prices slightly. She asks for your advice. Write a short report to advise Margaret what to do.

Limited companies

The main drawbacks of sole trader businesses or partnerships are:

* There is only one or a few owners and they do not have much money to grow or expand.

- The owners have unlimited liability which puts their personal possessions at risk.

Therefore, the need might arise to form a limited company to overcome the two common problems associated with sole traders and partnerships.

The word 'company' suggests a group of owners who have come together to set up a business. In practice, many companies are not like this today because the owners (shareholders) may be quite far removed from the decision-making. Shareholders are rewarded with profit for the risk they take in investing their money into the business. The share of the profit the shareholders receive is called a dividend.

By forming a company, limited liability can be obtained for all members.

Limited liability can be applied to the shareholders of a private or public limited company and partners in a limited partnership.

Facts to remember about a limited company

1 Shareholders are the owners. They invest (put money) into the business.
2 Shareholders are rewarded with profit.
3 Shareholders have limited liability.
4 Shareholders vote for a board of directors.
5 The board of directors runs the company on behalf of the shareholders.
6 Employers are appointed to carry out instructions.

There are two main types of limited companies:

1   private limited company.
2   public limited company.

Setting up a limited company

To set up a limited company (Ltd or PLC), two important documents are needed:

1 Articles of Association
2 Memorandum of Association.

Once these documents are ready, they are sent to someone who is appointed by the Government and called the Registrar of Companies. He or she makes sure that that above two documents are accurate and issues a Certificate of Incorporation which the business needs to start trading.

Private limited company

A private limited company is a limited company in the private sector. Shares are not sold on the Stock Exchange, and shareholders are often made up of family and friends. The company is run by a board of directors who are elected by the shareholders. No minimum (capital) investment is required to set up a private limited company. The minimum number of owners required to set up a private limited company is two. Examples of private limited company are Littlewoods and River Island (which is owned by the Lewis family).

River Island is a private limited company (Ltd)

CASE STUDY — Joseph Dobson & Sons Ltd
Makers of fine quality boiled sweets since 1850

Joseph Dobson & Sons Ltd is one of the largest privately owned confectionery manufacturers in Yorkshire. Dobson's sweets are loved and well stocked in almost all local shops. The advent of the humble polythene bag has enabled the company to increase the distribution of its products more widely and to new outlets such as supermarkets.

The company still runs a traditional sweet shop in Elland, West Yorkshire.

The company is owned and managed by direct descendants of Joseph. The business continued to be passed down from father to son, providing continuity and passing expertise and experience of five generations to the current great-great-grandchild, Miriam, and her husband Stephen.

Dobson & Sons have always been famous for sweets with distinctive flavours and, to add to originality, each type of sweet has its own special shape. Dobson Sweets have always been known as a sweetie manufacturer and the company have always been active in marketing their products at carnival processions, and in mounting displays centred around the giant antique glass jars in shops, supermarkets and museums in the area.

The famous 'Yorkshire Mixtures' sweet was named entirely by accident. The story is that while Joseph's son, Thomas John, was carrying some sweets downstairs, he slipped and the sweets became mixed. Thomas John was inspired to name the jumbled mess "Yorkshire Mixture".

Source: the business website address www.dobsons.co.uk

Read the case study and answer the following questions:

1   What is the type of business ownership for Dobson & Sons?

2   What are the main advantages of this type of ownership?

3   Where did the business name come from?

4   Where is the business located?

5   Where is the business's main market?

6   Where is the product distributed?

7   What is the brand name of Dobson & Sons sweets?

8   Where did the brand name come from?

9   How did the new packaging of the sweets affect sales?

10   Where does the company market the sweets?

11   How has the quality of the sweets contributed to the success of the business?

A private limited company must show the letters Ltd at the end of the company title.

Facts to remember about a private limited company (Ltd)

Many of these facts apply to all limited companies, whether they are private or public. Facts that are only true about private limited companies are highlighted in bold.

1   It is in the private sector.
2   There are two or more owners.
3   Board of directors run the business.
4   Shareholders own the business.
5   Shareholders have limited liability.
6   **No minimum investment.**
7   **Business affairs are private.**
8   Death or illness of shareholders does not affect the running of the business.
9   **Shares are not exchanged or sold on the Stock Exchange.**
10   **Shares are not sold to the general public. They are sold only with the permission of all shareholders, often mainly to family and friends.**

Public limited company

A public limited company (PLC) is a limited company in the public sector. It is owned by shareholders from the public, so shares are sold on the Stock Exchange. The company is run by a board of directors who are elected by shareholders.

Examples of public limited companies are:

- Marks and Spencer PLC
- Barclays Bank PLC
- Halifax PLC.

ACTIVITY

Find out five more examples of public limited companies. You can look at the Stock Market section in a local or a national newspaper.

Facts to remember about a public limited company (PLC)

Many of these facts apply to all limited companies, whether they are public or private. Facts that are only true about public limited companies are highlighted in bold.

1   It is in the private sector.
2   There two or more owners.
3   Board of directors run the business.
4   Shareholders own the business.
5   Shareholders have limited liability.
6   **Minimum investment is £50,000.**
7   **Business affairs are public.**
8   Death or illness of shareholders does not affect the running of the business.
9   **Shares are exchanged or sold on the Stock Exchange.**
10   **Shares are sold to the general public.**

ACTIVITY: PUBLIC OR PRIVATE

Finish off the following statements using only one of the words, **public** or **private**.

1 A sole trader business is in the .... sector.

2 A Ltd company is in the .... sector.

3 For a PLC, business affairs are ....

4 A partnership is in the .... sector.

5 For a sole trader, business affairs are ....

6 A PLC is in the .... sector.

7 For a Ltd company shares are sold in .... to family and friends.

8 For a PLC shares are sold in .... on the Stock Exchange.

CASE STUDY – Chey International

'We are the little fish that swim around amongst the sharks. Anything that is going we take.' That is Chey's comment on how a beginner can move into a field like the rag trade, where struggling small businesses are normal, and still do well.

Nature of business: Manufacturer of leather garments
Location: East End of London
Business ownership: private limited company
Proprietor: Aiyub Ebrahim (nickname Chey)

Chey was born in India but came to Britain when he was 11. He was educated here and went on to university, studying biology. Then he made a basic mistake – he went travelling for about ten years.

'I did odd jobs to survive – everything you can think of, from dish-washing upwards. Then I decided to do something more positive. It is pure coincidence I ended up in this business', Chey said.

He knew a friend who wanted some CMT work done. CMT is contract work in the clothing industry. The major wholesalers gave Chey the materials and he just made it up. They paid him for the labour charges, so he did not need capital to start.

Location

Chey saw some premises that were empty, got second-hand sewing machines and recruited a few machinists from amongst people he knew.

Chey's father was a tailor, so he had some background in the rag trade. Chey himself had no personal experience of the industry, he just picked it up as he went along. 'My goal was to make as much money as possible and get out. I planned to work all hours of the day, get the money, get back to Germany and open a shop.'

Chey opened a leather shop in Munich in Germany, but unfortunately that failed. He had to come back to Britain and the firm has been going now for four years.

'With contract work, everything is done for you – all the designing, all the selling, you just supply the labour.' It took Chey a year or two to learn the tricks of the trade. Chey International Ltd became the King of the CMT trade for a time. Wholesalers were chasing them to make up garments for them.

It did not take Chey long to realise this was a mugs' game. It was the wholesalers who decided which firms they would give work to and how much they would pay. The flow of work could suddenly stop or reduce to a trickle that was not enough to survive. They were not really concerned to pay good enough rates to develop their suppliers to a level where they would be stable.

The wholesalers were keen to pay as little as possible, so that the percentage they added on when selling to the stores could be as high as possible.

Therefore, Chey thought if he could sell directly to the stores, he could offer a lower price and still make enough profit to pay his employees.

Chey's company has now reached the stage where they do not do CMT work any more. They make their own garments. Chey has a friend who does the designing and the sales. He goes to the shops and takes the concept he has designed. He explains, 'We can make anything you want exclusive to you, all you have to do is to tell us what you want.' So the customer gets a better service.

Chey's company can make better products and more quickly. For example, if a shop phones up and says 'I want 50 jackets' the business can produce them in two days. The big wholesaler wants at least six weeks.

Competition

Chey International can also react to changes in fashion, whereas the big firms cannot. They import most of their materials from the Far East. They have to place big orders months in advance, and take the risk that changing fashion will make it unsaleable.

However, Chey recognises the danger in taking business from under the wholesalers' noses. If he grows too big he feels they will cut their prices to a very low level to drive

him out of the market. That is why he tends to stay clear of the big department stores which are the wholesalers' major customers.

How the company is run

On friendly terms with all employees, Chey believes in being closely involved in the work. He has done most of the tasks himself, except the machining. He usually inspects the finished garments, ensuring they are up to the quality he wants.

Chey admits to being a workaholic, with little relaxation apart from watching videos when he gets home in the evenings. Now the company has reached a more stable level and can take on specialists to handle different aspects of management, Chey feels he may be able to take a bit more time for himself.

Read the case study carefully and answer the following questions:

1 What type of company ownership is Chey International?
2 What are the main advantages of this type of ownership?
3 Who are the owners of the business in this type of ownership?
4 What are Chey's main personal skills which contributed to the success of his business?
5 What are Chey International's main business activities?
6 Chey said that the attitude of wholesalers put him in a 'mugs game'. Explain what he meant.
7 Who are Chey's main customers?
8 Who are Chey's main competitors?
9 How does Chey respond to the competition?
10 Who are the stakeholders who influence Chey International's activities?

Co-operatives

Co-operatives are a special type of ownership in the private sector.

How co-operatives developed

People organising themselves together as a co-operative is not a new idea. It dates back several hundred years in many areas of the world, although we usually think of the Co-op Movement in this country developing from the 19th century. It was a time of rapid industrialisation, low wages and poor living conditions. Therefore, the consumer co-operatives were set up by the Rochdale Pioneers to provide a cheap source of food for themselves. Around the same time, the first worker co-operatives were established.

There are several different types of co-operatives which share the same basic principles of:

- democratic control
- ownership by members.

The most popular co-operative in the United Kingdom is the Co-operative Wholesale Society (CWS). It is the modern successor of the co-operative movement founded in Rochdale in 1844.

Co-Op is Britain's best known co-operative business

Facts to remember about a co-operative

1   A co-operative is in the private sector.
2   A co-operative is a special type of ownership.
3   There are many types of co-operative, e.g. consumer co-operative, worker co-operative and producer co-operative.
4   The most common type of co-operative is a worker co-operative, where workers run and own the business.

Co-operatives and the law

Businesses can register as co-operative societies under the Industrial and Provident Societies Acts of 1965-1975. The Co-operative Development Agency (CDA) and the Industrial Common Ownership Movement (ICOM) assist with the setting up of co-operatives; for example, by providing advice, training and business information.

 **ACTIVITY: WHO ARE THE OWNERS?**

The main principle of co-operatives is that members have a democratic say and control over the business.
Read the above information carefully.
Fill in the gaps in the following sentences, stating who are the owners and who are the runners in each type of the following co-ops.

1   In a consumer co-operative .... own the business and .... run the business.
2   In a worker co-operative .... own the business and .... run the business.
3   In a producer co-operative .... own the business and .... run the business.
4   In a retailer co-operative .... own the business and .... run the business.

CASE STUDY – Speedy M & V

A good basis for your own business is often the skills and experience you have acquired in your paid employment. That was what Monica and Violet decided, but they didn't like the idea of being bosses. In preparing for the future when they expected their business to expand, they opted for a co-operative structure rather than that of a partnership.

If you would like to know why, read the following case study.

Nature of business: Word processing/ typing bureau
Location: Central London
Business ownership: co-operative
Proprietors: Monica Butcher and Violet Fearon

Violet did secretarial training after school and worked as a secretary for various companies. When she joined an insurance company in the City, she met Monica Butcher. They became friends and discussed the idea of starting their own business. They liked the idea of working for themselves.

In the next few years, Violet did a three-year course in Business Studies at a Technical College and Monica took a short business course. Finding time to plan your own business project properly can be a problem. Violet's course helped there. 'At the end of my course, we had to do a project about starting our own business and mine was about starting a secretarial agency.'

Type of business ownership

Monica and Violet went on a weekend course at the City University about small businesses. Different business structures were discussed. They liked the sound of a co-operative. It seemed to offer the possibility of financial and other assistance, and everybody is equal in a co-op.

Monica and Violet then went to Islington Co-operative Development Agency (one of the many CDAs around the country). There they were helped to write a business plan and a cash flow forecast over three years.

Setting up a co-operative

Monica and Violet registered through ICOM (Industrial Common Ownership Movement Ltd) and they liaised with Companies House on the Memorandum and Articles of Association. That is the formal document needed to register as a company limited by guarantee, one of the ways becoming a co-operative.

Market research

Monica and Violet carried out market research to find out how easy it would be to get customers. They drew up a questionnaire, and telephoned firms from the *Yellow Pages*.

Finance

The CDA suggested that they should apply to Islington Council's Economic Development Unit for a grant. 'They were keen on supporting co-ops,' explained Monica.

Premises

The next step was finding premises. Monica and Violet went to estate agents, and to the Council which had a list of vacant business properties. They chose premises which were near to the City of London and all those potential customers.

Speedy M & V has its office on a busy road on the first floor over a bookmaker's. The main office has enough space to add more desks and equipment, if required. It also has a small kitchen and toilet and a separate reception area.

Monica and Violet worked very long hours during the week and sometimes they came in on Saturdays to finish a rush job.

There were bad weeks too, with only one or two jobs. The work consists mostly of letters and reports for companies, theses for students at the nearby university, copy typing, audio typing and typing up accounts.

Promotion

To get customers when they started Monica and Violet promoted their business in different ways:

1 They printed leaflets and business cards which they designed themselves.
2 They did a mailshot with the leaflets – went around putting leaflets through the letter boxes of local firms.
3 They put a small advertisement in the local newspaper, which produced the best results.
4 They put business cards up on notice boards in the university.

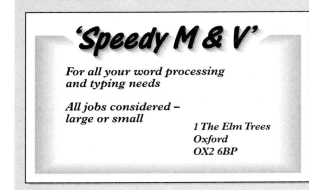

'Speedy M & V'

For all your word processing and typing needs

All jobs considered – large or small

1 The Elm Trees
Oxford
OX2 6BP

5 They advertised in the *Yellow Pages*, the local telephone directory and business directories.
6 They also made a point each morning, when they were not too busy, of selecting 10 companies each from the *Yellow Pages* and ringing them up.

Business future

Violet does the book keeping and they both do invoicing. They split all the other tasks between them. They also have a management meeting, just the two of them, to discuss what order to tackle the jobs in.

Monica and Violet are now getting to the stage where they have to submit the annual accounts for the first year. Therefore, they are looking for an accountant to audit those.

The current debate is whether they can buy more equipment and afford to start doing desktop publishing.

They also see themselves expanding into photocopying, and recruitment. Of course, it would take more people to handle all that, so they would have to take other people into the co-operative as equals.

Monica and Violet still keep in touch with the CDA. They tell them how they are doing and the CDA has helped them with tax problems, cashflow forecasts and with getting rate reductions.

Monica and Violet are now well into their second year. They have needed most of the income from the business to buy extra bits of equipment and furniture. They are much happier than being employed as secretaries by a company.

Read the above case study carefully and answer the following questions:

1 Why did Monica and Violet choose a co-operative type of ownership?
2 What are the disadvantages of this type of ownership?
3 How did Monica and Violet manage to raise money (finance) for their business?
4 What are Speedy M & V's main objectives?
5 How did the government help Monica and Violet?
6 In which industrial sector does Speedy M & V operate?
7 Get in touch with the Economic Development Department in your local council. Find out examples of co-operatives in your local area.

Franchise

Franchising is a type of business ownership which allows the owners to enjoy the benefits of running their own business without the risk of failure.

How does it work?

- In franchising, a big company, such as Kentucky Fried Chicken or Body Shop, allows someone to buy the right to use their products or techniques under their trade name.

- Franchising offers a 'ready-made' business opportunity for those who have the capital and are willing to work hard.

- Franchising is one of the fastest growing sectors of the economy and accounts for 20 per cent of retail sales.

Facts to remember about a franchise

1 A franchise business is in the private sector.
2 A franchise business is a special type of ownership.
3 The franchisee could be a sole trader, partnership or a company.
4 The franchisee is the person or business which buys a ready made business name
5 The franchiser is the person, business who sells a ready business name.
6 The franchisee pays the franchiser a sum of money to buy the business name.
7 The franchiser offers advice and training to the franchisee.
8 The franchisee pays a share of the profit at the end of the year to the franchiser.

Public sector ownership

The UK has a mixed economy. This means that, as well as many businesses being privately owned, there are others which are run by the government. These government-run enterprises make up what is known as the public sector. The public sector is made up of government departments (e.g. The Department of Education) and local council services (e.g. libraries and sport centres).

The public sector offers many goods and services to consumers. Some of these goods and services are financed entirely by money the government obtains from taxes or by borrowing (e.g. Education or National Health Service). They are offered to the consumer free of direct charge at the point of use.

The government produces goods and services that it is believed the private sector cannot or will not produce efficiently.

Why a public corporation?

There are number of reasons why public corporations have been set up:

1   To avoid waste of resources and confusion. For example, just imagine if more than one bank was allowed to print notes and coins in England and Wales!!

2   To protect jobs and key industries. Many people feel that the government has a responsibility to protect jobs, even if this means lower profits, for example, in the mining industry.

3   To set up and run important but non-profitable services. For example, although the BBC makes sure that most of its programmes are profitable and popular, it also operates a loss-making service in some areas, for example, producing special programmes for minority groups.

The BBC is a public corporation

> **Facts to remember about a public corporation**
> 1   It is in the public sector.
> 2   It is owned by the government.
> 3   It is controlled by the government.
> 4   It is run by a board of directors.
> 5   It provides a service to the national economy.
> 6   It protects jobs.

ACTIVITY

Find out examples of businesses which are owned by the local council in your area. You might need to ring the Economic Development Department in your local council.

ACTIVITY: WHAT IS THE TYPE OF OWNERSHIP?

Find out the type of ownership for each of the following businesses. Choose one of the following: sole trader, Limited Company, partnership, franchise, PLC, co-operative.

1   Keith Ellis owns a plumbing business called 'Quality Plumbing, Bathrooms and Tiling'. The business was established 21 years ago and offers 24-hour service. Keith makes all the business decisions and takes all the profit. However, everything he owns is at risk.

2   James and Asif own 'Happy Motoring Garage'. They have owned the business for 13 years. James and Asif know that if the business does not succeed everything they own is at risk. Therefore, although they employ 7 mechanics to work for them,

they run the business themselves, and make all the decisions. The business is going from strength to strength and James and Asif enjoy sharing the profit.

3   Smith Gordon and Sons is a removal business. It is a family business which was established in 1958 and since then it has been run and owned only by the Gordon family. Robert Gordon is the managing director and has shares in the business. There are also another four managers.

4   The Golden Arms Co, Ltd provides training. The Carter family take 15% of the profit every year.

5   Global Telecom is a large company which operates in the communication and telecommunication sector. The company is owned by hundreds of shareholders who share the business profit at the end of each year.

Business size (scale)

The European Commission has introduced one method of defining business size by numbers employed. For example:

Micro	1–5 employees
Small	6–99 employees
Medium	100–250 employees
Large	250+ employees

The market share of a business is its total sales as a percentage of the total sales of the industry in which it operates. For example, Marks & Spencer holds 15% of the UK clothing market.

It is important to point out that if a business employs fewer than 100 people, but has a 90 per cent share of the market in which it operates, the influence it exerts on that market will be greater than the influence exerted on its market by a business employing thousands, whose market share is only 20 per cent.

Some businesses can never grow very large because their market is small or geographically limited. Craft or luxury goods producers cannot become mass producers or they lose the essential features of their production. For example, Rolls-Royce cars, which are still partly hand made, remains a very small company when compared to Ford or Nissan.

Key Terms

Articles of Association One of the legal documents that the Registrar of Companies requires for the setting up of a company. It contains the day-to-day rules about how the company will operate and how the shareholders will be involved in the business.

Certificate of Incorporation A certificate issued by the UK Registrar of Companies at the stage of setting up a business when all the other required documents have been drawn up and registered.

Competition The idea that in a market one producer should always be rivalled by another producer to ensure that prices are kept low and the customer is not exploited.

Consumer A person who buys goods and services for his or her own use or consumption.

Deed of partnership The legal contract which controls how a partnership will be owned and organised.

Franchise A special type of ownership in the private sector, where a franchisee (a person or a business) buys a ready made business name/opportunity from a franchiser, such as McDonald's or Pizza Hut.

Franchisee The business or person that buys a franchise (a ready made business name or opportunity) from a franchiser.

Franchiser The business or person that sells a ready made business name or opportunity, e.g. Kentucky Fried Chicken and Body Shop.

Limited company A registered company where the liability of its members is restricted to the amount of capital they have put into the business.

Limited liability The owners of a company are liable for only the amount of capital that they have put into a company in the event of that company being wound up.

Memorandum of Association One of the documents that the owners of a company have to place with the Registrar of Companies when the company is formed. It contains the external affairs of the business, i.e. address, name, capital raised.

Mixed economy In this type of economy the government and the private sector share the ownership of resources. In a mixed economy, as in the UK, there is a private and a public sector.

Objective The particular goal that an organisation is trying to achieve.

Partnership A type of legal organisation for a business which has between two and twenty owners, and each partner has unlimited liability.

Private limited company A limited company that does not issue shares for public sale and its shares cannot be sold or transferred in the Stock Exchange, for example, Littlewoods.

Private sector That part of a mixed economy in which decisions about what to produce, how to produce it and where to produce it are made by private individuals. Virtually all businesses in the UK are now in the private sector.

Profit It is what the business has left after it has paid all the costs of producing its goods and services.

Public corporation A limited company which is owned by the government and is in the public sector, for example the BBC. A public corporation is run by a board of directors.

Public limited company (PLC) A form of limited company where that public are invited to buy shares on the Stock Exchange. Two people are the minimum number needed to set up a PLC, for example, Halifax PLC.

Public sector That part of a mixed economy where decisions about what to produce, how to produce it and where to produce it, are made by central government rather than being left to private individuals.

Public services Those services which are provided by the state, either free of charge or below the market price, to all members of the public, for example, the National Health Service.

Registrar of Companies The government official who is responsible for recording details of companies established in the UK.

Risk All business decisions involve an element of risk because there are a number of possible outcomes from a decision.

Scale The size of a business, which is sometimes measured by the number of people who work in the business.

Sales income The money that a business receives as a result of selling its products.

Sole trader A type of business organisation where one person is the owner and where that person has sole responsibility for the decisions in the business. He or she has unlimited liability.

Stock Exchange It is the place where buyers and sellers trade in shares, for example, London Stock Exchange.

Unlimited liability A form of liability in which the owners of a business are personally responsible for all the losses of the business, irrespective of the amount of capital they have invested in it, i.e. sole trade or partnership.

Chapter 6 Business activities

Introduction

Every business will have a key activity. Body Shop develops and sells beauty products. Even within an organisation as diverse as Richard Branson's Virgin (from airlines to soft drinks), there will be different divisions with their own focus. Someone working in the Cola part of the business will not be involved in developing financial services.

When you collect your evidence for this unit for your portfolio it is very important that you choose two contrasting (different) organisations. The pages that follow describe different types of business activity and will help you understand your chosen organisation.

Business organisations can be classified according to their production activity into three main sectors:

- primary sector
- secondary sector
- tertiary sector.

CASE STUDY – Boots Contract Manufacturing

Boots Contract Manufacturing (BCM) develops and manufactures a wide range of quality cosmetics and toiletry products. It is the largest contract manufacturer in Europe. It manufactures over 450 million units and produces over 4500 different products a year. The main product ranges are:

- over-the-counter medicines
- prescription medicine
- colour cosmetics
- suncare
- baby toiletries
- skincare
- haircare and styling
- vitamins
- oral hygiene.

BCM has seven factories and one major development laboratory. These are located on the company's main site at Nottingham and in Airdrie, Scotland.

Read the above case study carefully and answer the following questions:

1 What are the main advantages for BCM of producing more than one product?

2 In which industrial sector does BCM operate?

3 In which side of manufacturing is BCM specialised?

4 Find another 5 examples of manufacturing businesses or companies. You might find the information in the *Yellow Pages* or your local library.

Primary sector

The primary sector is concerned with the extraction (digging out) of basic raw materials provided by nature which are either above or below the earth's surface. Examples are farming, fishing and mining.

Secondary sector

The secondary sector consists of the manufacturing and construction industries; These products include: capital goods (goods purchased by businesses to make other products, e.g. a car manufacturer needs to buy metal products in order to be able to make cars); and consumer goods (products which you can buy in high-street shops). Raw materials are made into end products.

Tertiary sector

The tertiary sector is also called the service sector. The service sector includes retailing (selling clothes, food, furniture, computers etc), leisure and entertainment (cinemas, clubs, theme parks, hairdressers etc),

CASE STUDY – Northern Foods PLC

Northern Foods PLC is a leading UK food producer, focused on two distinct operating areas:

1 chilled foods
2 convenience foods.

Their Prepared Foods business is Britain's foremost supplier of high quality chilled foods under their own labels or those of major retailers. The company also has a strong branded presence in biscuits, fresh chilled dairy products, frozen food and savoury pastry products. The business brands which include Fox's, Ski, Goodfella's and Pork Farms, account for one-third of their sales.

The business has a very strong and competitive position in all markets, based on a consistent investment in high quality, low cost production facilities.

The company also owns the Smiths Flour Mills, which has five mills supplying wheat and other flours to Northern Foods companies and food manufacturers.

Read carefully the case study and answer the following questions:

Examples of some of the branded foods Northern Foods PLC makes

1 What are Northern Foods PLC's main business activities?
2 Which business activities take part in the primary sector?
3 How important are primary sector activities for the business?
4 Which business activities take part in the secondary sector?
5 Which business activities take part in

activities such as banking and insurance and public services such as education, the police and the fire service.

ACTIVITY

In your groups, identify three businesses in the primary sector, three businesses in the secondary sector, and three businesses in the tertiary sector. You can use the *Yellow Pages* to help you to find out about businesses.

ACTIVITY: WORKFORCE IN THE INDUSTRIAL SECTORS

1   Make a list of the occupations of 15 adults who are known to you (members of your family or neighbours).
2   With your tutor, decide how many of the 15 belong to the primary, secondary and tertiary sectors.
3   Present the numbers of the adults working in different sectors in a spreadsheet.
4   Combine your totals with those of other members of the group.
5   Draw a diagram or bar chart to present the percentage of people working in each sector.
6   How do you think this diagram might look in 50 years' time?

Wholesale activities

A wholesaler is the person or business which is the middle person between the manufacturer and the retailer. The wholesaler buys goods from a manufacturer in bulk to sell on to retailers.

A manufacturer will normally seek the services of wholesalers. They carry the cost of storing goods and transporting them to the final customer. The wholesalers bear some of the risk of non-payment which a manufacturer might otherwise run. The wholesaler has to pay the manufacturer of the goods and then try to get the money back when the goods are re-sold. The wholesaler may make a loss if the goods involved go out of fashion. As well as advising retailers about new products, the wholesaler will inform the manufacturer of changes in taste and demand by adjusting their own purchases.

There has been a growth of wholesalers which sell direct to the general public. These large discount stores sell furniture and other household products with relatively poor customer facilities. This is often the case for building materials or consumer durable goods such as furniture.

Wholesales markets exist throughout the country where goods such as meat, fruit and

Smithfield's Market is a wholesale meat market

fish are sold in the very early hours of the morning. The most popular wholesale markets are:

- Meat – Smithfields Market, London
- Fish – North Quay, Isle of Dogs, London
- Fruit- Nine Elms, London.

Despite the advantages of the wholesale service, the manufacturer may not use it if it believes it is possible to provide the same service itself at cheaper prices.

ACTIVITY

1 What are the advantages of wholesaler services for manufacturer and customers?
2 Find out five examples of wholesalers in your local area.
3 Find out on which day in your local area the wholesale market for fish or fruit takes place.

Other service activities

Services are the commercial activities that assist trade in its job of selling goods and services. Examples include banking, finance, insurance and transport. Financial services now account for one-fifth and services in general for two-thirds of all UK output.

Banking services

Commercial or 'high street' banks such as Barclays, Lloyds TSB and NatWest, are public limited companies, and one of the institutions which provide business capital. They can offer both long-term capital, in terms of loans and mortgages, and short-term loans, for example, overdrafts. The

commercial banks also provide a wide range of other services to businesses.

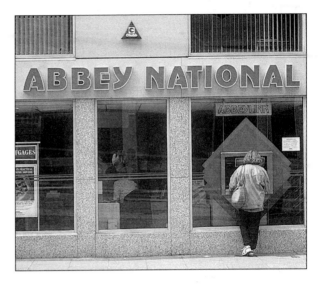

The main business activity of a bank is to provide a service

Healthcare services

Some businesses exist mainly to provide healthcare services to customers. You learned early on in this unit in chapter 5 that the public sector is made up of public corporations, nationalised industries, central government departments (e.g., Department of Health) and local government services (e.g., council-run leisure centres). The main aim here is not to make profit, but to provide a service for the community.

The UK healthcare service is provided mainly by the government, and called the National Health Service. It is paid for through taxes and national insurance contributions. Many organisations work together to provide the total service, for example, hospitals, family planning clinics, and General Practitioner Clinics (GPs).

However, there are still healthcare services on a smaller scale which are provided by the private sector, for example, BUPA.

ACTIVITIES

1 Look in the *Yellow Pages* (under the hospital and clinic sections) for the list of organisations which provide healthcare services to the local community in your area.
2 Find out how many private hospitals there are in your local area which provide private healthcare services.
3 Interview 10 of your friends, neighbours or relatives to ask them about their views on the healthcare service they get.
   a How many of them have private health insurance?
   b What are their views about the quality of the services which are provided by the National Health Service?
4 Collect a leaflet from one of the private hospitals in your local area. Check what services it offers and how much they cost.

Leisure and sport

Some businesses are mainly set up to provide leisure and/or sports services. Stadiums and leisure centres are mainly owned by the local council to provide these services for the local community.

Charity activities

Charities are part of what is called the voluntary sector. Their purpose is very different from most other private sector organisations. They exist to promote and support a cause or activity and, as such, do not have a profit motive. This is not to say that they do not make profits. In fact, many charities have subsidiaries that sell goods or services but their profits are re-invested to support the main charitable aim.

ACTIVITIES

1 Collect an article which describes a charitable event in your local area. Find out who organised the event and what the main purpose was.
2 Visit your local library and find out the addresses of the charitable organisations in your local area.

Transport activities

Businesses use transport to distribute their products to customers. Whether the manufacturers deliver products to wholesalers, retailers or directly to customers, they need some sort of transport. Therefore, all businesses one way or another have transport activities as part of their trading activities.

There are a number of conflicting pressures on a firm when it comes to choosing how to deliver or distribute its product to customers. Final decisions will be based on the:

• cost of transport
• type of market
• type and the image of the product.

The cost of transport depends on the method of transport to be used. In choosing which method of transport to use a firm must consider the cost, urgency, distance, the product, and the safety and security of this product.

Once again the firm is faced with a range of conflicting pressures when making its choice. For example, the safest method of transport might be too slow or too

(contd. on page 80)

CASE STUDY – Calles and Cakes

Maggie Smith and Joan Curtis design and make cakes for special occasions such as weddings and birthdays. Their business is run from Maggie's home. They spend a lot of time in the kitchen, baking and decorating, but they also have to order and collect the ingredients, keep accounts and deliver the finished cakes to customers.

Until a few months ago, most of their business came from family and friends. However, when they started advertising in the local paper, the orders came flooding in, mainly by telephone. They also received an offer from a top department store for them to supply 'designer' cakes for their customers.

Joan and Maggie were delighted that their business was growing but it gave them a problem. With all the increased orders they were, inevitably, spending more time out and about. They realised that they could lose customers, or potential customers, who rang and found the phone unanswered or engaged. Their families were out at work or school all day, so they couldn't help. Their income, although growing, would not stretch to employing staff. They had to rethink their communications needs. They found some simple and inexpensive solutions:

1   installing telephone extensions into Maggie's kitchen and into her spare room which doubles as their office
2   having a telephone in the kitchen with a memory to store numbers which they ring regularly

3   having a telephone answering machine which picks up calls whilst they are out or too busy to answer the phone
4   making use of relatively new telephone network services, 'Call waiting' and 'Call diversion'.

Read the above case study carefully and answer the following questions:

1   How can the new telecommunication techniques help Maggie and Joan to run the business?
2   Find out from your local BT shop the services which each of the above telecommunication options can provide Maggie and Joan.
3   How do you think this could help their business?
4   What other telecommunication solutions can Maggie and Joan use for their business?

expensive. In a business operating for profit the main consideration will usually be to keep costs as low as possible.

- fleet of cars
- fresh bread.

ACTIVITY: WHICH METHOD OF TRANSPORT?

1 Sort out the following methods of transport, starting with the most expensive one first: road transport, rail transport, sea transport, air transport, inland waterway.
2 Suggest the best method (quickest, safest, cheapest) method to transport the following products:
   - oil and gas
   - timber or coal
   - fresh flowers
   - bricks

Communication and telecommunication

Some businesses specialise in communication and telecommunication products and services. For example, CableTel and BT are the most popular businesses in this sector. The two companies are in competition and each of them is trying to attract more customers.

Communications are becoming increasingly important in our modern life. With a fast style of life and people becoming more time-conscious, the use of communication services and products is increasing rapidly. For example, the mobile phone market is growing rapidly and prices are becoming lower and more affordable.

CASE STUDY – In touch with BT

'Keeping in touch has always been our business at BT. That, after all, is what telephone networks are made for. But to our mind, there is much more to it than giving you a fast and simple way of contacting your family and friends. We constantly provide our customers with the latest communication products and services. Telephones and answer machines with the latest technology, fax machines and mobile phones are examples of our communication products. Our network service includes high quality services which BT provides to customers, for example, Call Waiting, Call Diversion, Three Way Calls and Call Reminders, etc. But the improvements to our communication service don't end there. We also recognise that we need to be in touch with what customers want from us.'

Read carefully the above case study about BT and answer the following questions:

1 What are the main communication activities for BT?
2 Who are BT's main competitors?
3 What other communication services does BT offer? You can get in touch with your local BT shop or ring 0800 622302 to find more information about BT communication products.
4 Find from the *Yellow Pages* other businesses which operate in the communication sector. Make a list of them.

Key Terms

Charities Any of the organisations, such as those often found in the voluntary sector of an economy, for example, Oxfam. They exist to promote and support a cause or activity and, as such, do not have a profit motive.

Consumer A person who buys goods and services for his or her own use or consumption.

Goods A general term used for the wide variety of visible items which are produced by a business, e.g. cars, computers etc.

Primary production The stage of economic activity that involves the extraction of natural resources from the land so that they can be used in the secondary stage of production, for example, mining, farming and fishing.

Production Describes the way a business uses financial and human resources to make raw materials into an end product that is consumed by someone else.

Recession Period of time when the economy is slowing down or output is falling.

Retailing The last stage in the channel of distribution which involves the final selling to consumers of the goods and services that have been produced.

Secondary production The manufacturing of products from raw materials or other manufactured products, for example, wood into tables.

Service A term used to describe invisible items, such as banking, insurance, education, which are provided by a business or person.

Tertiary production The provision of services which help to support the other two sectors of economic activity, the primary and the secondary sectors. It includes professional services, administration transport, banking, insurance and the public services, including health and education.

Wholesaler The middle person between producers and consumers. The wholesaler plays the important role of breaking down the bulk of what is produced by the manufacturer, and delivering the goods in smaller quantities to retailers which then sell them to customers.

Chapter 7 The location of businesses

No matter where you live in Britain it is extremely probable that the type of industries in your area have changed considerably over the last 50 years. Traditionally, the North of England was renowned for the heavy industries: steel, ship building, coal mining, and for cotton and wool manufacture. The Midlands were famous for car production, pottery and engineering. The South East had a range of manufacturing companies plus canneries, refineries, tobacco companies and warehouses near the docks. Cornwall and South Wales were mining communities, the first for tin and the second for coal.

Current industrial trends

The trend today is for newer industries to emerge, for example, in computers and electronics, light engineering and telecommunications, together with a growth in the service industry.

Automation (the use of modern technology) has reduced the number of people employed and the size of factories and in nearly all areas industries have moved out of town and inner city areas to new industrial areas and parks on the outskirts – away from residential areas.

Factors affecting location

One of the earliest decisions any entrepreneur (owner) has to make is where to locate his or her business in order to be successful. To do this, he or she has to make a careful assessment of costs. The ideal location would be the one where costs are minimised. The entrepreneur would need to look at the benefits which each area has to offer as well as any government help which might be available.

Factors affecting the location of a business can be divided into three main areas:

*   costs of location
*   benefits of location
*   government influence on location (help and constraints).

Costs and benefits affecting location

For every potential site, the business needs to look at a combination of factors to weigh up the advantages and disadvantages of each. The site chosen will be the one that provides the best overall result, and not necessarily the best in every category. All of the factors which are going to be mentioned below have to be considered, assessed and ranked in order of importance to make the final choice about where to locate the business.

I The need to be close to customers

The market is made up of the customers of a particular product or service. The market will almost always be a crucial factor in deciding location. Service industries (such as shops) need to locate near their customers, and large shopping centres need to locate near to major centres of population. For example, the Metro Centre outside Newcastle and Meadowhall outside Sheffield are both located near large cities and the motorway network.

Meadowhall, Sheffield, is conveniently located near the motorway

2 Nearness to raw materials and natural resources

Businesses in the primary sector generally need to be close to the natural resources which they use, for example, coal mining in Yorkshire, quarrying in North Wales. Likewise, fishing and forestry can take place only near their raw materials. The primary sector includes farming which takes place where there is arable or grazing land for crops or livestock.

Businesses in the secondary sector, i.e. manufacturers, sometimes locate near their raw materials or near the ports through which the raw materials are imported. This is especially true when the raw materials are bulky and, therefore, expensive to transport. For example, Britain's steel industry was located in towns such as Scunthorpe because these places are close to the iron ore which is an essential ingredient of steel production. Businesses which need to be located near the raw materials they use are known as bulk-decreasing industry. This is because the raw materials are bulky but the final product is not. Bulk-increasing industries, on the other hand, need to be located near their markets, because their final product is either bulky or fragile.

3 Transport costs

Different industries have different transport needs. Two major influences are the pull of the market and of the raw material. These depend on whether the industry is bulk increasing or bulk decreasing. However, many industries' markets are spread out and raw materials come from several suppliers, for example, the car industry.

4 Land costs

Land costs vary considerably nationally and some firms might need a large square footage. They might, therefore, be influenced by the cheaper rents and property prices found in some areas. For example, the cost of land is higher in the South of England than in the North.

5 Cost of premises

Firms generally need to buy or hire premises on which to carry out their business. Shops will pay high rents for premises only if the location brings sufficient revenue. For example, a jewellers' shop might be profitable enough to be sited on a town's most expensive street, but a less profitable store selling second-hand motor parts probably could not afford such a site.

6 Supply of skilled and experienced labour

The availability of labour might attract firms to an area, particularly if that labour force has the skills the firms require. Increasingly, a key factor for many businesses is the availability of a supply of labour that is skilful and experienced. It is important for a company to know that it will be able to employ workers who are capable and competent. For example, there is no point in McDonald's opening a new restaurant in an area where there is a shortage of people available to work in the business.

Certain areas have colleges which offer training specifically for local industry, for example, agricultural colleges in rural areas that specialise in farming, or engineering courses in colleges near manufacturing plants.

7 Safety

Some industries have to locate their premises well away from high density population levels and their location is limited, for example, nuclear power industries.

8 Waste disposal

Certain industries produce considerable waste and the costs associated with the disposal of this might affect location. Some plants are on rivers or the coast so that waste products such as hot water can be pumped away. Also, large chemical plants and nuclear power stations are sited away from towns and cities so that, if there is an accident, fewer people will be affected.

9 Communication

The accessibility of motorways, ports and airports have become increasingly important locational factors over recent years. A sound infrastructure (the term is used for network, bridges, building, motorway) creates the opportunity to trade with ease, for example, South East England.

In the last century many businesses located near the railways for the same reason. Some specialist companies which produce small, expensive goods with a worldwide market locate near airports.

10 Regional advantages

A number of facilities for certain industries might be concentrated in particular regions. A concentration of similar industries and subsidiary industries could well attract a firm, as could skilled labour, local research facilities and commercial markets.

11 Government influence

In the UK, some areas have higher levels of unemployment than others. The main reason the government may wish to influence the location of industry is to improve the regional balance of employment; in other words, to move production into regions of high unemployment and areas where industry has declined. These areas of the country, such as Newcastle (its shipbuilding industry declined, creating high unemployment), receive investment aid from the UK government and from the EU.

The government also restricts the areas where businesses may locate in order to protect the environment.

12 History and tradition

Some businesses are located where they are because they have a long tradition of being in that place. For example, some of the finest makers of quality pottery, such as

Wedgwood, have always been located in Staffordshire. This has meant that the name Staffordshire itself has come to be associated with quality pottery. Also, the fact that pottery has been made in this area for a long time means that there is a good supply of people with the sorts of skills needed to work in this industry. Therefore, a pottery business located in Staffordshire would probably be reluctant to move from the area, and the owners of a new pottery business might be attracted to locate their business there.

Other factors affecting location

1 The personal preference of the owner

In some cases, the personal decision of the owner will be the deciding factor. It is said that Detroit became the motor car capital of the USA because Henry Ford chose to live near there. This factor can be equally important if a location has a negative image, i.e. depressed and contain declining industries. In this case, owners of new businesses might not wish to locate there.

2 The location of other businesses

In some cases, such as shoe shops and estate agents, businesses cluster together because customers 'shop round'. Any shop or business not near the others will be at a disadvantage because most potential customers will visit only the main cluster. On the other hand, businesses such as newsagents tend to locate away from rivals. If they are too close together they will split the market and lose sales.

Businesses with more than one location

For some businesses, even though the head office is located in a particular area, they operate in other areas. For example, the Boots Head Office is in Nottingham but the company has stores everywhere in the UK. This means that the Boots market is national. Boots and Marks & Spencer might have more than one site or store in the same town. Marks & Spencer's Head Office is in London and the business not only expands nationally but also internationally. The business trades in over 683 locations across the UK and 30 locations abroad. Ford, ICI, IBM, Shell and Coca-Cola sell their products worldwide.

ACTIVITY

Find out from the *Yellow Pages* the following:

1 a business which has more than one site in your local area.
2 a business which has different sites and location throughout the country.

Key Terms

Bulk-decreasing industry An industry which is located near the natural resources, because the raw material is bulky, for example, stainless steel in Sheffield.

Bulk-increasing industry An industry which is located near the market because the final product is bulky or fragile, for example, biscuits and garden furniture.

Chapter 8 How competitors affect business activities

Any business that hopes to be successful needs to be aware of the needs and wants of its customers and to work hard to satisfy and meet these needs and wants.

In a mixed economy such as the UK, where the ownership of resources is shared between the private and the public sectors, there are elements of competition. Businesses in the private sector are in constant competition to attract more customers by using a variety of methods.

BP (British Petroleum) is a very large business which operates nationally and internationally. Internationally the business's main competitors include Shell, Esso and Texaco, and at the national level, state and independent oil companies. In Europe, the company is in competition with supermarkets and hypermarkets, e.g. Tesco and Sainsbury's petrol stations, for fuel sales among customers.

ACTIVITY: TYPE OF COMPETITION

Fill in the following sentence using one of three words: **local**, **national**, **international**

1   A grocery business in Huddersfield which is owned by two partners mainly faces .... competition.
2   River Island is a private limited company which has different stores throughout the UK, and it therefore faces .... competition.
3   Marks and Spencer has stores not only in the UK but also in Europe and the USA.

Therefore it faces .... and .... competition.

Methods of competition

In order to satisfy the wants and needs of the customers the business must carefully combine the following elements: the right **Product**, at the right **Price** in the right **Place** with the right **Promotion** methods. This is known as the 4 Ps.

Businesses compete in different ways:

1   developing new products
2   improving existing products
3   changing their prices
4   developing new packaging and design
5   improving customer service and building up a new reputation.

Businesses compete by making their products look and sound different from those made by their competitors. This is called adding value to the product. Value can be added in various different ways, for example: improving the packaging and design of the product; giving the product an attractive brand name and image; displaying the product on the shelves in an exciting way; providing better customer service.

Developing new products

For a business to be successful and able to compete it needs to respond to changes in:

• customer needs and wants
• customer attitudes

- customer tastes
- the environment
- economic conditions
- the climate
- competition
- supplier attitudes
- the law
- fashion
- technology.

Improving customer service

Having sold a product to the customer, all of the departments in the business must see that the consumer is content with the product.

Changing their prices

The actual prices that a business charges for its products will depend on whether it is trying to win a massive share of the market, or whether it wants consumers to buy its product because it is different to, or better than, a rival's products. Setting the right price is important to:

- attract more customers
- compete with rival businesses (competitors)
- make a healthy profit.

ACTIVITY

1 In your group, choose 20 different products, and find out the price of each in three different supermarkets. Enter your findings in a table.
   a Add up the total prices for the 20 products for each supermarket.
   b Which supermarket is the cheapest?
   c Which supermarket is the most expensive?
   d Find out if people you know who regularly shop in these places agree with your findings.

2 Choose one of the products which is sold at different prices by different supermarkets, for example, bread.
   a Find out which firm charges the lowest price.
   b Find out which firm charges the highest price.
   c Find out which firm charges an average price.
   d Ask people you know who regularly go shopping which price they would be prepared to pay from the above range of prices for this product.

CASE STUDY — Boots and the competition

John Boot was born in Radcliffe-on-Trent in 1815 and his early life was spent as an agricultural worker on local farms. He travelled to attend services at the Wesleyan chapels in the Lace Market area of Nottingham. It was a poor area and John Boot became involved in chapel affairs and local schemes to improve living conditions within his community.

At that time, herbal remedies were

popular among poor people who could not afford the services of a physician. In 1849, with the assistance of his mother, father-in-law and the support of the local Methodist Community, John opened the British and American Botanic Establishment at 6 Goose Gate, hoping to provide comfort to the needy, as well as a reasonable living for his family. John and his wife Mary gave consultations to poor people and prepared many remedies themselves. However, in 1860, after hard work and ill health, John died at the age of 45. His wife Mary and their son Jesse took over the management of the shop.

When Jesse Boot reached the age of 21, he became a partner in the business, which then began to trade under the name of M & J Boot, Herbalists. To beat his competitors, Jesse cut his prices and asked customers to pay cash rather than take credit. He advertised extensively and began to sell an ever wider range of stock; 'over 2000 articles' as one advert claimed. In 1877 Jesse took sole control of the shop and became the largest dealer in herbal medicines and one of the busiest shopkeepers in Nottingham.

The business needed more space. With financial support from several local business contacts, Jesse took on a lease, and converted a property at 16-20 Goosegate into a shop. It contained the retail and wholesale shops, workshops, stockrooms, office and living accommodation. In 1883 the business became a private limited company.

Following the expansion of the Goosegate shop, Jesse wanted to repeat its success elsewhere in Nottingham. He bought up vacant properties across the city – often

sites in poorer areas where properties were reasonably cheap. To beat his competitors, and to promote the business further, each new shop was opened with a great deal of publicity.

The success of the business provoked a hostile reaction from many fellow chemists, who criticised the cut-price tactics and tried to cast doubt on some of Boots' products.

In 1879 the House of Lords supported the right of general stores and companies, as well as traditional chemists, to dispense medicines. Jesse therefore sought a qualified pharmacist in order to offer dispensing services. To build up public confidence in the quality and purity of his products, in 1888 Jesse renamed the business Boots Pure Drug Company.

Read the above case study carefully and answer the following questions:

1   What were the main business objectives for Boots?

2   Who were Boots' main competitors?

3   Why do you think the local community supported John Boot?

4   What was Boots' main product?

5   How did John Boot come up with the idea of developing this product?

6   When Jesse Boot took over the management of the business, one of his main aims was to beat the competition. Explain how John responded to his competitors.

7   What were the main factors which Jesse considered in choosing the location of his shops?

Key Terms

Competition The idea that in a market one producer should always be rivalled by another producer to ensure that prices are kept low and the customer is not exploited.

Competitive business Where a business is more able to compete to attract more customers.

Demand The desire or need of a consumer backed up by the ability to pay over a period of time.

Efficiency The effective use of a business's resources without waste of time or materials.

Price The market value of goods and services that are bought by consumers and firms.

Product development The process of a business bringing new products into the market or adapting and improving upon existing products.

Value added Adding value to a product to make it look more attractive for customers without adding too much to the cost.

Want The desire or need of a consumer to buy goods or services; if backed up by the ability to pay, this becomes demand.

Chapter 9 Businesses and their stakeholders

Businesses make decisions regarding their objectives, activities and location. Stakeholders are the people who can influence these decisions. You are going to learn:

- who they are
- how they can influence businesses
- how businesses react to this influence.

All organisations have a responsibility to their stakeholders. Stakeholders are individuals and groups who have a stake in the running of the organisation. Stakeholders may include shareholders, suppliers, customers, employees and managers, as well as the government and society as a whole. Stakeholders can influence business decisions in a variety of ways, such as the following.

- Customers need to be satisfied; they have a choice as to where they buy products.
- Employees can choose whether or not to work for a certain business organisation.
- Shareholders carefully select organisations in which to invest their money.
- The government can impose rules and regulations on businesses to ensure that customers are not exploited and employees are working in safe conditions.

Therefore, to satisfy stakeholders, a business needs to develop codes of conduct, stating clearly the way in which the business will carry out its activities.

Shareholders

The main role of shareholders in a business is:

- to vote or elect directors who make

decisions on their behalf
- to invest in the business, so they have a right to a share in the profits.

Shareholders will play no part in the day-to-day running or management of the organisation.

ACTIVITY

Discuss in your groups the following sentence.

'Shareholders exercise influence on businesses to increase and maximise the profits.'

The Government

The government can impose rules and regulations on business activities to ensure that:

- business activities are legal
- business activities are safe and do not harm the community
- customers are not exploited
- the product which a business sells is safe
- employees are protected in the workplace
- business activities do not harm the environment.

Employees

Employees are the workforce which is employed by a business. Employees could be either the management team, supervisors, or the rest of the workforce.

Employers could be sole traders, partners in a partnership or a limited company.

With the extension of education and improvements in living standards,

The employees of a bike shop are stakeholder's in the business's activities

employees demand more than financial rewards. As people spend a large part of their life at work, it is important that they get some satisfaction from their jobs.

Not all jobs can give satisfaction, and people have different ideas of what constitutes a good job. For some people pay is the most important factor, while others will have some other priority. Often it is a combination of many factors which makes a job satisfying.

The following are just some of these factors:

- pay and opportunity for wage increases
- promotion prospects
- working hours and times of attendance
- holiday arrangements
- conditions in which work is carried out
- style of management
- communication in the workplace
- training.

Management

Managers are employees in the business who act on behalf of shareholders (who elected them), and their main role is to protect shareholders' interests.

CASE STUDY – Business Council planning action

The staff and workforce at Harwood PLC have created a joint council to discuss industrial action. The move at one of the companies in West Yorkshire is a direct result of a pay offer they labelled "miserly". One of their first tasks will be to co-ordinate industrial action at the company next week.

Ms Janet Ayton, the trade union representative in the company and chairman of the new group, said 'This is the second year that staff had been offered a pay rise below inflation. Over the same two years the Managing Director has seen his pay rise by a staggering 47%.'

The workforce in the company are among the lowest paid in the country and all are seriously overworked.

Read the case study carefully and answer the following questions:

1 What is the workforce at Harwood PLC angry about?

2 What sort of action are the workforce threatening to take?

3 How does the workforce in Harwood PLC exercise pressure on management?

Customers

A successful business is a business which identifies customer needs and wants and works hard to satisfy these needs and wants. Therefore, customers exercise constant pressures on businesses to make them develop, and supply, the right **Product** at the right **Price** in the right **Place**.

ACTIVITY: CUSTOMERS AND PRESSURES

Customers are very important stakeholders who influence businesses. In this activity you are going to learn how businesses should respond to customer pressures.

Using your business knowledge and the information above, try to complete the following statements with the words in the box.

Customers can influence businesses to:

1 .... existing products.

2 .... new products.

3 .... that they need and want.

4 .... to changes in lifestyle.

| develop |
| respond |
| provide |
| improve |

Competitors

Businesses are in constant competition to satisfy customer needs and wants. Competitors influence business decisions in one way or another. For a business to survive in the market it must be able to compete by offering lower prices, better quality products, or produce new products.

ACTIVITY: THE ROLE OF COMPETITORS

Using your business knowledge, complete the following statements with the words in the box.

Competitors influence businesses to:

1 .... their prices.

2 .... the quality of their products.

3 .... new products.

4 .... new technology.

| reduce |
| improve |
| provide |
| develop |

ACTIVITY

In your groups, think of two or three businesses which are in the same area of production, for example, supermarkets, car manufacturers, hairdressers, etc. Discuss how these businesses compete with each other and who benefits from this competition.

Local community and its concerns for the environment

The local community can be a very important external influence on business decisions. For example, the local community might protest against the building of a new supermarket, a pub or an industrial estate in the local area. Businesses are also aware that their customers are the local community. Therefore, one of the prime aims of any business is to gain local community support for their activities.

Promoting businesses' image in the local community

Most businesses seek to establish good relations with the local community through such activities such as sponsoring schools' computers, raising money for charitable events, and participating in school and college activities.

Inviting employers to participate in group activities at school or college doesn't only strengthen the links with local firms but also:

1   enables you to engage actively with new subject matter

2   challenges and encourages you to participate in practical activities

3   adds a touch of reality to group activities

4   promotes your communication and presentation skills

5   adds more fun to the learning environment, as students usually like to see and work with different people

6   allows you to explore opportunities for short-term work placement

7   enhances your confidence in working with strangers.

ACTIVITIES

1   Look in your local newspaper for an example of a pressure group in your local area; for example, local residents protest at the building of a new road, supermarket or an industrial estate near where they live. Express your views on the problem.

2   In your groups describe briefly an event in your school or college where employers from local firms were invited to take part. Try to evaluate their contribution to the event and to the school or college.

CASE STUDY –
Battle win for noise row hotel

A hotel owner has won his battle for a new entertainment licence after a row with local residents over noise.

Mr Robert Grey, the owner of Come Inn Hotel, says he is doing all he can to reduce noise and has employed a noise consultant in a bid to end complaints. Mr Grey's entertainment licence has been renewed by Calderdale Council Licensing sub-committee, despite objections from local residents. Six people wrote letters asking councillors to pull the plug on the permit because of loud music, late night parties, rowdiness and door slamming.

Some residents from the recently built development near the hotel said the situation was making their lives a misery.

Mr Grey who has owned the premises for 15 years said he was also working closely with the council's environmental department and the noise has always been monitored.

Mr Grey said he had received no complaints before the development was built last year.

Read the above case study carefully and answer the following:

• What did the local residents complain about?

• Why do the local residents put pressure on Mr Grey's business?

• How might this pressure affect Mr Grey's business?

• Why did the local council permit Mr Grey to continue his business?

Other examples of businesses' involvement with the local community

CASE STUDY – McDonald's and the environment

McDonald's is very aware that the local communities in which it operates are an important stakeholder in its business activities. Because many of these communities are concerned with the environmental issues, McDonald's is keen to let them know about its commitment to helping the environment. McDonald's produces literature about its policies on subjects such as diet and the preservation of the rain forests and also sponsors a number of environmental initiatives, many in local communities. Examples of McDonald's environmental work include the following.

Conservation

McDonald's does not purchase beef whose production threatens tropical rain forests anywhere in the world. It does not use any South American or Central American beef for hamburgers sold in the USA or Canada. Only 100% pure USDA-inspected domestic US beef is used. McDonald's also monitors suppliers' plants and checks government stamps to make sure that suppliers do not sell any beef that has been imported from another area.

Litter control

Since 1988, McDonald's, in partnership with the Tidy Britain group, has sponsored the 'Bin it for Britain' and 'National Spring Clean' campaigns. 'Bin it for Britain' is designed to encourage good litter behaviour in young people. Every day McDonald's staff regularly collect all rubbish (not only McDonald's packaging) dropped in the vicinity of the restaurant.

Many of McDonald's restaurants organise their litter-related competitions with local schools, colleges and youth groups.

Recycling

McDonald's, in line with its stated policy of fostering quality environmental practices, helped to promote recycling of aluminium cans in Staffordshire by working with the local authority, community groups, schools, colleges and the Aluminium Can Recycling Association (ACRA).

Built environment

McDonald's takes a sensitive approach to its built environment, working closely with planning and conservation officers to preserve buildings of architectual merit and to improve the townscape.

McDonald's has successfully integrated into many listed buildings and conservation areas including restaurants in Windsor, Cambridge, York and Shrewsbury as well as Tower Hill and Fleet Street in London.

In many towns McDonald's has invested considerable sums in restoring old buildings, often putting back architectural details that have been lost. York, Chester and Stratford-upon-Avon are prime examples.

After reading this case study with your tutor, answer the following questions:

1 Many of McDonald's restaurants organise their litter-related competitions with local schools, colleges and youth groups. Visit McDonald's restaurant(s) in your local area and find out if any are or have been involved in litter-related competitions with local schools and colleges.

2 Find out if your school or college has been involved in any of the litter-related competitions with McDonald's or other businesses.

3 Find out examples of other businesses which support the environment.

Stakeholders and conflict of interests

It is obvious that stakeholders have different interests and see business success in different ways. The criteria for success vary from one group to another, depending on their interests and the role they play to influence the business.

CASE STUDY — The Body Shop approach to stakeholders

In 1976, Anita Roddick opened the first Body Shop in Brighton, selling 25 naturally based skin and hair care products. The Body Shop International PLC has over 1500 shops in 47 countries selling more than 400 different products. The Body Shop, however, is not just a highly successful manufacturer and retailer of toiletries and cosmetics. The whole organisation is committed to issues such as respect for human rights, animal and environmental protection.

Although the business's main objective is to maximise profit and look after the environment, The Body Shop recognises that there are a number of different groups in society with an interest in its performance. These groups, or stakeholders, may have different priorities. The way the business operates affects them, and their interests may influence the way the business sets its objectives and how it seeks to achieve them.

The management team of The Body Shop must run the business in such a way as to satisfy the different groups of stakeholders. This may not be easy and conflicts of interest may develop.

1 Employees

The Body Shop directly employs 2500 staff at the headquarters in Littlehampton and all company-owned facilities and shops in the UK. Fair income, promotion and training opportunities are methods of motivating employees to work hard.

Workers' rights include a safe, healthy working atmosphere, fair wage rate and no discrimination on the grounds of race, gender, or sexual orientation.

2 Customers

In the 52 weeks to 28 February 1997, The Body Shop recorded 87 million customer transactions. This means that every 0.4 seconds, someone, somewhere buys something from The Body Shop. Customer care therefore has become a crucial part of the trading policy. The Body Shop customers demand not only high quality, value-for-money products, but also recognise the need for environmental responsibility. The customer needs to be well informed in order to make responsible choices.

3 Suppliers

The Body Shop has hundreds of suppliers, all of whom have their own stakeholders to satisfy. For smaller suppliers, profit and income may be significant, but also discounts and payment periods may be important.

4 Community Trade suppliers

This is a group of 25 suppliers in 13 countries (as at May 1997), such as Brazil, Ghana and Bangladesh, specifically chosen because they are struggling economically. The Body Shop believes that this trade should be more than the simple exchange of goods and currency (money). It wants to help create livelihoods and support development in those countries. The Body Shop offers its knowledge and training in exchange for materials from these countries. These communities clearly have a stake in the future success of the organisation.

5 Shareholders

The Body Shop is a public limited company and its shareholders are the legal owners. Although the shareholders recognise the company's social and economic commitments, the share price remains important. A falling share price can wipe millions of pounds off the value of a company. In theory, if the shareholders are dissatisfied with the performance of the company, they can remove the Board of Directors at the Annual General Meeting.

6 Local community

Although The Body Shop has many objectives, it is part of a local community and, therefore, has a responsibility to the community in which it operates and the local economy. For example, in a town with unemployment above the national average, The Body Shop is the second largest employer. Job creation is therefore very important to the town. The Body Shop also allows its employees paid time off to do voluntary work in their local community.

With your tutor, read the above case study carefully and answer the following question:

The above case shows that The Body Shop has several stakeholders who have an interest in the business. In this task you are going to match the following statements (the interests of a stakeholder) with the right stakeholder.

Statements

1 'I want to be heard, I have questions I need answering. I ensure that my voice matters.'

2 'So you don't test your products or ingredients on animals, but how do I know your suppliers are not doing it?'

3 'I want to know what I have in common with other suppliers to The Body Shop. I want to share my experience and learn how we can improve together.'

4 'What I want is a livelihood that will last. So that my daughters can live a life that is better than mine.'

5 'How do I balance concern for human rights with my financial return?'

6 'Everybody is trying to tell us about the community – politicians, business people, everybody. Instead of telling us, why don't they include us? Don't we all belong?'

Stakeholders:

a local community

b customers

c shareholders

d suppliers

e employees

f community trade suppliers.

Unit 2 Test your knowledge

This is a quick test to help you check how much you have understood.

In the following statements, there are some right and some wrong answers. Circle only the **wrong** answer/answers.

1   In a sole trader business:

    a   the owner has limited liability
    b   the owner runs the business
    c   the owner can employ other people to work for him
    d   the owner takes all the profit.

2   The scale of a business refers to:

    a   the type of market the product is sold in
    b   the size of business
    c   the location of the business.

3   In the UK the private sector:

    a   is owned by the government
    b   is owned by private individuals
    c   is controlled by private enterprises.

4   The public sector in the UK mainly exists:

    a   to provide services to the local and national community
    b   to compete with the private sector
    c   to make profit.

5   A public limited company is:

    a   owned by the public
    b   in the public sector
    c   in the private sector.

6   For a private limited company:

    a   business affairs are public
    b   business is privately owned by family and friends

    c   the ownership is in the private sector.

7   A bulk-decreasing industry is an industry which:

    a   is located near the raw materials
    b   is located near the market
    c   could be located anywhere
    d   involves a low transport cost for the final product.

8   A business scale could be measured by:

    a   the number of its employees
    b   the number of business sites
    c   the size of the market share
    d   the amount of capital invested.

9   The primary sector is concerned with:

    a   the extraction of raw materials from the ground
    b   the manufacturing of raw materials
    c   the distribution of raw materials
    d   the distribution of the final product.

10   Banks and building societies are:

    a   in the secondary sector
    b   in the primary sector
    c   in the tertiary sector.

11   Toyota car manufacturer mainly operates in:

    a   the primary sector
    b   the secondary sector
    c   the tertiary sector.

12   Dobsons & Sons Ltd is an example of:

    a   a private limited company
    b   a public limited company
    c   a public corporation.

13   A public corporation, for example, the BBC is:

a   in the primary sector
b   in the public sector
c   owned by the government.

14 Declining industries, for example, mining and fishing, mainly exist in:

a   the secondary sector
b   the primary sector
c   the private sector
d   the tertiary sector.

15 In a sole trader business the number of owners are:

a   1–5
b   only 1
c   more than 5.

16 A sole trader business is a small business because:

a   there is only one owner
b   it is in the private sector
c   the site of the business is usually small.

17 In a partnership business, partners might draw up a legal agreement which is called:

a   a job contract
b   a contract of employment
c   a deed of partnership.

18 In a partnership, partners usually have:

a   limited liability
b   unlimited liability
c   active role in the running of the business.

19 In the public sector the entrepreneur (owner of resources) is:

a   the government
b   public
c   The board of directors.

20 Customers are the group of people who:

a   run a business
b   own a business
c   buy a product.

Unit 2 Assessment

Check with your tutor what you need to produce for your portfolio. If you do the assignment below, you will be on your way to completing the work you will need to do.

1   Choose two businesses to find out about. Make sure that you pick two different kinds of business. For example, one could be a business that provides a service while the other could produce goods. Or, one of the business could be a large, well-known company, while the other could be a small family business.

2   Find out the following information about each business.

   a   How is the business owned, e.g., is it a sole trader, a partnership, or a PLC? What are the main features of this type of ownership? Why is this type of ownership suited to the business? Can you say how another form of ownership would make the business different?

   b   What does the business do? Describe its main activities. How does it carry out these activities?

   c   Where is the business located? What are the reasons for its location, e.g., how easy is it to get to?

   d   Who are the business's main competitors? What do these competitor businesses do and where are they located?

   e   Who are the business's main stakeholders? Describe them. Why is the business important to these people? Who do you think are the business's most important stakeholders?

3   Use your word processing skills to write a report about everything you have found out about each of your two chosen businesses. Base the report on your answers to question 2. As well as describing each business's ownership, location and stakeholders, try to write about how things like the business's location and stakeholders affect what happens to the business and how it is run.

Finance in business

All businesses need accurate financial information in order to succeed. This can be achieved only by effective communication and organisation between different departments.

When businesses communicate with other businesses or customers, they will need to use financial documents. Businesses use some of these documents when they make purchases from suppliers, others when they sell products to customers.

It is very important for a business to record its financial transactions in the most effective way. In this unit you are going to learn about:

- business costs and revenues
- how to work out a business profit
- financial documents and what they are for
- how financial documents are used
- how payments are made
- methods of making and receiving payments.

Chapter 10 Investigating cost and revenue, profit and loss

Money is an important resource for a firm. Without it, the firm will be unable to pay its workers, buy raw materials or purchase machinery. Money flows through the organisation as it is received from customers and is passed on to workers or suppliers.

A successful business will need to control both the inflow and the outflow of money. In large firms this will be done by a finance department headed by qualified accountants. The job of the finance department is to keep records of payments and receipts and to make information available to help in decision making.

Many owners get the money to start a business by arranging a bank loan

Flow of money

Somebody provides the money to start up the business in the first place. Extra finance may have to be introduced into the business if it is to develop and expand.

Where does the money come from?

- The owners of the business can provide funds themselves from their own savings.
- Money or funds can be provided from profits which are not taken out of the firm but used instead to buy more resources.
- There are also a number of possible sources of finance available to a firm from people outside the organisation, for example, arranging loans from banks.

Money is used to pay for the following:

- raw materials
- wages
- replacement of old equipment

- dividends (share of profits to shareholders)
- taxes
- retained profits for future investment.

Because firms will often have to pay for labour and raw materials before they sell their goods or services, there is always a risk that the money coming into the firm (revenue) will be less than the money that is being paid out (costs). Those people providing finance (e.g. banks) will therefore want a reward for taking the risk of not being repaid.

What is the reward?

Profit is the reward that goes to the owner of the business if it succeeds.

Interest is the reward that is paid to the lender (for example, a bank) for lending the money to the business.

ACTIVITY: BUSINESS REVENUE AND COSTS

Sort out the information below into the following two groups:

1 business revenue
2 business costs.

Cash   Rent   Wages   Cost of raw materials   Advertising expenses   Interest on loans   Insurance premium   Transport expenses   Payment for market research   Income from ice cream sales   Heating   Electricity   Income from selling   Insurance policies   Petrol

Factors which affect a business's sales income and costs (spending)

Revenue and spending vary from one business to another. It depends on many factors such as:

* size of business
* what the business sells, e.g. goods or services
* the number of employees in the business
* the number of business premises
* the number of products which a business sells
* the price of the product.

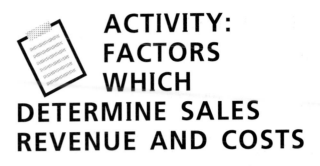

ACTIVITY: FACTORS WHICH DETERMINE SALES REVENUE AND COSTS

Fill in the following statements using one of two words, **costs** or **revenue** (sometimes you can use both words):

1 The bigger the business size the higher the .... and the ....
2 The more employees a business has the higher the ....
3 The more a business sells the more .... it receives.
4 The more premises a business has the higher the ....

Profit

Profit is the money left from sales revenue after taking away all costs.

Profit = Revenue − Costs

Working out costs and revenue

Most, if not all, businesses in the private sector work for profit, whether they are selling goods or providing services. Each business should be able to work out its:

1 costs
2 income
3 profits/losses.

For a business to make profit, it needs to generate income that is greater than its costs.

Types of costs

There are two different types of costs that a business has to estimate and then work out accurately.

1 Start-up costs (non-trading expenses)

These are costs that a business pays on any non-trading expense, i.e. paying for market research, buying premises and capital items such as machinery or computer equipment which must be bought before the business can start trading.

2 Running costs (trading expenses)

These are the expenses that relate to business trading activities, including VAT (Value Added Tax). Examples of trading expenses are:

- cost of raw materials
- salaries and wages
- rent
- council tax
- bills
- VAT
- petty cash.

Types of running costs – fixed or variable?
Fixed costs are costs that do not change from one month to the next, no matter how many goods or items the business produces or how many clients to which it provides its services. For example, the cost of renting, heating and insuring premises for a hairdressing business will not be affected by the number of customers whose hair is blow-dried or trimmed.

Variable costs do change from one month to the next, depending upon the quantity of goods or items produced by the company or the number of clients to which it provides a service. For example, in a hairdressing salon, the cost of shampoo, conditioner and styling products will depend on how many customers are seen.

Do your calculations in stages
Stage 1: Fixed costs or overheads
These are costs that have to be met regardless of whether a business sells its product or service. When the Light Delight Ice Cream business was set up, Liz and Margaret needed to think about the following:

1 the cost of hiring or renting a place to work from

2 the cost of running this place, e.g. heating, water rate, electricity etc.

3 the cost of employing people to work for them.

Margaret and Liz were aware that they would have to pay the above costs regardless of the amount of ice cream they produced and sold every day.

Stage 2: Variable or direct costs
When Margaret and Liz set up the Light Delight Ice Cream business, they knew that there were other costs that they had to pay on top of the monthly fixed costs. They needed to buy raw materials to make the ice cream, for example, sugar, fruit, cream, etc. These costs change depending on the amount of ice cream they make. The more ice cream they produce, the more raw materials they need to buy. These costs are called variable costs.

Stage 3: Total running costs
You can now work out exactly what costs a business such as Light Delight would face:

Total running cost = fixed costs + variable costs

ACTIVITY

Steve Howe, the owner of Pine Tree Furniture, realised that the business total cost (fixed + variable) was too high.

1 Suggest two ways for a business to reduce its costs.
2 Which way is more practical and under the control of the business? Explain your answer.

Business income (revenue)

Income or revenue is the money a business makes from selling its products or seervices. For example, if Pine Tree Furniture sells 100 tables at £10 a table, the total sales income will be £1000. Therefore, to work out business income or revenue, we need to work out:

- the price per item or unit (this could be for a product or a service)
- the number of items or units a business sells.

ACTIVITY

Sarah Woodhead is a hairdresser who works from home. Work out her total revenue in January if she has 10 regular customers, 4 of whom have their hair cut and blow-dried and 6 of whom have their hair coloured. She charges £8 for a cut and blow dry and £15 for colouring.

Working out the price

Every business needs to decide on a reasonable price to charge its customers.

Here they will have to use some business judgement:

- If they charge more than their competitors, they may not sell anything.
- If they charge too little, they may not cover their costs.

The owner or the management of a business must make sure that whatever they suggest is a reasonable price. It should be enough to cover the variable costs plus enough to make a contribution towards paying their fixed costs.

Revenue = Number of sold items
× Price

ACTIVITY

1 From the above information fill in the gaps in the following sentences using only one of two words, **higher** or **lower**.

The .... the number of sold items, the .... the price the more the business income.

The .... the number of sold items, the .... the price the less the business income.

2 From the above information suggest two ways to increase Pine Tree Furniture's income (revenue).

Working out a business profit or a loss

In its simplest terms, a business profit could be worked out from the formula below:

> Profit = Income (Revenue) − Total
> running costs

Remember: to calculate a business profit, you have to consider the total running costs (fixed and variable), and the total revenue. A business makes profit if the total revenue covers the running costs. The cost of machines and equipment (start-up cost) is not added to the total cost.

In the first few years of a business's life, it might make enough income to cover its running costs. Even so, the start-up cost is not yet covered.

 **ACTIVITY**

Fill in the gaps in the following sentences using one of the words **bigger** or **smaller**.

1 A business will make profit if its income is .... than its costs.

2 A business will make losses if its costs are .... than its income.

3 A business will make profit if its costs are .... than its income.

4 A business will make losses if its income is .... than its costs.

 **ACTIVITY**

1 If a business makes losses, from the information above suggest two ways to reduce its losses and perhaps to change them into profits.

2 What happens if a business income equals its costs?

 **ACTIVITY**

1 Will the business make a profit if its total income equals total revenue?

2 Will the business make a loss if its total income equals total revenue?

 **ACTIVITY**

Delicious Bakery is a business that was set up in January 1997. Peter Davies, the owner, invested £10,000 to buy new equipment and computers for the business. During the year, Peter had to pay for the following items:

Wages	£5,500
Heating	£1,500
Electricity	£750
Leaflets	£500
Advertisement in the local newspaper	£250
Insurance	£500
Transport	£650
Rent	£3,500
Council tax	£750

Peter also had to pay £3,500 for flour, sugar, milk and other ingredients to make bread, cakes, muffins, sandwiches and buns.

At the end of the year the business made £15,500 revenue from selling bread, sandwiches, cakes, muffins and buns.

1 Work out:

  a the total start-up cost for Delicious Bakery

  b the business's total fixed costs in 1997

  c the business's total variable costs in 1997

  d the business's total running costs in 1997

  e the business's losses or profit at the end of the year

2 Peter had to pay the following costs during the year 1998:

Wages	£5,500
Heating	£1,500
Electricity	£750
Insurance	£500
Transport	£650
Rent	£3,500
Council tax	£750

Peter also had to pay £4,500 for flour, sugar, milk and other ingredients to make bread, cakes, muffins, sandwiches and buns.

At the end of the year the business made £20,500 in revenue from selling bread, sandwiches, cakes, muffins and buns.

    a What is the business's start-up cost?

    b What is the business's total fixed costs?

    c What is the business's total variable costs?

    d What is the business's total running costs?

    e Compare the business's running costs for 1998 with the running costs for 1997. Why do you think this is the case?

    f What happened to the business's sales revenue in 1998? Why do you think this is the case?

    g What is the business's loss or profit at the end of 1998?

ACTIVITY

The Pine Tree Furniture business manages to reduce its monthly fixed costs to £1,000, and the selling price per table is to be £55. The business sells 100 tables. The cost of wood to make each table is £50.

1 Work out the business's total income.

2 Work out the business's total variable costs.

3 Work out the business's total running costs.

4 Work out the business's losses or profits.

5 If the business does not make a profit, suggest two ways for the business to make enough income/revenue to cover (equal) its total cost.

ACTIVITY: WORKING OUT A BUSINESS'S TOTAL COSTS AND INCOME

This activity helps you to learn and understand:

- the meaning of fixed costs
- the meaning of variable costs
- the meaning of income (revenue)
- reasons for a business being unable to generate income.

Output	Fixed costs	Variable costs	Total costs	Revenue	Profit/ Loss
0	1000	0	1000	0	(1000)
1	1000	500	1500	700	(800)
2	1000	1000	2000	1400	(600)
3	1000	1500	2500	2100	(400)
4	1000	2000	3000	2800	(200)
5	1000	2500	3500	3500	0
6	1000	3000	4000	4200	200
7	1000	3500	4500	4900	400

- The business's monthly fixed costs = £1000.
- The cost of raw materials (wood) per table = £500.
- Total costs = Fixed costs + Variable costs.
- The selling price for each table is £700.

Formulas to remember:

    a Variable costs = Price of raw material per unit × No. of units

b Revenue = Selling price per unit × No. of units.

Look carefully at the table above and tick the correct statement at each level of production:

At level 0 of output:
1 Total costs are less than Revenue.
2 Total costs are more than Revenue.
3 Total costs equal Revenue.

At level 1 of output:
1 Total costs are less than Revenue.
2 Total costs are more than Revenue.
3 Total costs equal Revenue.

At level 2 of output:
1 Total costs are less than Revenue.
2 Total costs are more than Revenue.
3 Total costs equal Revenue.

At level 3 of output:
1 Total costs are less than Revenue.
2 Total costs are more than Revenue.
3 Total costs equal Revenue.

At level 4 of output:
1 Total costs are less than Revenue.
2 Total costs are more than Revenue.
3 Total costs equal Revenue.

At level 5 of output:
1 Total costs are less than Revenue.
2 Total costs are more than Revenue.
3 Total costs equal Revenue.

At level 6 of output:
1 Total costs are less than Revenue.
2 Total costs are more than Revenue.
3 Total costs equal Revenue.

Key Terms

Competition The idea that in a market one business should always be rivalled by another business to ensure that prices are kept low and the customer is not exploited.

Consumer A person who buys goods and services for his or her own use or consumption.

Costs The money a business spends in order to produce goods and services for its customers.

Fixed costs or overheads Those costs of a business that remain unchanged whatever the level of output the business is producing over a period of time.

Profit What is left when all costs incurred in making and selling a product are deducted from the revenue gained from that sale.

Risk All business decisions involve an element of risk because there are a number of possible outcomes from a decision. For example, there is a risk in setting up a business because it might fail. Owners are rewarded with profit for taking this risk and investing their money in the business.

Running costs These are the expenses that relate to business trading activities, including VAT.

Sales revenue The income that a business receives as a result of selling its products.

Sales revenue = Price × Quantity sold

Start-up costs These are costs that a business pays on any non-trading expenses, i.e. capital items such as machinery or computer equipment.

Turnover The value of sales over a period of time (sales revenue). Total sales.

Variable costs Those costs that change directly with the output of a business, i.e. raw material cost, overtime cost, fuel and power cost.

At level 7 of output:

1 Total costs are less than Revenue.
2 Total costs are more than Revenue.
3 Total costs equal Revenue.

From your findings answer the following questions:

1 At which levels of production (output) are there profits?
2 At which levels of production (output) are there losses?
3 At which level of production is there is no loss and no profit? Why do think this is the case?

Book keeping

You have learnt a simple way to work out a business's losses and profit. In reality it is more complex than that. This is because other factors need to be considered, for example:

1 Business revenue from selling products is not the only source of revenue. There are other sources, for example, interest received on savings or investment.

2 Businesses, when working out whether they have made a profit or a loss, need to consider the start-up costs. Start-up costs are costs that need to be met before the business can start trading, for example, the cost of market research and buying machines and equipment.

3 Not all sales revenue arrives in cash. Businesses sometimes sell products to customers on credit.

4 The above simple analysis does not show the change in sales revenue and cost from one month to another.

5 The above simple analysis does not show the period of time, for example, a week or a month, when these revenues and costs were made.

Why keep accounts?

Businesses need to keep track and record their financial transactions. This is the most basic part of any system of accounts. It is a record of all payments by the business and the money it receives. Small businesses can buy books already set out for this purpose.

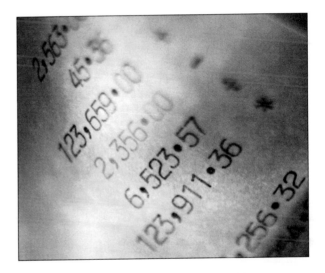

What financial information must be kept?

All businesses must keep records of their sales revenue and the costs that they have paid to make and sell their products. To do this all businesses should do the following:

1 keep all invoices raised on behalf of the business
2 keep all sales invoices numbered sequentially
3 keep all purchase invoices received and listed
4 record all wages and salaries paid
5 keep all cheque-book stubs, paying-in slips/books and business bank account statements
6 keep a full record of VAT, whether paid by or to the business.

Business budget

Businesses need to plan and estimate their income and costs. This plan is called a budget. It is a statement of the estimated income and expenditure (spending) of a business over a particular period of time, usually one year. A budget enables the business to:

1 work out the total business expenditure and income

2 find out if there are any liquidity problems (if a business's cash income is less than its cash expenditure)

3 show how the business managed to cover its shortage of cash, e.g. arranged for a short-term loan or an overdraft.

ACTIVITY: SETTING UP A SPREADSHEET FOR A BUSINESS BUDGET

Setting up a spreadsheet for a business budget

Below is the cash budget for Trading Ltd.

a Set up a spreadsheet with 13 columns and 12 rows.

b In the spreadsheet, enter the text for each column and row heading, as shown below.

c Enter the figures shown below for the months January to December.

d Using the spreadsheet, calculate the totals for the column so you have the total monthly costs (expenditure) for all the items, such as purchases, wages, rent, etc.

Item	Jan	Feb	March	April	May	June	July	August	Sept	Oct	Nov	Dec
Sales	0	5,000	6,000	5,000	8,000	9,000	10,000	9,000	7,000	7,000	5,000	8,000
Grant	2,000	0,000	0,000	0,000	2,000	0,000	0,000					
Owner's capital	10,000	0,000	0,000	0,000	0,000	0,000	0,000					
TOTAL REVENUE												
Purchases	5,000	3,000	5,000	6,000	4,000	3,000	4,000	4,500	3,500	3,500	3,000	5,000
Wages	1,000	1,000	1,000	2,000	2,000	2,000	2,000	2,000	1,000	1,000	1,000	2,000
Rent	500	500	500	500	500	500	500	500	500	500	500	500
Electricity	0	600	0	0	650	0	0	500	0	0	0	750
Petrol	100	150	200	150	250	250	250	200	150	150	100	200
TOTAL COSTS/ SPENDING												
PROFIT/ LOSS												

   e Calculate the total costs (expenditure) for the year.

2 a Work out the profit and loss at the end of each month.

   b Work out the profit and loss at the end of the year.

Key Terms

Accounts The financial records of a business that are used by managers, owners, employees, creditors and others to show how well the business is doing.

Budget A plan showing the expected sales revenue over the coming month or year, matched against the estimated costs that will be incurred.

Cash The most liquid of all the assets that a business has. Businesses need cash to pay for the day-to-day running of the business, e.g. to pay wages, bills and for raw materials from suppliers.

Cash flow The flow of money into and out of a business.

Cashbook It is a book that is used to record the sources of income and recipients of money paid out.

Drawings The amount of money withdrawn from the business (sole trader or a partnership) for personal use.

Overdraft More cash allowed by a bank to a business or personal customer, by permitting the withdrawal of more from a current account than is in it, up to a certain limit.

NORTHUMBERLAND COLL
LIBRARY
OF ARTS & TECHNOLOGY

Chapter II Investigating financial documents for buying and selling

Buying and selling are at the heart of business and it is very important that all sales and purchases are recorded accurately. A customer may have been very impressed with the layout of the shop, the goods on display and any help or advice that they may have received from the sales staff. The customer may have spent some time in the shop and have been very satisfied with the goods that they have chosen. But this favourable impression of the shop will soon be destroyed if there is then a long delay or a problem of some kind at the check-out.

Therefore, the way a business handles and organises its financial documents is very important for the following reasons:

1   to provide permanent and secure records

2   to provide accounts for tax purposes

3   to provide records for transactions with customers

4   to provide records for transactions with suppliers

5   to provide records for the inflow of money

6   to provide records for the outflow of money

7   to provide records for profits and losses

There are many financial documents that any business would use to control:

• the movement of goods or services and cash out of the business

• the movement of goods or services and cash into the business.

ACTIVITY: IN OR OUT?

This activity should help you to understand the movement of transactions in and out of a business.

Fill in the gaps in the following sentences using only **out of** or **into**.

1   Goods and services move .... the business when they are sold to customers.

2   Goods and services move .... the business when they are bought from suppliers (wholesaler or a manufacturer).

3   Cash moves .... a business to pay for wages, fuel, rent, equipment and raw materials.

4   Cash moves .... a business to pay for sold products.

5   When goods and services get .... a business, this could mean cash getting .... the business.

6   When cash gets .... a business, this will pay for the cost of producing the products, e.g. wages, electricity, rent, raw materials, etc.

You are going to learn all about the following documents:

- Purchase orders
- Delivery notes
- Invoices
- Credit notes
- Statements of account sent by the business
- Remittance advice slips
- Cheques
- Receipts
- Petty cash vouchers.

A business like Light Delight Ice-cream Ltd, the fictional business you learnt about in Unit 1, would use these documents every day.

Light Delight **sends** financial documents such as delivery notes and invoices when it sells ice-cream to customers.

Light Delight **receives** financial documents such as delivery notes and invoices when it buys the materials to make ice-cream from its suppliers.

We will look at what happens at Light Delight to find out how these documents are used and to practise filling them in.

Light Delight as a supplier

The following process would take place if Sava Stores – one of Light Delight's main customers – wants to buy some Light Delight ice-cream:

a Sava Stores makes an enquiry about the price of the different flavours of ice-cream. Light Delight sends them a **price list**.

b Sava Stores makes an order by filling in an **order form**.

c Light Delight receives the order and lets the customer know that it has been received.

d Light Delight delivers the order to Sava Stores.

e Sava Stores also receives a **delivery note** from Light Delight to say that the ice-cream has been delivered.

f Sava Stores receives an **invoice** from Light Delight, asking them to pay for the ice-cream.

g Sava Stores makes their payment for the ice-cream either by **cash**, **cheque** or a **credit** or **debit card**.

h Once Light Delight receives the payment, they issue a **receipt** which says that payment has been received and send it to Sava Stores.

Light Delight as a customer

On the other hand, this is what happens when Light Delight wants to buy some items or goods from a supplier. North Dairy Milk Products Ltd is one of Light Delight's main suppliers. It supplies the business with fresh and powder milk. If Light Delight decides to order milk, they would have to go through the following process:

a Light Delight makes an enquiry about the price of the full fat, semi-skimmed and skimmed milk. They receive a **price list**.

b Light Delight makes an order by filling in an **order form**.

c North Dairy Milk Products receives the order and lets Light Delight know that it has been received.

d North Dairy Milk Products delivers the order to Light Delight.

e Light Delight also receives a **delivery note** from the supplier to say that the milk has been delivered.

f Light Delight receives an **invoice** from North Dairy Milk Products asking them to pay for the milk they have purchased.

g Light Delight pays for the milk either by **cash**, **cheque** or a **credit** or **debit card**.

h Once the payment is received by North Dairy Milk Products, they issue a receipt and send it to Light Delight saying that payment has been received

First of all, it is important to learn about the order in which these documents are usually used.

Now you are going to learn about each of the above financial documents and how to fill them in.

Catalogues or price lists

Before making an order to buy ice-cream, Sava Stores would ask for a catalogue or a price list from Light Delight. In response to a telephone call or letter of enquiry Light Delight may send a catalogue showing the full range of ice cream offered for sale and how much they charge. A price list usually shows current prices and recent

amendments, and should be referred to before placing an order.

The order (purchase order form)

To make an order, Sava Stores sends Light Delight an order form, which lists all the details of the range, flavour and prices of the ice-cream they want to buy.

Like many other businesses, Sava Stores has many checks and controls to ensure that only 'authorised' people can make orders. Many businesses use pre-printed order forms, on which there is usually a reference number. This reference number is included so that, when the goods and demand for payment are received, they can easily be checked against the original document.

LIGHT DELIGHT ICE-CREAM LTD

Unit 28 Penraven Industrial Estate
Mean Wood Road
LEEDS
LS7 2AP

Selected Price List

Ice-cream

Qty.	Item	Catalogue no.	Price
Large box	Vanilla ice-cream	CL/234	£3.25
Large box	Strawberry ice-cream	CL/235	£4.10
Large box	Chocolate ice-cream with nuts	CL/236	£5.10
Large box	Chocolate ice-cream without nuts	CL/237	£4.20
Large box	Banana ice-cream with nuts	CL/238	£5.45
Large box	Banana ice-cream without nuts	CL/239	£4.75
Large box	Raspberry ice-cream	CL/240	£4.10

Sava Stores

22 Thorncliffe Street
Fixby
Huddersfield
HD1 1GH

Order Form

From: Paul Corp
Address: As above
Order Number: ERG 6554

To: Light Delight Ice-Cream Ltd
Unit 28 Penraven Industrial Estate
Mean Wood
Leeds
LS7 2AP

VAT Reg No: 2334
Date: 26/6/2000

Order No. JH/1009

Item Required	Quantity	Unit price	Ref.	Total price
Vanilla ice-cream (large box)	10 boxes	£3.25	CL/234	£32.50
Strawberry ice-cream (large box)	10 boxes	£4.10	CL/235	£41.00
Chocolate ice-cream without nuts	5 boxes	£4.20	CL/237	£21.00

Signature: Diana Woods   VAT at 17.5. %

Light Delight will also need to order items from its suppliers, and will have to send the supplier an order form with details of what they want to buy.

LIGHT DELIGHT ICE-CREAM LTD

Unit 28 Penraven Industrial Estate
Mean Wood Road
LEEDS
LS7 2AP

Tel. No.: 0113 234543   **Order**   VAT Reg No: 680 73842 88

Date: 3/7/200

Order No. DF/1315

To: **The North Dairy Milk Products Ltd**
14 Dockland Road
Leeds
LS3 3DT

Please supply

Quantity	Description	Ref	Unit Price
10 Kg	Full fat milk powder	K/123	2.13 per kg
10 kg	Semi-skimmed milk powder	K/124	2.13 per kg
10 kg	Skimmed milk powder	K/125	2.13 per kg

Delivery: asap
Signed by *Renata Ottolini*

ACTIVITY

Several items of office stationery are required for the stationery counter at Light Delight Ltd. The required items are included in a memo from Gillian Ward to Renata Ottolini.

Emma Jebson, the other administration clerk, asks you to order the above items and gives you a blank order form (your tutor will give you a photocopy of the order from the back of the book). She asks you to make sure that:

MEMO

To: Renata Ottolini

From: Gillian Ward

Can you please arrange for the following items to be ordered as soon as possible from Business Supplier Ltd, 14 Dockland Road, Leeds, LS3 3DT?

1 10 boxes of blue ballpoint pens (12 per box) ref. BB/3 – cost 90p per box.

2 150 A4 writing pads ref. WP/16 (10 per pack) – cost £9.50 per pack.

3 10,000 10 × 7 White envelopes ref. WE/27 at 26 per 1000.

We get a discount from the above supplier.

GW.

---

1 The name and the address of the supplier and all of the other details on the order are correct.
2 The order numbers are in sequence. The last order number was 25/125.
3 Delivery is requested as soon as possible.
4 All order forms are signed by Renata Ottolini.

ACTIVITY

Renata Ottolini gives you a copy of an order which has been received from a new customer, Frozen Food Ltd, Newhey Road, Huddersfield HD1 2PJ (see page 116). She has noticed several errors on the order but does not have time to check these in detail. She asks you to check the order against Light Delight's price list on page 114. and to make a written note of any errors. After you have done that, she wants you to send a fax to Frozen Food Ltd to let them know about the errors: ask Frozen Food Ltd to get back to you to tell you what they need. Renata gives you the price list for different ice-cream flavours:

Vanilla ice-cream @ £3.25 a box (large)
Strawberry/Raspberry ice-cream @ £4.10 a box (large)
Chocolate ice-cream with nuts @ £5.10 a box (large)
Chocolate ice-cream without nuts @ £4.20 a box (large)
Banana ice-cream with nuts @ £ 5.45 a box (large)
Banana ice-cream without nuts @ £4.75 a box (large)

ACTIVITY

Renata Ottolini asks you to order a new printer from Electronic Speed Ltd, 15 Highway Park Leeds, LS3 2FE. She gives you an order form (your tutor will give you a photocopy of the Light Delight order form at the back of the book). The printer you need to order is a Desk Jet 500 printer, Ref. No. L20, retail price £355 plus VAT.

Receiving an order

Once a business order has been received the sales department in Light Delight will:

1 Find out if there is enough ice-cream in stock.

2 Inform the production department if more ice-cream needs to be made.

3 Inform the distribution department or the person who is in charge of distribution that they have to deliver the ice-cream.

4 Inform the finance department that an invoice needs to be made out.

While all of the above is happening the sales department in the business will send the customer an **acknowledgement of order** form to show that the order has been received and is progressing.

Frozen Food Ltd

Newhey Road
Huddersfield
HD1 2PJ

Order Form

To: Light Delight Ice-Cream Ltd   From: Aisha Hassan
       Unit 28 Penraven Industrial Estate   Sales manager
       Mean Wood Road
       Leeds
       LS7 2AP

Order No. DF/1245   Date: 4/7/2000

Quantity	Description	Cat No.	Unit Cost	Total Cost
5	Boxes of banana ice-cream without nuts (large)	CL 239	£4.25	£21.25
10	Boxes of strawberry ice-cream (large)	CL 235	£4.10	£31.00
10	Boxes of chocolate ice-cream without nuts (large)	CL 236	£5.10	£51.00
	Subtotal			£123.25
	VAT at 17.5%			£ 21.57
	Total including VAT			£144.82

Delivery: ....   Signed by: ....
Authorized by: ....

LIGHT DELIGHT ICE-CREAM LTD

Unit 28 Penraven Industrial Estate
Mean Wood Road
LEEDS
LS7 2AP

ACKNOWLEDGEMENT OF ORDER

Date   Order No.:   Order Date

Value of order   Expected Delivery Date

Description of Order

COMMENTS

Once Light Delight receives the order form from Sava Stores, they will do their best to deliver the ice-cream as soon as possible. Once the ice-cream is delivered, Light Delight gives or sends Sava Stores a delivery note.

When North Dairy Milk Products has received the order from Light Delight they will send them the required milk powder with a delivery note.

LIGHT DELIGHT ICE-CREAM LTD

Unit 28 Penraven Industrial Estate
Mean Wood Road
LEEDS
LS7 2AP

DELIVERY NOTE

To Sava Stores   VAT REG NO 680/7384288
22 Thorncliffe Street
Fixby
Huddersfield
HDI IGH

Your order DF/1245	Invoice date	Invoice No	Dispatch date 10/7/00
Quantity	**Description**	**Cat No**	
10 boxes	Vanilla ice-cream	CL/234	
10 boxes	Strawberry ice-cream	CL/235	
5 boxes	Chocolate ice-cream without nuts	CL/239	

Received by....... James Bond   Date: 10/7/2000

Delivery note

A delivery note is a list of the products which have been sent by a business. It can either be included with the goods being delivered or it can be sent separately by post. It is a useful document for checking the quantity and condition of the products when they are received by the purchaser. Quantities ordered are numbered so goods can be checked. The delivery note often has a space for the recipient's signature. Businesses receive delivery notes from their suppliers when they order goods, and businesses send delivery notes to customers when they send them finished products.

Delivery Note

NORTH DAIRY MILK PRODUCTS LTD

14 Dockland Road
LEEDS
LS3 3DT

Date 9/07/2000

Our Ref. 9643

To: Light Delight Ice-cream Ltd
      Unit 28 Penraven Industrial Estate
      Mean Wood Road
      Leeds
      LS7 2AP

Your order No. DF/1315

Quantity	Description	Price per kg.
10 kg	Full fat milk	£2.13
10 kg	Semi-skimmed milk	£2.13
10 kg	Skimmed milk	£2.13

Received by Emma Jebson   **Date: 19/5/2000**

3   The despatch or delivery date is mentioned in the note.

BROWN STORES LTD

Main Road   •   HALIFAX   •   HA1 5HG

Order Form

To:
Light Delight Ice-Cream Ltd
Unit 28 Penraven Industrial Estate
Mean Wood Road
Leeds
LS7 2AP

Delivery address:
Brown Stores Ltd
Main Road
Halifax
HA1 5HG

Date required 12/4/00   Date of order 28/3/00   Order number BS/9340

Quantity	Please supply the following	Unit Price	Total AMOUNT
5 boxes	Strawberry ice-cream	£4.10	£20.50
10 boxes	Banana ice-cream without nuts	£4.75	£47.50
15 boxes	Chocolate ice-cream without nuts	£4.20	£63.00

ACTIVITY

On 29 March 2000, Light Delight receives the following order from one of their customers, Brown Stores Ltd. The ice-cream is going to be delivered to Brown Stores on 12 April 2000. Emma asks you to prepare a delivery note. (ask your teacher to make you a copy of a blank delivery note from the back of the book). She also asks you to make sure that:

1   The order is correct and without any errors or mistakes.
2   The name and the address of the supplier are correct and match what is on the order form.

Remember: The order number must appear on all invoices and delivery notes

Invoice

The sales invoice is the bill, i.e. the demand for payment. Businesses receive invoices from suppliers asking for payment, they send invoices to customers at the same time as the goods. The invoice states what has been delivered, the price and terms. The 'terms' are the amount of time allowed for payment; many businesses allow 30 days from receipt of the invoice.

Key facts about invoices

1 The invoice or bill is the main document used in business.

2 It tells the business which has bought the goods what it owes and when payment is due.

3 If the invoice is sent by a supplier to a business it will be called a purchase invoice because it is sent by the supplier to the business which has made the purchase.

4 Invoices must be paid by the purchaser once they have been received from the supplier.

Information in an invoice

Various items of information are included on an invoice, for example:

a quantity, type, size and colour of the products

b final total

c value added tax (VAT).

d terms of delivery, e.g. carriage paid

e the order number.

Most businesses have a system for checking each invoice against a goods received note or delivery note. For example Emma Jebson, the administration clerk at Light Delight, checked the invoice from North Dairy Milk Products against (below left) their delivery note with reference number 9643 (page 118).

On the other hand after Light Delight delivered the ice-cream to Sava Stores, they sent them the invoice below:

NORTH DAIRY MILK PRODUCTS LTD

Light Delight Ice-cream Ltd
Unit 28 Penraven Industrial Estate
Mean Wood Road
Leeds
LS7 2AP

14 Dockland Road
LEEDS
LS3 3DT

No 451   Date 10/7/2000

INVOICE

To The purchase of

10 kg of powder full fat milk	£21.30
10 kg of powder semi-skimmed milk	£21.30
10 kg of power skimmed milk	£21.30
SUBTOTAL	£63.90
VAT 17.5%	£11.18
TOTAL DUE	£75.08

E&OE

LIGHT DELIGHT ICE-CREAM LTD

Unit 28 Penraven Industrial Estate
Mean Wood Road
LEEDS
LS7 2AP

INVOICE

VAT REG NO 680/7384288

Customer Sava Stores
22 Thorncliffe Street
Fixby
Huddersfield
HD1 1GH

Customer Ref. No:
Despatch Date: 10/7/00

Invoice No: 10202
Date 18/7/00

Quantity	Description	Unit Price	Total
10 kg	Large boxes of Vanilla ice-cream	£3.25 a box	£32.50
10 kg	Large boxes of Strawberry ice-cream	£4.10 a box	£41.00
10 kg	Large boxes of Chocolate ice-cream without nuts	£5.10 a box	£51.00
E&OE		Subtotal	£124.50
		VAT (17.5%)	£21.88
		Total	£146.38

Special notes in an invoice

1 The letters "E and OE" are found on every invoice and stand for **Errors and Omissions Excepted**. This means that if there are any mistakes or items missed off, the supplier has the right to send a **supplementary invoice** to charge the extra amount still owing.

2 **Value Added Tax (VAT)** is added to the total cost of the goods (after any discounts have been subtracted). The current rate is 17.5%.

How to work out VAT in an invoice

The invoice on the previous page, sent by Light Delight Ice-cream to their customer Sava Stores, shows you how VAT is worked out.

1 The subtotal of the invoice is £124.50 (no discount is offered).

2 VAT on goods is 17.5% of £124.50 = £21.88

3 Total amount due is £124.50+ £21.88 = £146.38

Remember that sometimes businesses give a discount to encourage prompt payment. For example, in the above invoice Light Delight Ice-Cream might offer Sava Stores a 10% discount off the subtotal if payment is made within 14 days. Therefore, if Sava Stores pays quickly, the total amount which they will have to pay will be less. Look at the invoice at the top of the right-hand column.

LIGHT DELIGHT ICE-CREAM LTD

Unit 28 Penraven Industrial Estate
Mean Wood Road
LEEDS
LS7 2AP

INVOICE

VAT REG NO 680/7384288

Customer **Sava Stores**
22 Thorncliffe Street
Fixby
Huddersfield
HD1 1GH

Customer Ref. No:
Despatch Date: 10/7/00

Invoice No: 10202
Date 18/7/00

Quantity	Description	Unit Price	Total
10 kg	Large boxes of Vanilla ice-cream	£3.25 a box	£32.50
10 kg	Large boxes of Strawberry ice-cream	£4.10 a box	£41.00
10 kg	Large boxes of Chocolate ice-cream without nuts	£5.10 a box	£51.00
	E&OE	Subtotal	£124.50
		Discount 10%	£12.45
		Amount after discount	£112.05
		VAT (17.5%)	£19.60
		Total	£131.65

ACTIVITY: WORK IT OUT YOURSELF

In each of the following situations, calculate the final cost of the goods.

a 6 bottles @ £35.75 per bottle with 6% trade discount + VAT.

b 5 cartons @ £31.15 per carton with 10% trade discount + VAT.

c 8 dozen @ £58 per dozen with 8% trade discount + VAT.

ACTIVITY: WORKING OUT VAT IN AN INVOICE

Look at the invoice below and work out:

a   The amount of VAT
b   The subtotal
c   The total amount due.

1   Remember that there is a 5% cash discount if the invoice is paid within 10 days.
2   Follow the same steps which are shown above.

ACTIVITY

On 15/4/00 Renata Ottolini at Light Delight asks you to invoice Brown Stores for the ice-cream which was delivered on 12/4/00. The order number is BS/9340. There is a discount of 12.5% for prompt payment (ask your teacher to give you a blank copy of an invoice). Renata has asked you to write and carefully check the invoice before you have it signed and authorised. She has also drawn your attention to the following components, e.g. **goods, terms, date, amount of money etc.** Before you have the invoice signed, check the following.

LIGHT DELIGHT ICE-CREAM LTD

Unit 28 Penraven Industrial Estate
Mean Wood Road
LEEDS
LS7 2AP

INVOICE

VAT REG NO 680/7384288

Customer Frozen Food Ltd
Newhey Road
Huddersfield
HD1 2PJ

Customer Ref. No:
Despatch Date: 14/8/00

Invoice No: 10231
Date 24/8/00

Quantity	Description	Unit Price	Total
15	Large boxes of Vanilla ice-cream	£3.25 a box	
5	Large boxes of Strawberry ice-cream	£4.10 a box	
10	Large boxes of Chocolate ice-cream with nuts	£5.10 a box	
7	Large boxes of Banana ice-cream without nuts	£4.75 a box	
	E&OE Subtotal
Discount 5%
Amount after discount
VAT (17.5%)
Total		

Invoice checking procedure

Component	What to check	How to check it
Name of business	Brown Stores Ltd	Their order form and delivery note
Address of business	Brown stores Ltd, Main Road Halifax HA1 5HG	Their order form and delivery note
Delivery address	Does it relate to your business Brown Stores?	Ask and check files (order form and delivery note)
Order no.	Does this match their order number?	Check against order
Despatch date	Whether the goods have been delivered	Check the Delivery Note
Quantity	Has the right quantity been delivered?	Check Goods Received Note or Delivery Note
Description of catalogue no.	Is this what they ordered?	Check order form
Price	Is this as quoted?	Check quotation or order

Component	What to check	How to check it
Total price	Are calculations accurate?	Check them!
Trade discount	Is this the discount agreed?	Check quotation or order
VAT rate	Is this correct/is VAT calculation correct?	Work it out
Delivery charges	Are you liable to pay these?	Check quotation or order

ACTIVITY

Explain in your own words what would happen if you sent the wrong invoice to Brown Stores Ltd.

Settling an invoice or account (making payment)

When businesses send an invoice or a statement of account, they like payment to be made as soon as possible. Sometimes customers are given a period of time (2–3 weeks, for example) to send this payment. As was explained above, in the process of making purchases businesses agree that immediate cash is the most favourable option or method of paying a bill! However, there are other options available to customers, e.g. cheques, credit, hire purchase etc.

Whenever payment is made, there will be a system for recording the amount and the date. This system provides evidence that the transactions have occurred and can be used to check against other financial records.

One of the most common payment methods is the cheque and you will find that most businesses use cheques a lot. The following pages will tell you how to write cheques and what happens when a business receives a cheque. You will find out about other methods of making and receiving payments on pages 141–145.

Cheques

Cheques provide a favoured method of paying bills and are one of the most common forms of payment. Businesses generally count payment by cheques as a 'cash sale' because they receive money into their bank account as soon as the cheque has been cleared. Businesses also send payment to other businesses by cheque.

A cheque is simply a written instruction from a customer to a bank to pay a certain sum of money to another named person. If you pay by cheque for something which you are going to take out of a shop straight away, then the shopkeeper takes it on trust that you have the money in your account so that the cheque will be paid.

For more expensive goods, you may have to wait for the cheque to be 'cleared' (i.e. the money transferred from your account to the retailer's). This usually takes about five days.

On the above cheque there are the names of two people:

1 The person who is paying the cheque. He/She is called the **Drawer**.

2 The person to whom the cheque is payable to (the receiver of the money). He or she is called the **Payee**.

The drawer's bank (the bank where the person who is paying for the cheque has his account) is called the **Drawee**.

**SPENDALOT
BANK PLC**

Date _6 September 2000_ 25-72-10

Pay _Cheap Sports Ltd_   or order

Twenty-nine pounds and ninety-nine   £ _29.99_

pence only   _Patrick O'Brien_

538125 25 7210: 1 6213338   PATRICK O'BRIEN

What a cheque looks like

How to safeguard a cheque

The most common way of safeguarding a cheque is to cross it, by drawing or printing two vertical or sloping lines across its face. This means that the cheque can only be paid into a bank account of the payee, and not in cash across the counter by anyone.

1 Is the above cheque well safeguarded? Explain your answer.

2 Who is the account holder?

3 At what bank is the account held?

4 What is the cheque being used for?

5 There are numbers which can be read on the above cheque?

    a Which of these numbers is the account number?

    b Which of these numbers is the cheque number?

    c Which of these numbers is the bank or the branch identifying number?

ACTIVITY

Imagine that your friend has sold you his second-hand computer game for £25.75.

1 Ask your teacher to run you 2 copies of the blank cheque at the back of your book.

2 Fill in the blank spaces in the cheque to instruct your bank to pay your friend £25.75

When writing a cheque you must remember to:

1 **Write** the date in full.

2 **Write** the payee's name (in full) clearly on the top line.

3 **Write** the amount to the left of the lines to make alterations or addition difficult.

4 **Add** the word 'only' after writing the amount.

5 **Write** the amount of pence in figures.

6 **Write** the amount in words so that it is the same as the amount in figures.

6 **Cancel** any blank spaces remaining by drawing a line through them.

7 **Sign** the cheque.

Cheque guarantee cards

If you pay for something in a shop with a cheque, the shop assistant will usually ask to see your cheque guarantee card. The assistant will write the card number on the back of the cheque and check that the card has not expired (i.e. is still in date).

A cheque guarantee card gives the shopkeeper a guarantee that the bank will pay the shop the amount written on the cheque, up to the amount the cheque guarantee card says – usually £50 or £100.

ACTIVITY

1 Why do you think shopkeepers should not accept a cheque without a guarantee card?
2 Ask someone who has recently paid for some goods with a cheque the following questions:
   a Did the checkout operator or the sale assistant at the shop ask them to present the guarantee card?
   b Where did the checkout operator write the number of the card on the cheque?
   On the reverse side.
   On the top corner of the front side.
   On the bottom corner of the front side.

ACTIVITY

1 Find out the type of information which is printed on the front of a cheque guarantee card.
2 Find out what is on the back of this card.

ACTIVITY

Find out if the following statements are true or false:

When writing a cheque:

1 Customers can use either a pencil or a pen.
2 Customers should write the amount in words and figures as close to the left as possible.
3 Customers don't have to sign against any alteration.

4 Only one line should be drawn after the name of the person, to whom the cheque has to be paid.

ACTIVITY

Renata Ottolini at Light Delight Ltd passes you two invoices which she wants you to check. She wants you to check the calculations on the invoices. If they are correct then you have to make out a cheque for the amount due. Use today's date, then pass it to Ismat Niaz (the Finance Manager) for signature and authorisation.

If any of the invoices is incorrect, note the details in a brief memo to Renata Ottolini.

◣◢ **Delta Plastic Manufacture**

23 River land Road
Leeds
LS2 1JB

Light Delight Ltd,
Unit 28,
Penraven
Industrial Estate,
Mean Wood Road
Leeds
LS7 2AP

VAT Reg 456 543

Invoice no 4765

Date 30/11/00

INVOICE

12 plastic packaging boxes (small)	£50.00
12 plastic packaging boxes (medium)	£70.00
12 plastic packaging boxes (large)	£95.00
Subtotal	£225.00
Plus VAT (17.5%)	£39.38
Total Due	£274.75
E&OE	

KEITH PLUMBING

17 Greenaway Rd
Leeds
LS4 6HD

INVOICE

Light Delight Ltd,   VAT Reg 225 762
Unit 28,   Invoice no 446
Penraven Industrial Estate,   Date 30/11/00
Meanwood Road
Leeds
LS7 2AP

INVOICE

TO

Replacing leaking radiators:

1 600mm *2000 mm radiator	£83.25
1 600mm *1000 mm radiator	£50.90
1 thermostatic radiator valve	£7.25
7 hours @ £10.50 per hour	£5.50
Subtotal	£136.90
VAT 17.5%	£23.96
TOTAL DUE	£160.86
E&OE	

ACTIVITY

Describe what would happen if you wrote the cheque to Keith Plumbing Ltd without first checking the invoice number 446.

ACTIVITY: SPOT THE ERROR

Emma Jebson is a new clerk in the administration department at Light Delight Ice-cream Ltd. Emma's main job is to receive and check the cheques which suppliers send the company to pay for the ice-cream they have purchased. In her first few weeks Emma found the work difficult and confusing. On a few occasions she was not sure if she was doing things right. The Administration Manager Renata Ottolini called Emma to her office to draw her attention to some errors.

Emma was not told what she did wrong in each of the following situations. Your task is to find the error(s) which Emma has made and to tell her what she should have done instead.

1 On 1/2/00 Emma accepted a cheque value £57.89 with no signature.

2 On 13 April 2000 Emma accepted a cheque from a customer which is dated the 13/6/1998.

3 On 23/5/00 Emma accepted a cheque from a customer with the amount of money, 75.99p. Nothing was written on the back of the cheque.

4 On 2/5/00 Emma accepted a cheque for £57.95, which does not have a payee's name.

5 On 7/5/00 Emma accepted a cheque with the written words for the amount Twenty three pounds and 95p. The amount in figures was £7.95.

6 On 8/5/00 Emma accepted a cheque for £65.95. Jean wrote the guarantee card number on the front side of the cheque.

7 On 16 May 2000 Emma accepted a cheque for £72.12. She wrote the card number 0002346567 and the expiry date 30/4/00 on the back of the cheque.

ACTIVITY

One Monday morning Renata is worried that some of the following cheques (all payable to Light Delight) have not been checked properly. Renata asks you to:

1 Check the following cheques.

2 Note any errors and,

125

3 Advise her what action she should take in each case.

Luckily the cheques were accepted with a cheque guarantee card.

Happy Bank plc	Date 2/7/00	92-12-20
Pay Light Delight Ltd		or order
One hundred and thirty-two	£ 123.95	
pounds and ninety-five pence only		
243620 92 1220: 1 1436789		SAVA STORES

Northern BANK PLC	Date 7/7/00	67-22-15
Pay Light Delight Ltd		or order
Two hundred and one pounds and	£ 201.45	
forty-five pence only		
172235 67 2215: 1 7533826		FROZEN FOOD LTD

Happy Bank plc	Date 4/9/00	92-12-20
Pay Light Delight Ltd		or order
Sixty-seven pounds and seventy-	£ 76.67	
six pounds only		
243621 92 1220: 1 1436789		SAVA STORES

Northern BANK PLC	Date 4/10/01	67-22-15
Pay Light Delight Ltd		or order
One hundred and thirty-two and	£ 96.63	
95p only		
172235 67 2215: 1 7533826		FROZEN FOOD LTD

ACTIVITY

The following week Renata asks you to write and sign all of the following cheques, using today's date (print out copies of the blank cheque at the back of the book):

1 A cheque for £42.65 payable to North Dairy Milk Products Ltd.
2 A cheque for £238.29 payable to Speed Manufacturer Ltd.
3 A cheque for £89.98 payable to Juicy Fruity Ltd.
4 A cheque for £101.10 payable to Keith Plumbing Ltd.

ACTIVITY

Because of the errors that Emma made with the cheques last week, Renata Ottolini asks you to type a note for her which states exactly what procedure should be followed when accepting cheque payments.

ACTIVITY

On 3/5/2000 Light Delight Ice-Cream Ltd. receives the following order from one of their regular customers, Frozen Food Ltd.

1 Check all the prices and the arithmetic on the purchase order against the price list. Correct any errors.
2 Check all the items on the delivery note against what is required in the purchase order. Correct any errors.
3 Check all the items on the invoice against the accurate copy of the delivery note.
4 If you think that the invoice is correct and should be paid, sign it and complete a cheque ready for signature.

5 If you think the invoice is not correct, make the required correction, sign it and complete a cheque ready for signature.

LIGHT DELIGHT ICE-CREAM LTD

Unit 28 Penraven Industrial Estate
Mean Wood Road
LEEDS
LS7 2AP

Selected Price List

Ice-cream

Qty	Item	Cat No	Price
Large box	Vanilla ice-cream	CL/234	£3.25
Large box	Strawberry/Rasberry ice-cream	CL/235	£4.10
Large box	Chocolate ice-cream with nuts	CL/236	£5.10
Large box	Chocolate ice-cream without nuts	CL/237	£4.20
Large box	Banana ice-cream with nuts	CL/238	£5.45
Large box	Banana ice-cream without nuts	CL/239	£4.75
Large box	Raspberry ice-cream	CL/240	£4.10

Frozen Food Ltd

Newhey Road
Huddersfield
HD1 2PJ

Order Form

To: Light Delight Ice-Cream Ltd   From: Aisha Hassan
     Unit 28 Penraven Industrial Estate   Sales manager
     Mean Wood Road
     Leeds
     LS7 2AP

Order No. DF/1245   Date: 30/4/00

Quantity	Description	Cat No.	Unit Cost	Total Cost
15	Boxes of vanilla ice-cream	CL/234	£3.25	£48.75
10	Boxes of strawberry ice-cream (large)	CL/235	£5.10	£51.00
20	Boxes of chocolate ice-cream (large), no nuts	CL 236	£4.25	£85.00
	Total			£184.75
	VAT at 17.5%			£32.33
	Total including VAT			£217.08

Delivery: within 2 weeks
Signed by: ------------------
Authorized by: Aisha Hassan

The above order was delivered on 9 May 2000, and the following delivery note was issued.

LIGHT DELIGHT ICE-CREAM LTD

Unit 28 Penraven Industrial Estate
Mean Wood Road
LEEDS
LS7 2AP

DELIVERY NOTE

To: Frozen Food Ltd VAT REG NO 680/7384288
Newhey Road
Huddersfield
HD1 2PJ

Your order	Invoice date	Invoice No	Dispatch date
DF/1245	13/5/00		9/5/00

Quantity	Description	Cat No
15 boxes	Vanilla ice-cream	CL/234
10 boxes	Strawberry ice-cream	CL/235
20 boxes	Chocolate ice-cream with nuts	CL/236

Received by....... James Bond   Date: 9/05/200

LIGHT DELIGHT ICE-CREAM LTD

Unit 28 Penraven Industrial Estate
Mean Wood Road
LEEDS
LS7 2AP

INVOICE

VAT REG NO 680/7384288

Customer Frozen Food Ltd
Newhey Road
Huddersfield
HD1 2PJ

Customer Ref. No:
Despatch Date: 9/5/00
Invoice No: 12134
Date 13/5/00

Quantity	Description	Unit Price	Total
15	Large boxes of Vanilla ice-cream	£3.25 a box	£49.74
5	Large boxes of Strawberry ice-cream	£4.10 a box	£41.00
10	Large boxes of Chocolate ice-cream with nuts	£5.10 a box	£102.00
E&OE	Subtotal		£192.75
	Discount 5%		£9.60
	Amount after discount		£202.35
	VAT (17.5%)		£35.35
	Total		£237.70

Statement of account

Statement of account Light Delight Ice-cream Ltd usually receives a statement of account from their supplier. Sometimes suppliers send the statement at the end of each month to show what is owed and what has been paid. Light Delight also sends statements of account at the end of the month to their own regular customers, mainly supermarkets. A statement lists payments as **credits** and the amounts owed as **debits**. Opposite is a statement from Light Delight to Sava Stores.

LIGHT DELIGHT ICE-CREAM LTD

Unit 28 Penraven Industrial Estate
Mean Wood Road
LEEDS
LS7 2AP

FAX: 0113 234543
TEL: 0113 234544

VAT REG NO 680/73842/88

STATEMENT

To: Sava Stores
22 Thorncliffe Street
Fixby
Huddersfield
HDI IGH

Date: 31/7/2000

Account no 2327

Date	Details	Debit	Credit	Balance
10/7/2000	10 boxes of chocolate ice-cream (invoice number 10202)	£146.38		£146.38
22/7/2000	6 boxes of vanilla ice-cream and 4 boxes of strawberry (invoice number 10221)	£35.90		£35.90
29/7/2000	5 boxes of chocolate ice-cream with nuts (invoice number 10267)	£25.50		£25.50
Total outstanding balance				£207.78

ACTIVITY

In October 2000, Sava Stores buys the following from Light Delight:

1 2/6/00 – 8 boxes of Vanilla ice-cream at £3.25 a box.

2 13/6/00 – 12 boxes of Chocolate and nuts ice-cream at £5.10 a box.

3 26/6/00 – 6 boxes of banana ice-cream without nuts.

On 27 October Sava Stores paid £35 of their outstanding balance

Prepare a statement for October to be sent to Sava Stores using a copy of the blank statement from the back of the book. Work out their total outstanding balance.

What should a business do when it receives a statement?

When the statement is received the purchaser should check it against all invoices, credit/debit notes and payments made since the last statements, and if it is correct send payment to the supplier.

What happens if the statement is not settled?

Settling a statement simply means sending the payment to the supplier. If the payment is not sent, the supplier will send another copy to the business (purchaser).

Light Delight receives the following statement for July from their supplier North Dairy Milk Products Ltd.

STATEMENT

NORTH DAIRY MILK PRODUCTS LTD

Light Delight Ltd,
Unit 28, Penraven
Industrial Estate,
Meanwood Road
Leeds
LS7 2AP

Date 3/07/00

Account No 668750

14 Dockland Road
LEEDS
LS3 3DT

Date	Item Description	Debits	Credits
2/7/00	5kg of full fat milk	£10.65	
	10kg of full fat milk	£21.30	
15/7/00	payment received thank you		£10.65
19/7/00	20kg of fat free milk	£42.60	
23/7/00	7kg of semi skimmed milk	£14.91	
Total outstanding balance			**£78.80**

Payment received after 30 July is not included

ACTIVITY

Check the above statement to make sure that the outstanding balance is correct.

ACTIVITY

The following transaction took place in September 2000 between Light Delight Ltd and its customer Frozen Food Ltd. The customer account number is 2355.

1   Use a blank copy of the Light Delight statement to record the following transactions.

2   Work out the total outstanding balance at the end of the month.

   a 4/9/00 Frozen Food Ltd bought 15 large boxes of Chocolate ice-cream flavour without nuts @ £4.20 a box

   b 12/9/00 Frozen Food Ltd bought 8 large boxes of Vanilla ice-cream @ £3.20 a box.

   c 27/9/00 payment of £60.00 was received from Frozen Food Ltd.

   d 29/9/00 Frozen Food Ltd bought another 5 large boxes of vanilla ice-cream.

Remittance advice slips

The supplier will send businesses a document called a remittance advice slip at the same time as a statement of account. It is often attached to the statement.

The remittance advice slip is designed to be detached from the statement and returned with the payment. It gives details of how to pay the balance of the account (the amount that is owed).

Just as businesses receive remittance advice from suppliers and other businesses, which they return with the payment, they go through the same process with customers. Businesses also send a remittance advice slip to customers at the same time as a statement of account. It is often attached to the customer's statement of account.

Customers should detach the remittance advice slip from the statement of account and return it with the payment.

A remittance advice slip generally includes the account number and address to which payment must be sent.

REMITTANCE ADVICE

Ref No 2232

Please send payment to: Customer name:

LIGHT DELIGHT ICE-CREAM LTD

Unit 28 Penraven Industrial Estate
Mean Wood Road
LEEDS
LS7 2AP

Customer Account No: Cheque:..............................

Amount due: Cash:...................................

Total amount paid..............

ACTIVITY

Sava Stores sends Light Delight their outstanding balance for July (go back to the July statement on page 129). Obtain a blank copy of the remittance advice slip (at the back of your book) and fill it in.

Why do you think it is useful to return this document with payment to Light Delight?

Evidence of payment: receipts

When a customer pays for goods or a service, a receipt is provided. A copy of the receipt is kept for the supplier's own records and this receipt is also the customer's evidence of paying for the product, and it proves his or her ownership of the product.

A receipt is vital if goods have to be returned; otherwise the supplier might refuse to accept them.

Businesses might provide customers with one of the following receipts.

Hand-written receipts

This is usually the case with small businesses that do not have the facility to make printed receipts. Looking at the receipt below, it was issued by the Light Delight business to their customer Sava Stores in settlement of the invoice number 10202.

LIGHT DELIGHT ICE-CREAM LTD

Unit 28 Penraven Industrial Estate
Mean Wood Road
LEEDS
LS7 2AP

RECEIPT   No 121

RECEIVED FROM: Sava Stores

the sum of one hundred and forty six

pounds and 37p   £146.37

the payment of invoice number 10202

Received by Emma. J   Date 17/7/00

Printed receipts

These are usually printed out by a cash register and are offered to customers by large businesses, e.g. supermarkets, retailers and petrol stations. Receipts usually show the following information:

- date
- the number of items which were purchased
- how they were purchased
- the name of the store or the shop
- any discount the customer received.

RECEIPT   **NORTH DAIRY MILK PRODUCTS LTD**

14 Dockland Road
LEEDS
LS3 3DT

Number: 7001   **Date:** 15/7/00

Received from: Light Delight Ice-cream Ltd

The sum of: Ten pounds and thirty p only.

£10.65

For: milk powder

```
                                        ┌──────────┐
              RECEIPT                    │ NORTH    │
                                        │ DAIRY    │
                                        │ MILK     │
                                        │ PRODUCTS │
                                        │ LTD      │
Number:  7002           Date: 1/8/00    └──────────┘
                                        14 Dockland Road
Received from: Light Delight Ice-cream Ltd   LEEDS
                                             LS3 3DT
The sum of: Forty-six pounds and sixty p only.

        £40.65

For: milk powder
```

ACTIVITY: READING RECEIPTS

Read carefully the information on the above receipt

1 Which business issued this receipt?
2 Why was the receipt issued?
3 What other information can you read there?

ACTIVITY

1 Renata Ottolini gives you blank copies of the business receipt (ask your tutor for a copy of the receipt from the back of the book) and asks you to write and send the two receipts for the settlement of the following payments:

   a payment of £60.00 received from Frozen Food Ltd on 27/9/00

   b payment of £35.90 received from Sava Stores on 3/8/00.

2 Check the two receipts received from North Dairy Milk Products on page 131 and 132. Can you spot any errors?

ACTIVITY

Brown Stores Ltd sent a cheque on 23/4/00 to pay for their order no. BS/9340. The ice-cream was delivered on 12/4/00. In previous activities you have prepared and sent them a delivery note and an invoice. Renata Ottolini asks you to write and send a receipt to acknowledge that payment has been received (ask your teacher for a blank copy).

ACTIVITY

Collect three different receipts from different businesses for three different products, which you or your family have purchased in the last few weeks. What information can you find on each receipt?

Receipts	Information

Draw a table like the one above. Stick the three receipts on it and write down the relevant information which is included on each one.

ACTIVITY

Brown Stores is a regular customer of Light Delight. On 4 March 2000 they buy 2 boxes of vanilla ice-cream at £3.25 a box and a box of chocolate ice-cream at £4.20 a box. On 25 May they pay the total amount due by cheque. Renata Ottolini asks you to check the following cheque – if it is correct, write and send Brown Stores a receipt (you can ask your tutor to photocopy a blank receipt from the back of the book)

If you think that the cheque is not correct, make the required correction and write a receipt.

Credit notes

When a customer is overcharged or returns unsuitable or damaged products, a credit note may be issued by the supplier.

- Credit notes let the purchaser know that he or she is entitled to a full refund of the cost of the returned items.

- Credit notes give the customer the right to spend at a future date in the shop (for some businesses a credit note must be used within 3 months).

- It is within the customer's rights to refuse the credit note and insist on a cash refund if the goods are faulty.

For example, the following credit note was issued by North Dairy Products Ltd. on 1/10/00. Light Delight ordered 10kg of fat-free milk. The wrong order was delivered. Therefore, a credit note with the amount of £21.30 was issued.

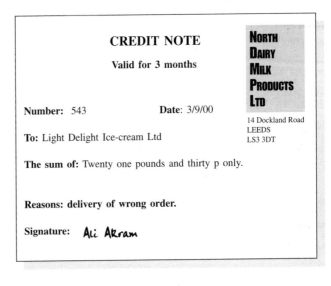

ACTIVITY

Discuss with your partner if the customer has the right to refuse a credit note and to insist on a cash refund in the following situations:

1 Mary has recently bought new dress, without trying it on in the store. When she got home she realised that the dress was too small.
2 Carly received a brown leather handbag as a present from her husband on her birthday. Carly did not like the colour and wants to exchange it for a black one.
3 John recently bought a pair of pyjamas. When he washed them for the first time, at the right temperature, they shrunk.

4   Louise bought a new pair of shoes two months ago. After she wore them only a few times the heel wore out.

ACTIVITY

Sava Stores orders five boxes of vanilla ice-cream from Light Delight Ltd at £3.25 a box. When the order is delivered, Hussain Ahmed, the owner of the supermarket, finds that it is the wrong flavour. He telephones Light Delight to complain. Louise, the Customer Service Manager at Light Delight, is very understanding and apologises to him for this error. She tells him that she will send him a credit note including £5 extra as an apology. Louise asks you to write the note immediately and send it to Sava Stores with a letter of apology. (Ask your teacher to provide you with a blank Light Delight credit note from the back of the book.)

ACTIVITY: THE PURCHASE AND SALE PROCESS

You have learned from the information above that businesses need to make purchases and sales when they trade with suppliers and customers. In this trading process of buying and selling, more or less the same documents are used. When businesses buy from a supplier they receive financial documents and when they sell to customers they send them.

WORD	OPPOSITE
Customers	Sell
Purchase	Receive payment
Send invoice	Receive delivery note
Make payment	Suppliers

Send statement	Receive invoice
Send delivery note	Receive statement

1   Match each of the above words/processes with the opposite one.
2   Rearrange some of the above words into two main headings:
    a   The purchases process for a business.
    b   The sales process for a business.
3   Write in the right order the financial documents which a business sends or receives when it purchases goods from a supplier.
4   Write in the right order the financial documents which a business sends or receives when it sells goods to a customer.

Some businesses purchase (buy in) goods from suppliers to sell them to customers. Others purchase raw materials and equipment to make and sell a final product.

There are two flows: goods flow into the business and goods flow out of the business.

In these buying and selling transactions there are two processes:

a   The process of making purchases.

b   The process of making sales.

ACTIVITY

Fill in the gaps in the following statements by using only opposite words to the underlined ones (use the opposites from the activity above).

The first one is done for you.

1   The first stage of a purchase process is to place an order with a supplier.

The first stage of a <u>selling</u> process is to <u>receive</u> an order from a <u>customer</u>.

Word	Opposite
purchase	selling
deliver	receive
suppliers	customers

2 The second stage of a **purchase** process is to **receive** goods and a delivery note

The second stage of a .... process is to .... goods to customers and a delivery note.

3 The third stage of a **purchase** process is to **receive** an invoice.

The third stage of a .... process is to .... an invoice.

4 The fourth stage of a **purchase** process is to **receive** a statement of account with remittance slip.

The fourth stage of a .... process is to .... a statement of account with remittance slip.

5 The fifth stage of a **purchase** process is to **make** payment and to **send back** the remittance slip.

The fifth stage of a .... process is to .... payment and .... the remittance slip.

5 The final stage of a **purchase** process is to **make** payment and **to send back** the remittance slip.

The final stage of a .... process is to .... payment and .... the remittance slip.

 # ACTIVITY

Draw two separate charts to illustrate the financial documents, which are used with Light

Delight Ltd in their purchases process from a supplier and sale processes to a customer.

ACTIVITY: PURCHASE OR SALES!

As you have already learnt, the following documents record the financial transactions for the purchases function or the sales function.

Financial documents:

*   order (purchase order form)
*   delivery note
*   invoice
*   statement of account
*   remittance advice
*   cheque
*   receipt

This activity will help you to understand when the each of these documents is used in the two business processes of making a purchase and making a sale.

Fill in the gaps in the following sentences using only one of two words, **sale** or **purchase**.

1   When a business **receives** a delivery note, this is a step in the process of making a

....

2   When a business **sends** an invoice, this is a step in the process of making a ....

3   When a business **sends** a statement of account, this is a step in the process of making a ....

4   When a business **sends** a customer a receipt, this is a step in the process of making a ....

5   When a business **receives** a remittance advice, this is a step the process of making a ....

6   When a business **sends** a cheque out to settle an account, this is the final step in the process of making a ....

7   When a business **sends** a purchase order form, this is a step in the process of making a ....

8   When a business **receives** a delivery note, this is a step in the process of making a ....

9   When a business **receives** a receipt from a supplier, this is a step in the process of making a ....

Petty cash vouchers

Most offices find that they need to make cash payments each day for items bought for the office, e.g. cleaning materials, light bulbs, tea, coffee, flowers and plants. Instead of asking the chief cashier each time cash is required, it is simpler to make these payments from petty cash.

What is the petty cash?

The petty cash is an amount of money made up of small notes and coins. This cash is kept in a lockable metal cash box.

It is sensible to have only one set of keys for the cash box and these keys are generally looked after by an accounts clerk or a senior secretary. The person may also be called the petty cashier.

What is a petty cash voucher?

Whenever an employee wishes to claim back money which has been spent on items for the office, they should complete a petty cash voucher with details of the items

purchased and the price paid. Receipts should always be obtained for these items and attached to the petty cash voucher as proof of purchase.

Petty cash voucher		No 103
		Date: 13/2/00
For what required	**Amount**	
	£	P
2 pints of fresh milk		76
2 cartons of fresh apple juice	1	98
Sandwiches for the Director's meeting	12	43
Total Cash Spending	15	16
VAT is included		
Signature Emma. J		
Authorised		
R. Ottolini		

Example of a petty cash voucher

Petty cash items are usually quite small purchases. Even so, the total amount of petty cash expenditure in a business over a year can be considerable.

This is particularly true for a large company with many employees. For every petty cash purchase, a petty cash voucher must be completed. Even for very small purchases (for example, of 50p or less), on each petty cash voucher a note should be made as to whether or not the price paid included VAT.

If more than one item has been purchased, the amounts are totalled on the voucher to show the full amount being claimed. The voucher should be dated and signed by the person claiming the money.

Things to remember about petty cash vouchers:

1 The receipts should be kept and attached to the voucher as proof of purchase and the amount of money spent.

2 The voucher would also be completed by the petty cashier before making payments to people who were being paid for a service they had given the company, e.g. milkman, cleaner and window cleaner.

3 All vouchers are numbered and should be issued in numerical order

4 The vouchers are usually issued before the money is spent.

5 Junior staff must obtain authorisation from a supervisor before spending any money on behalf of the company or claiming any money from the petty cash.

6 Completed vouchers must be filed safely in numerical or date order.

 **ACTIVITY**

On 3 August 2000 John Edward who works as a secretary in the company ordered some sandwiches (£8.98), 4 cartons of fruit juice (£2.97) and some fresh flowers (£1.99) for the Board of Directors meeting.

Petty cash voucher	No I
	Date:
For what required	**Amount** **£ P**
Total Cash Spending	
VAT is included	
Signature	....
Authorised	....

Fill in a copy of the petty cash voucher below, and consider the following:

1 What information should be filled in?
2 What is John's total spending?
3 Who should sign the above voucher?
4 Who could authorise the above voucher?

Checking petty cash vouchers

The petty cashier will check that the voucher has been correctly completed (dated, added up correctly, signed, authorised) and is supported by receipts for the purchase.

The petty cashier numbers the vouchers, in order, and they are filed in numerical order. The cash can then be handed over to the person making the claim.

Where petty cash vouchers are kept

All completed vouchers must be kept with the petty cash box as they will be needed at a later date when the petty cash is checked and balanced.

Question
Why do you think it is important that the petty cash voucher is completed and signed by the petty cashier before the money is given out?

 **ACTIVITY**

Renata Ottolini the Administration manager at Light Delight Ltd asks you to work out how much money should remain in the petty cash tin on the date given, and should be reported to the petty cashier:

1 3/11/00 – petty cash amount £100.
Vouchers paid out to date: £26.25, £4.50,
£12.75, 95p, £3.35, £2.25.

2 4/11/98 – petty cash amount £50. Vouchers
paid out to date: £17.25, £3.50, £1.75, 80p,
£10.35, £7.25.

3 10/11/98 – petty cash amount £25.
Vouchers paid out to date: £8.15, £5.50,
£2.25, £1.05, £5.35, 75p.

ACTIVITY

Renata asks you to complete a pretty cash
voucher for cleaning materials at £7.50 and
sugar for the office at £2.54. The amount in
the petty cash tin is £25, and she tells you
that the last petty cash voucher number was
3454.

1 Who should sign this voucher?
2 Who should authorise this voucher?
3 How much money should remain in the
petty cash tin at the end of the day?

ACTIVITY

Renata Ottolini gives Emma £40 from the
petty cash. Emma spends most of the money
on mailing two parcels, buying fresh milk,
computer disks and stationery items. Renata
asks you to check the following cash petty
voucher before she authorises it. Find out how
much money Emma should have left.

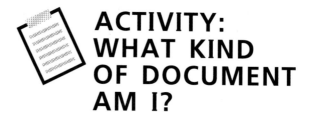

Petty cash voucher	No 776	
	Date: 29/9/00	
For what required	Amount £	P
fee for mailing 2 parcels	7	20
2 pints of fresh milk	0	75
computer disks	12	40
stationery items	10	35
Total Cash Spending	35	07
VAT is included Signature *Emma. J*		
Authorised		

ACTIVITY: WHAT KIND OF DOCUMENT AM I?

You have learned that businesses use a variety
of financial documents when sales and
purchases are made. Each of these documents
is simply a piece of paper with some
important information. The name and the
description of this piece of paper depends on:

1 **the nature** and type of written
information

2 **the purpose** of this information

3 **the user** of the information.

In this activity you have to find out the proper
name for each of the following pieces of paper.
The description of the information will help
you to identify the document

Before you do the activity revise the terms at
the end of this unit.

1 *I am a document* which firms have to
complete and send to a supplier to order

or buy a product. I contain full details of the quantity, type, size and colour of the goods required.

2   *I am a document* with a written order or instruction from someone to a bank to pay a specific sum of money to someone else.

3   *I am a document* which is issued by a business to a customer. I entitle the buyer of the product to a full refund of the cost of returned items, e.g. damaged items.

4   *I am a document* which is carried by the driver of a delivery vehicle. I am a list of the products which have been sent by a supplier.

5   *I am a document* which tells the business that has bought the goods what it owes and when payment is due. I am sent at the same time as the goods. I state what has been delivered, the price and terms.

6   *I am a document* which must be completed when a petty cash purchase is made.

7   *I am a document* which is sent by a business at the same time as a statement of account. I am often attached to the statement. I include details, e.g. account number, customer's name etc.

8   *I am a document* which provides a customer with evidence that they have paid for a product, and proves his or her ownership of it.

9   *I am a document* which shows a business what it is owed and what it has been paid. I list payments as credits and the amounts owed as debits.

ACTIVITY: WHY KEEP FINANCIAL DOCUMENTS?

All businesses need to record, store and keep information about their suppliers and their customers. This activity will help you to understand why a business needs to store these financial documents that were used to make sales or purchases.

1   Find out if each of the following statements is **true** or **false**.

   a   Businesses record and keep financial information about customers and suppliers in order to be able to work out how much they spend and how much they owe them.

   b   Keeping sufficient and accurate information and records about suppliers helps businesses to receive and organise customers' orders.

   c   Keeping sufficient and accurate information and records about customers helps businesses to work out their needs and wants.

   d   Keeping sufficient and accurate information and records about customers helps businesses to order the right level of stock from suppliers.

   e   Keeping sufficient and accurate information and records about suppliers helps businesses to work out their expenditure (spending) on suppliers.

   f   Keeping sufficient and accurate information and records about suppliers helps businesses to work out their income from sales.

   g   Keeping information about customers does not help businesses to communicate with them.

   h   Keeping information about suppliers helps businesses to offer a better customer service and after-sale service.

i Keeping sufficient and accurate information about customers wastes a business's time and resources in working out and claiming outstanding balances.

j Keeping adequate information and records about suppliers helps business to satisfy customers' needs and wants.

Methods of making and receiving payments

When you go to a supermarket to do your weekly shopping, or a shop to buy clothes or to a restaurant to buy a meal, usually you can pay for what you buy in different ways. Perhaps the most common ways nowadays to pay for what we buy are:

* cash
* cheques
* charge cards
* credit cards
* debit cards.

Cash

As we have said before, businesses agree that immediate cash is the most favoured method to pay a bill. The retailer gets the money immediately. Although cash is becoming less important it is still needed to make certain low-value purchases, for example, buying sweets or a newspaper from a corner shop.

Buying with a card

There are many different types of plastic cards but they all use a similar system at the point of sale – the situation where, having decided what you want to buy, you bring out a piece of plastic to pay for it!

The cashier or sales assistant will fill out a sales voucher which shows details of what you have bought and how much it cost. You hand over your card and the coded information on it is imprinted on to the sales voucher. In some cases this can be done electronically.

You check that the details are correct and then sign. A copy is given to you and this is your record that you have spent that money.

The shop or business from whom you bought the goods will make a number of sales during the day where people have paid with the same type of card as you used. They send all the sales vouchers off to the company which runs the card and at the end of the month they will be paid for all the sales made.

The card company sorts out all the vouchers belonging to your card number, and at the end of the month you will receive a state-ment showing all the purchases made using your card and the total amount you owe.

What you do now depends upon the type of card and how you are choosing to use it.

Charge cards

With a charge card, when you get your statement at the end of the month you have to pay the amount owing. Examples of charge cards are American Express and Diners Card.

Debit cards

Debit cards are used in the same way as cheques. The best known systems are called

Switch, Connect and Delta. Before the payment is made the checkout operator checks to see if there are sufficient funds in the customer's account.

The transaction requires the customer's own signature on the sales voucher to prevent fraud.

Did you know?

Some debit cards like Barclays Connect can not only be used as a debit card but also as a £100 cheque guarantee card, which allows you to withdraw money from thousands of cash machines in the UK and many more worldwide.

Credit cards

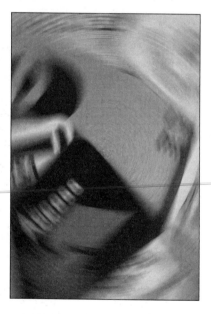

The best known credit cards are Access and Visa. With credit cards, customers buy the product now and pay later. Immediate payment is not required.

Once you are 18 or over, you can apply for a credit card.

With a credit card such as Access you are given a spending limit when you apply. When you receive your statement at the

end of the month, you can if you wish pay off all the balance outstanding. Your statements will show the date by which you must make the payment. If you make a purchase right at the start of your month then it may be 7 weeks before you pay the card company. In this way a credit card is rather like a free overdraft and many people use their cards in this way.

The risk of card theft and fraud is causing some banks to experiment with customer's photographs on cards.

Did you know?

1 VisaCard and MasterCard are accepted in 14 million outlets in over 200 countries worldwide.

2 Credit cards may be used to withdraw cash at any bank branch for a small fee (£1 – £1.50).

3 There is an immediate interest charge for this service. A credit card could be used as a guarantee card.

ACTIVITY

1 Ask three different people, preferably card holders, which method(s) they usually prefer to use when they purchase goods or services. Find out why they prefer this particular method(s).

2 Which methods of payment would you prefer to use to purchase each of the following items:

a a packet of sweets

b a bottle of wine

c a piece of home furniture

d the supermarket weekly shopping

e a winter coat

f paying a deposit for a holiday?

Explain your answers.

Store charge cards

Many major stores operate a charge card which can be used to purchase goods only in branches of the store, eg the Marks & Spencer Charge Card. It works both as a charge and a credit card. You can spend up to a certain amount and have the choice to repay in full or spread the payments over a number of months. If you don't repay in full at the end of the month then interest will be charged and added to your account.

Instant electronic payments

Banks have had to develop appropriate ways of making payments in these new systems, eg debit and credit cards. When customers hand in their cards to the shopkeepers or the checkout operators they give instructions to their bank to make payments for them via an electronic network.

Instant electronic payments using a wide range of payment and credit cards will increase. An electronic terminal reads a

Method of payment	Advantages		Disadvantages	
	Buyer	**Seller**	**Buyer**	**Seller**
Cash	• Knows how much money is left	• Gets money immediately	• Has to carry around a lot of cash, risk of losing it/being mugged etc	• Shops can become a target for robbery
Cheques	• Easy to carry around • Generally accepted	• Guaranteed up to £50 or £100 • Not attractive for robbers	• For expensive items retailer may not release goods immediately but wait until cheque has 'cleared'	• Takes about 5 days for money to reach seller's account • Cheques can 'bounce' after buyer has left with goods
Credit cards	• Easy to carry around • Not limited to amount in account • Gives some consumer protection	• Payment guaranteed (unless stolen) • Useless to robbers	• Easy to run up large debts • Easy to steal	• Credit card companies charge up to 5% • It takes – days for money to reach seller's account
Debit cards	• Easy to carry around • Spending limited to amount in account • Some stores give 'cash back'	• Payment guaranteed (unless stolen) • Usless to robbers • By giving 'cash back' can reduce amount of cash in tills • Payment instant	• Buyer is limited to amount so can't spread spending • Easy to steal	• A percentage is charged by banks to handle transaction
Store cards	• Offer the buyer 'perks' such as extra discount	• Encourages buyers to return to that store	• Rates of interest very high • Can only be used in named stores	

magnetic strip on the card when it is passed, or swiped, through it.

Can you be refused a card?

One day you might apply for a credit card or a store card and find that your bank or the business which you are applying to says no. The business or the bank has the right to refuse if they think you could be a bad risk. Your bank or the business does not have to say why, but the chances are they would have consulted a credit reference agency. There are a number of credit reference agencies throughout the country that collect information on people who may have not paid their debts in the past.

Stolen cards

Lost or stolen cards can be like losing money. But you can help to prevent other people from using your card by arranging a card protection scheme with your bank or building society. The schemes will cover all your cards, credit, debit, store and member fees cards. You can make one free call to cancel all missing cards and they will also replace the lost cards with new ones.

 ACTIVITY

1 Find 3 businesses in the high street which operate a charge card system. Write down the names of these businesses or stores.
2 What is the size of each of these businesses?
3 Write to or ring the customer service department in one of these businesses. Find out about the rules for applying for a charge card, eg age, occupation, etc.
4 Find out what you have to do if the card got lost or stolen.
5 Find out if local small shops issue charge cards to their customers. Why do you think this is the case?

 # ACTIVITY: BE SECURE

When you become a customer of a bank you are given items like cheque books and cards to help you make payments. If they fall into the wrong hands, money could be taken from your account by somebody else. You need to look after your 'financial instruments' and here are some words of advice.

Suggest what could happen if you don't listen to each of the following:

1 **Don't keep** your cheque card in the same wallet, pocket or bag as your cheque book.
2 **Don't leave** your cheque book and your cards in a changing room or cloakroom.
3 **Don't write** your cashpoint PIN number down on to a piece of paper and keep it with your card.
4 **Don't peer** over somebody's shoulder when you are at a cash point and don't let anyone look over yours.

Other methods of payment

The above methods of payment are not the only ones which customers can use to purchase a product. There are other methods of payment which some businesses allow customers to use. Other common methods include:

Standing orders

Sometimes a customer wants to make the payment for a fixed sum at regular intervals, eg a hire purchase instalment. To avoid having to remember to make a cheque on the right date, a standing order may be given to the customer's bank.

This instructs them to transfer from your account a stated amount at regular intervals to the bank of the payee.

Hire purchase

This is an older system than credit card sales. It is very similar in that the customer has the goods and pays for them over a long period of time (up to 3 years). With the hire purchase agreement you can spread the cost of buying a product over a period of time, 6 or 12 months. Customers have to pay interest to be able to obtain the facility.

However, the customer does not become the legal owner of the goods until the last payment. If the customer fails to keep up with the payments, the goods can be re-possessed.

Key Terms

Advice note A note that is sent from the supplier to the business (shop or warehouse) when an order is received.

Bank statement A statement that includes a summary of transactions over a period of time. It shows records of payments (debits) and receipts (credits).

Cheque IAn order written by the drawer (the person who writes the chequeto a bank to pay on demand a specific sum of money to someone else (the payee.

Cheque guarantee card A plastic, personal card with the name and account number of the holder and the expiry date. It guarantees that the banks will honour the cheque. There is usually a sued by a business to a customer. It entitles the buyer of the product to a full refund of the cost of returned items, e.g. damaged items.

Debit card A method of payment, e.g. Switch, Delta and Connect.

Delivery note A note that is carried by the driver of the delivery vehicle. It is a list of the products that have been sent by a supplier.

Drawee The drawer's bank where he or she holds an account.

Drawer The person writing the cheque.

Invoice A bill (demand for payment) which tells the business that has bought the goods what it owes and when payment is due. It is sent at the same time as the goods. It states what has been delivered, the price and terms.

Payee The person who receives the cheque.

Petty cash Cash that is available in a business for small purchases, e.g. coffee, sugar.

Petty cash voucher A piece of paper that must be completed when a petty cash purchase is made.

Purchase order form A form which firms have to complete and send to the supplier to order or buy a product. It contains full details of the quantity, type, size and colour of the goods required.

Receipt Customer's evidence of paying for the product, and it proves his ownership of the product.

Remittance advice A document that is send by a business at the same time as a statement of account. It is often attached to the statement. It includes details, e.g. account number, customer name etc.

Statement of account Statement that shows a business what it is owed and what it has been paid. It lists payments as credits and the amounts owed as debits.

Store charge card A card that is issued by a big store or retailer to customers, allowing them to make purchases only in that store. It acts like a credit card, so customers do not have to make immediate payment when they purchase the product. An example is Marks and Spencer Charge Card.

Value Added Tax (VAT) An indirect tax that is added to the total cost of the goods (after any discounts have been deducted). The current rate is 17.5%.

Unit 3 Test your knowledge

Activity I: Wrong or right answers

This is a quick test to help you check how much you have understood.

In the following statements, there are some right and some wrong answers. Circle only the wrong answer:

1   Costs are the money which a business:

   a   makes from selling its products.
   b   borrows from a bank or another business.
   c   spends in order to produce goods and services for its customers.

2   Fixed costs are costs which:

   a   remain unchanged at whatever the level of output the business is producing over a period of time.
   b   which change directly with the output of a business.
   c   an owner pays to start up the business.
   d   a business pays when it trades with suppliers or customers.

3   Profit is the money which is:

   a   paid to workers for doing their jobs.
   b   is left when all costs paid in making and selling a product are taken away from the revenue gained from that sale.
   c   made from selling a product.

4   Sales revenue is the money which a business:

   a   receives as a result of selling its products.
   b   pays for making and selling a product.
   c   receives from selling the products and after taking away all costs.

5   Variable costs are costs which:

   a   directly vary with the output of a business.
   b   don't change with the change in the level of production
   c   a business has to pay for making and selling a product

6   Running costs are costs which:

   a   a business pays on any non-trading expense.
   b   relate to a business's trading activities, including VAT.
   c   vary with the changes in the level of production.

7   A budget is:

   a   a statement which shows how much the business owes to others.
   b   an account which shows how much profit the business made last year.
   c   a plan showing the expected sales revenue and costs over the coming month or year.

8   Cash flow is the flow of money:

   a   into and out of a business.
   b   between suppliers and a business.
   c   between customers and a business.

9   A purchase order form is a form which:

   a   is sent from the supplier to the business (shop or warehouse) when an order is received.

b firms have to complete and send to the supplier to order or buy a product. It includes all the details about this product.

c includes a summary of transactions over a period of time. It shows records of payments and receipts.

10 A cheque is:

a the only method of payment for goods or services.

b an order written by the person who writes to the bank to pay on demand a specific sum of money to someone else.

c the quickest method of payment.

11 A cheque guarantee card is a card which:

a a retailer issues to guarantee the quality of a product.

b guarantees that the banks will honour the cheque.

c a bank issues to customers that guarantees the account will always have plenty of money.

12 A credit card is a card that is:

a used to pay for goods or services. It allows nearly six weeks for customers to pay for the goods.

b obtainable by anyone from a bank or building society.

c issued by a store or a retailer to customers to purchase goods.

13 The cost of new machinery and equipment is considered as:

a variable cost.

b fixed cost.

c start-up cost.

14 A credit note is a note that is:

a issued by a business to a customer. It entitles the buyer of the product to a full refund of the cost of returned items.

b carried by the driver of the delivery vehicle. It is a list of the products that have been sent by a supplier.

c completed when a petty cash purchase is made.

15 A receipt is:

a the customer's evidence of paying for the product, and it proves his/her ownership of the product.

b a document which is sent by a business at the same time as a statement of account.

c the order which is received by a business or supplier to check whether items are in stock and what price is to be charged.

16 The cost of renting business premises is considered as:

a start-up cost.

b running cost.

c variable cost.

Activity 2

Which financial document would you use in each of the following situations?

1 The manager of Speed Ltd asked you to order new machinery. You have to fill in and send a document to the supplier Engineering Manufacturing Ltd to order the new machinery. What is the document?

a a cheque
b a receipt
c a purchase order form
d an invoice.

2 Engineering Manufacturing Ltd send you a statement with:

a an invoice
b a purchase order form
c statement of account
d a cheque.

3 Your sales manager asked you to issue a document to a customer who purchased a faulty product to entitle her to a full refund of the cost of the returned CD player. What is the document?

a a receipt
b an invoice

c a credit note
d a petty cash voucher.

4 The administration manager of Speed Ltd asked you to record in a document the expenditure on milk. What is the document?

a petty cash voucher
b invoice
c statement of account
d remittance advice.

6 Your finance manager asked you to check if Engineering Manufacturing Ltd has sent a document to prove Speed Ltd's ownership of the new machinery. What is the document?

a receipt
b credit note
c invoice
d delivery note.

LIGHT DELIGHT ICE-CREAM LTD

Unit 28 Penraven Industrial Estate
Mean Wood Road
LEEDS
LS7 2AP

Tel. No.: 0113 234543   **Order**   VAT Reg No: 680 73842 88

Date: 3/7/200

Order No. DF/1315

To:

Please supply

Quantity	Description	Ref	Unit Price

Delivery: asap
Signed by

LIGHT DELIGHT ICE-CREAM LTD

Unit 28 Penraven Industrial Estate
Mean Wood Road
LEEDS
LS7 2AP

DELIVERY NOTE

To   **VAT REG NO 680/7384288**

Your order	Invoice date	Invoice No	Dispatch date
Quantity	**Description**		**Cat No**

Received by.......   **Date:**

LIGHT DELIGHT ICE-CREAM LTD

Unit 28 Penraven Industrial Estate
Mean Wood Road
LEEDS
LS7 2AP

INVOICE

VAT REG NO 680/7384288

Customer

Customer Ref. No:
Despatch Date:

Invoice No:
Date

Quantity	Description	Unit Price	Total
E&OE		Subtotal	
		Discount 5%	
		Amount after discount	
		VAT (17.5%)	
		Total	

LIGHT DELIGHT ICE-CREAM LTD

Unit 28 Penraven Industrial Estate
Mean Wood Road
LEEDS
LS7 2AP

FAX: 0113 234543

TEL: 0113 234544

VAT REG NO 680/73842/88

STATEMENT

To:

Date: Account no

Date	Details	Debit	Credit	Balance
Total outstanding balance				

REMITTANCE ADVICE

Ref No 2232

Please send payment to: **Customer name:**

LIGHT DELIGHT ICE-CREAM LTD

Unit 28 Penraven Industrial Estate
Mean Wood Road
LEEDS
LS7 2AP

Customer Account No: Cheque:.................................

Amount due: Cash:......................................

          Total amount paid ....

Petty cash voucher   **No**

          Date:

For what required   **Amount**
          £   P

Total Cash Spending

VAT is included
Signature   -------------------------------------

Authorised   -------------------------------------

LIGHT DELIGHT ICE-CREAM LTD

Unit 28 Penraven Industrial Estate
Mean Wood Road
LEEDS
LS7 2AP

RECEIPT   No

RECEIVED FROM:

£

the payment of

Received by   Date

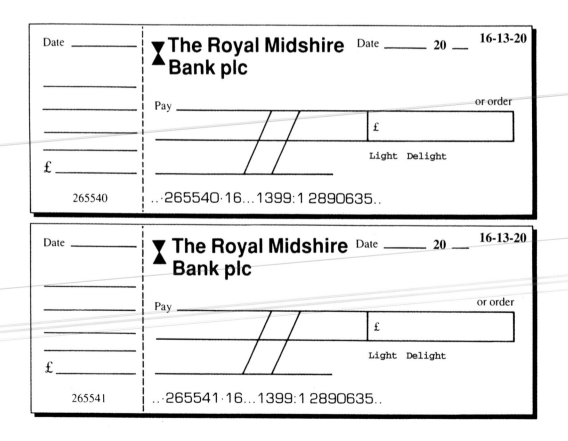

Date _____	▼ **The Royal Midshire**	Date _____ 20 __	**16-13-20**
	Bank plc		
_____			
_____	Pay _____		or order
_____		£	
		Light Delight	
£ _____			
265540	...265540·16...1399:1 2890635..		

Date _____	▼ **The Royal Midshire**	Date _____ 20 __	**16-13-20**
	Bank plc		
_____			
_____	Pay _____		or order
_____		£	
		Light Delight	
£ _____			
265541	...265541·16...1399:1 2890635..		

FAX MESSAGE

LIGHT DELIGHT ICE-CREAM LTD

Unit 28 Penraven Industrial Estate
Mean Wood Road
LEEDS
LS7 2AP

FAX NO: 0113 234543

TO:
DATE:

This unit introduces you to methods that can assist you in looking after your money effectively and to ways you can plan your spending to help make your future life more secure. You will find out about:

- sources of personal income and different ways of saving

- personal budget planning so that you do not pay out more money than you have coming in

- costs of borrowing and the benefits of saving

- financial institutions (such as banks and building societies) and how these can help you manage your money

- financial services and products that banks and building societies provide

- where to go for financial advice and help.

This unit is linked with Unit 3 ('Finance in business'), where the same principles are discussed but in relation to business finance.

This unit will be assessed through your portfolio work only. The grade awarded will be the grade for the unit.

When you leave school or college to start a new job, there are many questions you will have to ask yourself:

- Do I have enough money to pay my own way?

- Do I need a bank account and, if so, where and how do I open one?

- Will I be able to fulfil my ambitions to buy those things I have wanted for a long time?

- Should I save to get what I want or try to borrow money?

This unit is full of information that will help you to find answers to such questions as these. And remember to save all the information you collect while studying for this unit – it may be useful to you in the future!

Skills in managing personal finance

You have probably already handled many money transactions (e.g. buying magazines, clothes, CDs, etc.). You have probably also made decisions about whether you should spend your money or save it. You might also have worked on a part-time or a holiday basis and so will have learnt to manage a regular income.

You have probably made mistakes with your money. Many people know the feeling of having been given money only to realise that they have squandered it, spending it on things they did not really need.

Have you lent money to a friend and then lived through the difficult period when he or she has not been able to pay you back? Then there is the situation where you may have decided to commit yourself to going on a trip, believing you could save the money, only to find that, as the day draws near, you do not have the money and have to turn to parents or friends for help.

Through these experiences you will have learnt quite a lot about money and the problems of handling money, and some of you will have realised that, if you handle money sensibly, life is much less complicated.

Assessing your personal finance skills

This simple questionnaire will help you to assess your personal finance skills and will suggest further improvements you could make to your money-handling abilities.

1 I think carefully before I buy anything

  a always
  b usually
  c sometimes
  d occasionally
  e never

2 I borrow money from friends or family

  a always
  b usually
  c sometimes
  d occasionally
  e never

3 I shop around before I buy something

  a always
  b usually
  c sometimes
  d occasionally
  e never

4 I buy only what I need

  a always
  b usually
  c sometimes
  d occasionally
  e never

5 I look for bargains to save money

  a always
  b usually
  c sometimes
  d occasionally
  e never

6 I plan ahead about what to spend and when to spend it

  a always
  b usually
  c sometimes
  d occasionally
  e never

7 I try to save some of my money for a rainy day

  a always
  b usually
  c sometimes
  d occasionally
  e never

8 I learn from my spending mistakes

  a always
  b usually
  c sometimes
  d occasionally
  e never

9 I ask for help when I make mistakes with spending my money

  a always
  b usually
  c sometimes
  d occasionally
  e never

10 I ask for advice before I buy something

  a always
  b usually
  c sometimes
  d occasionally
  e never

Check your score:

1 a) 4, b) 3, c) 2, d) 1, e) 0
2 a) 0, b) 1, c) 2, d) 3, e) 4
3 a) 4, b) 3, c) 2, d) 1, e) 0
4 a) 4, b) 3, c) 2, d) 1, e) 0
5 a) 4, b) 3, c) 2, d) 1, e) 0
6 a) 4, b) 3, c) 2, d) 1, e) 0
7 a) 4, b) 3, c) 2, d) 1, e) 0
8 a) 4, b) 3, c) 2, d) 1, e) 0
9 a) 0, b) 1, c) 2, d) 3, e) 4
10 a) 4, b) 3, c) 2, d) 1, e) 0

Analysis

Score 25–32

Excellent/very good skills at handling money. This is an excellent start for the future. You have the right personality and attitude towards handling money matters. You will learn more from the unit to build on this.

Score 18–24

Good skills with handling money. A good start, but you need to learn more to improve these skills.

Score 11–17

Inadequate skills with handling your money. There is a lot for you to learn.

Score 4–10

Very poor skills in handling your money. You need to assess your attitude towards money and how it could be improved.

Sources of income

People receive their money from a variety of sources.

Earnings from a job

Once we have a job this is usually our main source of income. However, if you are still at school or college, your only chance to earn money will probably be through a summer or part-time job. You may not earn a great deal from part-time work but, remember, it is your window to life where you will learn a lot about what it means to work and, at the same time, how to communicate with other people.

In most cases, the money people earn from employment is taxable. They must pay a certain proportion of their incomes to the Inland Revenue. There are also other calls on people's incomes, which you will learn about later.

Benefit payments

Some people are paid benefits by the government for one reason or another – this will depend on individual circumstances. For example, unemployed disabled people receive extra benefit to help them with their higher living expenses. If you receive only supplementary benefit, unemployment benefit or a training programme allowance (or a student grant), these are not taxable.

 **ACTIVITY**

Find out from your local social security department about unemployment benefits (e.g. how much is usually paid and who is entitled to it).

1 Why do you think the government pays these benefits?
2 Do you think it is fair to give unemployed people benefits? Give your reasons.

Interest from savings

One of the things you will learn about in this unit is different ways of saving money. If you save your money in a cupboard it will not grow. If you save it in a bank or other financial institution you will earn extra money, which is called *interest*. If you are under the age of 16, the government will not tax your savings.

Pensions

Once you start work you must, by law, pay pension contributions. The maximum you can pay into a pension scheme is 15% of your annual income. Once you retire, you should enjoy a regular source of income from the scheme. The more you save in your scheme when you are young, the more income you will earn when you retire.

Allowances paid by the family

If you are still in school or college your family will probably pay your living expenses. You might also be receiving a weekly or monthly allowance. Some families introduce allowance schemes for their children for such items as clothing or stationery. Christmas and birthday money are other sources of personal finance you may receive from your family.

Borrowed money

Although borrowing is generally not a good idea, it does add to your sources of finance. Buying things on a credit card is a form of borrowing. This increases your finance in the short term but for few a few weeks only. If you do not pay the full amount you borrowed on credit before the due date, you have to pay the penalty (again, called interest).

ACTIVITY

Complete the following sentence:
Although borrowing will increase my . . . in the short term, it will . . . my spending in the long run.

Uses of personal income

You can spend your personal income in a variety of ways. Some of these you can choose, others you have no choice about. How much you spend depends on many factors:

- Your present income or earnings.

- Your plans for the future.

- How much is available to you from your regular savings (or, if you are older, from investments or pension payments).

- Your liability to pay income tax or national insurance contributions.

- Your plans for retirement (should you have already considered these!).

No matter what our personal income is or where it comes from, we must usually spend some of it in the following ways.

Everyday spendings

These are payments made to purchase everyday essentials such as food, rent and bus fares.

Spending on expensive items

We do not just spend money on essential goods. We buy expensive products that make our lives more pleasurable and easier – for example, washing machines, computers and microwaves.

Tax and national insurance

Unless you are self-employed, it is your employer's responsibility to pay your tax. Your employer does this by deducting the tax from the amount you earn. Your employer is told by the Inland Revenue how much to take out of your earnings.

ACTIVITY

Find out the address of your local tax office. Arrange to visit the office and ask them for a copy of the young person's guide to the tax system.

Most people in employment must pay a national insurance contribution. These contributions go towards paying for the services people receive under the National Health Service, for pension entitlements, etc.

> **? Did you know?**
>
> Everyone in this country has a national insurance number. When you are 16 years of age you will automatically receive your own number.

Insurance, pensions and savings

Another use of personal income is to buy

insurance against sickness or disability. The *premiums* (what you must pay to keep up your insurance policy) will be paid at regular intervals (e.g. monthly). Similarly, any arrangements someone has made for a pension scheme must be paid for, whether these come directly out of his or her wages or are paid directly by that person him or herself to the pension company.

If we are thoughtful about the use of our money, we are likely to be planning for the future. Hence our concerns about health insurance and pensions. However, we may want to have a special holiday, get married, or put down a deposit on a home of our own. These things can be very expensive and usually cannot be paid for outright – we need to save for them.

Saving is simply the decision not to spend money in the present in order to spend it in the future. Once you have decided to save part of your pay – for whatever reason and wherever you may decide to save it (a banks, building society, the post office or other financial institution) – this, too, will become an outgoing from your personal income.

Repayments for mortgages and loans

If you borrow money from a building society or bank in order to buy a house, you are taking out what is called a *mortgage*. You will need to repay the mortgage over a number of years (usually 25). Your home will be at risk if you do not keep up with your mortgage repayments. Hence, mortgage repayments are one of the most important considerations for most people when they are planning how they will spend their incomes.

Similarly, if you have borrowed money from a bank or a building society to purchase a new car or kitchen, you have to repay the loan (with interest) at fixed dates. Such loans can also be a major drain on our personal incomes. So too might be repayments for goods or services bought on hire purchase or by credit card.

The personal budget

From what you have learnt in the last section about all the demands on your personal income, it should come as no surprise to you that, if we are to manage our money effectively, we need to budget.

A *personal* budget is a similar to the statement a business makes about its profit, which we learnt about in Chapter 10. To prepare your own personal budget you need to record:

- The amount of money you have coming in from earnings and other sources each week.

- The amount of money you spend each week on items such as food, travel, clothes, entertainment and savings.

- Amounts you pay on a regular basis.

The first step in producing your personal budget is to try to work out how much money you have coming in each week or month and how much you must pay out each week or month.

ACTIVITY

Imagine you have left school or college and have started work. You earn £80 a week and out of this you have certain fixed weekly expenses:

	£
Rent to parents	20
Bus fares	5
Lunches	10
Weekends	22
Telephone	3
Total	60

1 What will be left over from your income at the end of the week?
2 If your expenses were to remain the same for the next six months, and your income also remained the same, how much would you have left over at the end of six months?

However, things are never as straightforward as this! Although our incomes may remain the same over a fairly lengthy period of time, our outgoings more than likely will not. There will inevitably be occasions when we would like to – or, indeed, may *have to* – spend more than we earn. In such circumstances we may have to consider borrowing money.

Borrowing money

It might be possible to ask your parents, friends or a bank to help you to sort out your financial problems by lending you money. Remember, though, they might be able and happy to help you some of the time, but not all the time!

We defined saving early as making a decision not to spend now in order to be able to spend more in the future. Borrowing is the reverse of this. You borrow a sum of money to spend now but have to put aside parts of your income to repay the amount you have borrowed. There is, however, one big difference between buying something with *borrowed* money and saving up your *own* money to buy it. Borrowing costs money because you will be charged a *rate of interest*.

 Did you know?

You must be over 18 years of age before you are allowed to borrow money from a bank or building society.

However, nearly all of us at some point in our lives you will be faced with the decision about whether to borrow money or not. This may be for something quite minor (such as borrowing money to buy a new hi-fi system) or for something that will commit us for many years to come (such as taking out a mortgage to buy a house). For whatever reason we want to borrow money, we must always ask ourselves three important questions:

1 Why am I borrowing this money?

2 Where can I borrow it from?

3 How am I going to repay it?

CASE STUDY — Repaying a loan

Look back at the activity you did earlier in this section where you worked out how much money you had left over at the end of the week and at the end of six months. Things have not worked out quite as simply as you expected:

- You borrowed £6 from your mother on 3 January because you knew your wages would not cover all your expenses for the week ending 7 January.

- You borrowed £10 from your father on 12 January to help you pay the £30 deposit for a holiday.

- You borrowed a further £20 from your father on 19 January to help you buy a new pair of shoes to wear for work.

- On 28 January you paid your father back £20 of the money he had lent you.

Read this case study carefully and then answer the following questions:

1 How much money do you still owe your *father?*

2 How much money do you still owe your *mother?*

3 Suggest items in your expenses you could reduce to repay your father and mother all the money you owe them.

The following is your personal budget for the first four weeks of January:

Week ending	7 Jan £	14 Jan £	21 Jan £	28 Jan £
Income	80	80	80	80
Expenses				
Rent to parents	20	20	20	20
Bus fares	5	5	5	5
Lunches	10	10	10	10
Weekends	22	22	22	22
Telephone	3	3	3	3
Clothes	15	-	-	-
Dry cleaning	2	-	-	-
Cinema	9	-	-	-
Holiday deposit	-	30	-	-
Shoes	-	-	40	-
Total	86	90	100	60
Net	(6)	(10)	(20)	20
Loan mother	(6)B			
Loan father		(10)B	(20)B	(20)R

B= borrowing; R= repayment; figures in brackets indicate shortfalls — either money you owe or have borrowed or money you need but which your wages will not cover.

So far we have looked at outgoings on a weekly basis. Things become more complicated when we have to consider outgoings that may occur on a monthly, quarterly or annual basis. For example:

- Monthly payments to repay a mortgage or bank loan.

- Monthly payments to pay the gas, water and electricity bills.

- Quarterly payments to pay for membership fees, to pay for a TV licence, etc.

- Annual payments to cover insurance premiums (e.g. for house contents).

CASE STUDY – Jason

Jason has just started work after leaving college. He has had to move to another town to find a job that suits him and has rented a bed-sit in a large old house. As he lived at home with his parents while he was at college, he has never had to budget before. After having tax, national insurance and pension contributions deducted from his wage, he takes home £150 per week. Out of this he pays £50 rent for his bed-sit. He must pay his own quarterly gas and electricity bills, as well as a monthly payment for water. He is also responsible for paying his own telephone bill.

To make new friends, Jason decided to join a local sports club. He pays membership fees of £40 per quarter for that. He has also joined a trade union at work and will pay £150 fees per year for membership of this. Jason has never had to cook for himself before and so, at the moment, tends to buy a great deal of take-away food. As he doesn't as yet have his own television, he tends to go to the cinema once or twice a week. As the job he does involves him coming into contact with members of the public, he must wear smart clothes, including a shirt and tie. He therefore has to go to the laundrette once a week to get his washing done (and he pays someone to do his ironing for him!).

At the moment he is managing on his money but, at the end of each week, he seems to have less and less left over. He is getting worried he may be spending too much and not putting enough aside to pay his bills. He says he is too busy to sit down with a calculator to work out his expenses but the real reason may be that he has never produced a personal budget for himself before.

If Jason were to ask you for help in setting up a personal budget for himself, what advice would you give him? The following are suggestions about the types of things you might tell him about:

- How to set out a personal budget (you could use the example given in the previous case study to help you with this).

- What items you should include in the budget (expenses, income, borrowings, etc.).

Remember, so far we have looked at budgets that set out income and expenses on a weekly basis. Jason also has outgoings that occur on a monthly, quarterly and annual basis. How could you set out his budget to accommodate these? (We don't know what his quarterly bills for gas and electricity are. Neither do we know how much he pays for water or for his telephone bills. You could make up *realistic* figures for these if you need to. If you are unsure about any of these bills, ask your teacher or tutor for help.)

Finally, Jason says he has less and less money left over at the end of each week. What advice would you give him about cutting down on his expenses? Is there any way you could budget for Jason so that he can save some of his money each week, rather than spend it? If he were able to save some of his money, what would be a good thing for him to save up to buy?

As we have already noted, most of us at some time in our lives need to borrow money from a financial institution (such as a bank or building society) so we can buy something we otherwise could not afford (e.g. a new car or a house of our own). Although you must be aged over 18 years before you can borrow money, it might help you if you practised now applying for a loan from a bank or building society.

ACTIVITY

Go to a local branch of a bank or building society to pick up a copy of a personal loan application form. (These may be kept in a rack somewhere in the office or you may have to ask for one.) Study this form carefully:

- What sort of information do you need to supply?

- Do you need to produce any documents to support your application?

- Will you need anyone else's help in order to obtain the loan?

When you have studied the form carefully, fill in as much as you can (there may be areas on the form you cannot fill in – just leave these blank for now). When you have filled in as much as you can and are happy with what you have entered, show the form to your teacher or tutor. He or she may be able to help you fill in those sections you are unsure about.

Financial institutions

There are many financial institutions we can use to help us manage our money. These institutions offer a wide range of services, from providing loans to offering us the facilities to save our money so that our money earns us interest.

Banks

These are the largest financial institutions. They are called 'clearing' banks because they handle the exchange and settlement of cheques between different customers' accounts. The biggest banks are the Halifax plc, Barclays, Lloyds TSB and HSBC.

The banks' most important roles include the following:

- Accepting deposits of money.

- Offering short- and long-term loans.

- The provision of a wide range of customer services (e.g. current accounts, standing orders, direct debits, etc.).

Building societies

Building societies were originally established to help people become house owners who would otherwise find it difficult to save the necessary money to buy their own homes. Because buying property involves such large sums of money, the loans are long term, with repayments over twenty to thirty years. These loans are called mortgages.

Building societies often compete with the banks. Recently, some building societies have converted to banks in order to offer their customers a wider range of financial services. (e.g. Abbey National plc and the Halifax plc).

The Post Office

The National Girobank is a state-run bank that operates through the Post Office. It was set up in 1968 and its computer centre is in Bootle in Merseyside. It offers most of the services other banks provide.

Credit unions

Credit unions are non-profit-making organisations (i.e. unlike most other financial institutions, they do not exist to make a profit from looking after their customers' money). They accept deposits and provide loans. Credit unions are really a form of co-operative (i.e. they are usually run by a group of people who have something in common – a group of workmates or neighbours, for example). Each member saves money regularly and his or her money

goes it into a pool. When someone needs to borrow money, he or she is given a loan out of this pool of members' money.

Insurance companies and insurance brokers

There are many types of insurance we can take out (e.g. against fire, accident, theft, etc.). The companies that provide these insurance policies have branches throughout the country to deal with the claims their customers make against their policies. If you wish to take out insurance cover, for whatever reason, you can approach an insurance company directly or you could go to an insurance broker.

CASE STUDY – Sainsbury's Bank

On 25 October 1996, J. Sainsbury's plc and Bank of Scotland announced they were to launch a joint bank. The bank would be 55% owned by Sainsbury's and 45% by Bank of Scotland. Sainsbury's became the first supermarket retailer to form its own bank.

On 19 February 1997, Sainsbury's Bank opened for business. It offered two Visa credit cards (Classic and Gold) and two savings accounts (Instant Access and Christmas Saver).

Sainsbury's Bank operates mainly through telephone banking and, therefore, incurs none of the costs of employing staff in branches nationwide. Hence the bank offers highly competitive rates of interest when compared with more traditional banks.

Sainsbury's Bank also has its own cash machines. In 1998, it had over 73

machines, and Sainsbury's customers can use their cards in around 14,000 Link cash machines throughout the UK.

In 1998 Sainsbury's Bank had over 800,000 customer accounts and it continues to add 10,000 new accounts each week. The bank also had in excess of £1.6 billion of customer deposits.

Read the case study carefully before answering the following questions:

1 Why do you think Sainsbury's Bank is able to offer a higher rate of interest on savings than other traditional banks?

2 What are the financial services Sainsbury's Bank offers its customers?

3 Find out if there are any other supermarkets that offer financial services. List these and compare their services with those offered by Sainsbury's Bank.

Insurance brokers work independently of the insurance companies and, therefore, they are able to give customers unbiased advice as to which is the best policy for them to buy from the many available through the various insurance companies.

Loan companies

These companies specialise in providing all types of loans. For example, they might provide personal loans and mortgages. They sometimes offer cheaper rates of interest than banks on long-term loans.

Supermarkets

The world of consumer finance is currently undergoing significant change. Large building societies have converted to banks and newcomers, such as supermarkets, are entering the banking market, offering a growing range of financial products.

Communicating with financial institutions

New and more convenient ways have evolved to make our communications with financial institutions less tiring and less time-consuming. In our modern society, people tend to employ the most convenient and easiest methods to carry out financial transactions.

Over-the-counter service

This is the oldest and the most traditional way of undertaking banking transactions. It simply means that, if you want to open a new account or to enquire about other financial matters, you call into your nearest branch. 'Over the counter', the cashier will be able to help you sort out very simple financial matters (e.g. enquiring about your balance, withdrawing cash or putting more money into your account).

By post

This is also a traditional way of banking that used to be very popular with customers. If you want to open an account or apply for a loan, you complete the application form enclosed in the bank's leaflet and post it back in a prepaid envelope.

By telephone

With telephone banking you can keep in touch with your bank account 24 hours a day, 365 days of the year by calling a special number from your telephone. This means you have the convenience of doing your banking at a time that suits you. You can do most routine things over the telephone, such as checking your balance or finding out what has gone in or out of your account.

By computer (online)

Most banks, building societies and other financial institutions offer online banking that gives customers 24-hour access to their accounts from their personal computer, either at home or in the office. In seconds you can check your balance on screen, view recent transactions and see what is going on in your account. You can also order cheque books and paying-in books, set up and pay all your regular bills and transfer money between your accounts – all at the click of the mouse!

Your calls are charged at the local rate, and most banks and building societies provide a 24-hour freephone help desk.

167

ACTIVITY

Visit a local branch of one of the big banks or building societies in your area and ask about the details of joining their online banking service. Alternatively, visit one of the following web sites to find more information about online banking:

www.natwest.co.uk
www.lloydsbank.co.uk
www.hsbc.co.uk
www.halifax.co.uk
www.barclays.co.uk

What are the benefits of using an online banking service?

Face to face at home

Banks and other financial institutions are quite happy to send their adviser to people's homes to give advice about their banking products. This is common practice for banks when they are selling long-term investments and insurance policies (e.g. life assurance policies or pension plans). However, the adviser is not independent – he or she cannot advise you about the products available from providers other than his or her own bank.

ACTIVITY

What are the advantages and disadvantages of communicating with financial institutions by the following methods?

- Over the counter.
- By post.
- By telephone.
- By computer (online).
- Face to face.

When working out the advantages and disadvantages, you might like to consider:

- convenience
- cost
- time
- effort
- the customer's age
- any disability a customer might have
- work and family commitments.

Which of the above methods do you prefer and which might you use in the future? Give reasons for your answer.

Financial services

Financial institutions offer their customers a wide range of financial products and services.

The main reason for having a bank account is that it gives you the means of receiving money from people and of paying money to others. There are two basic types of bank account – *current* (or cheque) and *savings* accounts.

Current accounts

A current account is for the money you want to have available now or for payments you wish to make to others in the near future. If you are over 18 and have opened a current account you will benefit from other banking services, such as:

- a cheque book
- a debit card (giving you access to your cash)

- personal loans

- bank statements

- your wages being transferred directly into your current account.

A current account can make your life easier:

- It is the easiest and the most convenient way to pay your bills. You can arrange for all you monthly bills to be taken straight from your account.

- You sometimes receive bills sent to you through the post that have a bank giro slip attached to the bottom. All you do is write out a cheque payable to the firm concerned and take it to your bank, who will make the payment from your account.

- Some employers pay their employees by making direct transfers of money into their employees' bank accounts. This is a far safer method of being paid than receiving cash or a cheque in a wage's envelope! On pay day you receive a pay-slip showing how much money you have earned and confirming this amount has been paid into your bank account.

Bank statements

Once you open a current account with a bank you will receive a monthly statement listing all the money that has gone into your account and all the money that has been taken out. You should check your bank statement against your cheque book and make sure all your standing orders have been paid.

You need to remember that you must not go overdrawn (where you spend more money than you have in your account). Under certain circumstances the bank will let you do this but you must be over 18 years of age and you must arrange it with the bank beforehand (see later in this unit).

 # ACTIVITY

Visit a bank or building society in your area. Obtain leaflets about their current accounts and find out if they offer current account facilities for students or school leavers.

You will probably find an application form enclosed in one of the leaflets for opening a student bank account. List all the information that is required to fill in this form. Describe what you have to do after filling in the application form.

Savings accounts

There are many savings schemes available, such as building society savings accounts and deposit accounts with banks.

Some banks now offer current accounts where interest is paid on the balance so that you can use these accounts for your daily financial transactions as well as for your longer-term savings.

Deposit means 'to put down' or 'leave'. A deposit account is for money you leave untouched in order to save it over a period of time. You may arrange to transfer a certain amount every month from your current account into a deposit account. Whilst the money is in the account it earns interest that is added to your savings. How much interest you get depends on:

- How much you have in your savings account.

- How long you are willing to leave the money in the account.

- The rate of interest you receive on your money.

Generally speaking, the longer you promise to leave the money in the account, the more interest you earn.

ACTIVITY

Visit a bank, building society or your local post office to collect leaflets about saving schemes. Make a list of all the saving schemes available and put them under two main headings:

1 Short-medium-term savings schemes.
2 Long-term savings schemes.

Which of these schemes offer the best rates of interest?

Which of these schemes do you think you might choose in the future? Give reasons for your answer.

Pension schemes

Banks, building societies and other financial institutions provide their customers with pension schemes. With these schemes, you should receive more money when you retire than you paid in to the scheme. The exact amount of money you will receive when you retire depends on:

- How much you have invested in the scheme.

- How long you have invested your money.

- The terms and the conditions of the scheme.

Even though most people will be eligible for a state pension when they retire, you should still make your own plans for your retirement. Without some kind of personal pension arrangement, you might face a drop in your living standards when you retire from work.

Life assurance schemes

Life assurance is a type of insurance that usually covers you up to the age of 60 years. You and your partner can join a scheme so that you are both covered by it. Should one of you die prematurely, the other one receives the agreed sum of money. When the scheme matures, but death has not occurred, you will be entitled to the full amount of money the scheme covers. Why do you think most banks and other financial institutions insist on customers completing medical declarations before they offer them a life assurance scheme?

Services for paying for goods and services

Banks and other financial institutions provide customers with other means (apart from cash) for paying for goods and services (e.g. cheques, debit cards, credit cards and standing orders).

Cheques

As you already know from Unit 3, the most common form of payment is the cheque. This is simply a written instruction from a customer to a bank to pay a certain sum of money to another named person. Millions of cheques are written every week.

Debit cards

Debit cards act like a cheques. The money is taken out of your account within a few days of you purchasing a product or service.

Credit cards

Credit cards (e.g. Visa) can be used in most shops as long as you do not exceed your credit limit. A credit card is convenient to use and offers financial flexibility. However, you must make sure you can afford to repay any amounts you run up on your credit card account by the date due. Otherwise, you will have to pay interest to the credit card company.

Store cards (or charge cards)

Store cards are issued by particular retailers or stores – usually the big ones. They can be used to make purchases from that particular retailer or store only, and not anywhere else (e.g. Marks & Spencer and River Island).

Store cards allow you to pay for a product six to seven weeks after you have made the purchase. If you pay the total amount owing by the date due, you do not pay interest.

Standing orders for hire-purchase agreements

If you have decided to buy goods or services on hire purchase, (i.e. paying the amount you owe in instalments), your bank or building society can arrange a standing order for your payments. With a standing order, the amount of money taken out of your account is fixed. Therefore, if the business or firm you have purchased the product from wants you to pay more, it has to write to you to ask you to sign a new standing order agreement to cover the new amount.

Using this service is a reliable way of remembering your repayment commitments and it avoids the embarrassing situation of suddenly discovering you owe someone money.

Loans

Providing loans is one of the most important financial services a bank or other financial institution can provide for its customers. In return for lending customers money, banks charge interest. The interest a bank or other institution charges depends on a variety of factors, including the current rate of interest, the amount of money borrowed and the length of time the money is borrowed for.

Short-term loans

Money borrowed over a short period of time is called a short-term loan (e.g. overdrafts and personal loans).

If you need to spend more than you have in your current account, you can negotiate an *overdraft* limit with your bank. This means you can spend up to a certain amount more than you have in your account. Overdrafts should be used only in an emergency or to cover a gap in your account for few days before your wage is paid in.

You may apply for an overdraft only if you are 18 years or over. To apply, you fill in a form, and only if your application is successful can you overdraw your account.

There may well come a time when you decide you want to buy something but you do not have the cash immediately available to do so (for example, you might need to buy a new kitchen or a new car). Under these circumstances you can approach the bank and ask them for a *personal loan*. Again, you need to be over 18 years of age and you must satisfy your bank manager that you can pay the monthly instalments.

Personal loans can be arranged over any period of time up to five years, and you can borrow money to buy most of the things that fall into the category of 'consumer goods' (e.g. a car, TV, computer, etc.). Bank charge interest on personal loans and the rate of interest is expressed as an annual percentage rate (APR for short).

Long-term loans

Money borrowed over a long period of time is called a long-term loan. The most common form of long-term loan is a *mortgage*.

Every year hundred of thousands of people will buy their homes with the help of banks or building societies. A mortgage is simply a long-term loan to help you buy a property. This means a mortgage cannot be used for other purposes (e.g. for buying a car or for going on holiday).

You can pay your mortgage instalments either by direct debit from your account or by sending a monthly cheque to your mortgage provider. Like all other loans, mortgages incur interest and you must keep up your repayments.

Insurance

When someone approaches an insurance company or broker for insurance protection (which is called *cover*), he or she does so to insure him or herself against a particular *risk*. The company quotes a price (which is called a *premium*) and sets out the terms of the insurance in a document called the *policy*.

There are many different types of insurance, but the most common ones are as follows.

Household contents insurance

This provides cover on your house contents and therefore compensation in the event that your house is burgled, set on fire or damaged by a water leak or burst in a pipe. You should always update your household contents insurance if you add an expensive item to your house.

Did you know?

Banks and other financial institutions offer contents insurance cover for students. It is valid for 24 hours a day, 365 days a year. It offers cover against fire and theft, storm and flood within your lodging or other temporary place of residence in the UK, including your parents' home.

Building and property insurance

This provides insurance cover on the actual structure of your house. Therefore, you should receive compensation in the event of any damage to the structure of your house caused by fire, flooding or a leak in the roof.

Motor insurance

When you get a motorbike or car, you must by law be covered by motor insurance. You cannot drive your motorbike or car without this insurance cover. Third-party insurance is the minimum the law will accept. It means that, if you are involved in an accident that is your fault, your insurer will pay for the cost of the damage to the other vehicle. Comprehensive insurance is more expensive, but covers the damage to your car as well.

Life insurance

If you buy a life (or endowment) insurance policy, it will pay out an agreed minimum sum of money in the event you die before a certain age (e.g. at 60 years). Should you not die by this age, the sum of money is paid to you anyway – plus any money the insurance company has managed to make for you by investing your money.

Life insurance is one of the most popular ways of saving money. You should give some thought to buying a policy when you are quite young. Remember, the younger you start, the cheaper the policy is.

Income protection/replacement insurance

This provides a cover and protection for your income. It will replace your income if you cannot work as a result of illness or disability. It goes on paying out each month until you are well enough to return to work or your policy ends, whichever happens first.

The most you can receive under an income replacement or protection policy is between 65 and 75% of your income (less any state benefit you can claim). Most income protection cover goes up in line with rises in your income.

Travel insurance

This type of insurance provides cover when you are on holiday. Travel insurance will cover any expenses you might incur or any money you might lose as a result of the following:

- Your holiday is cancelled because of events beyond your control (e.g. war or strikes).

- Your holiday is cut short (e.g. because of illness or death).

- You can incur medical expenses as a result of illness during your holiday.

- The temporary loss of your personal belongings.

- Delays in your flight.

ACTIVITY

What sort of insurance policies would you need to buy to obtain the following types of cover?

- Protect your family's finance if you died?
- Help look after you and your family if you suddenly became seriously ill or disabled?
- Plan for your retirement when you reach the age of 55 years?
- Help look after you and your belongings when you are away on holiday?
- Protect the contents of your home?
- Protect the structure of your house?

Financial advice and protection

At the moment your personal financial planning may be very straightforward. Later on, however, when you leave school or college and get a job, your circumstances may change and it may become important to review your needs and to know where to go for advice. Many financial institutions have financial advisers who give advice on their own products. There are also independent financial advisers who can advise you on products from a range of institutions and organisations.

Financial institutions are *regulated* (controlled) to make sure they carry out their business properly, and financial advisers must be qualified and authorised to carry out their work. These are safeguards to protect the consumers who use financial services.

Banks and building societies

All banks and building societies provide free financial advice to people who are interested in buying their products. Personal bankers (the people who look after individual customers' accounts) are happy to provide information and assistance on everyday aspects of money management. They provide advice regarding opening current or savings accounts, on standing orders, overdraft arrangements and personal loans. Personal bankers are trained to help you with the day-to-day running of your account.

If you need specific advice regarding long-term saving (e.g. life assurance or a pension scheme), your personal banker will put you in touch with someone who is qualified to help you. You can arrange to see expert advisers at the bank, can ring them or even arrange for them to discuss your needs in your own home.

Insurance companies

If you would like advice on insurance matters, get in touch with your insurance company. They will be happy to give advice about their own products.

Brokers

If you are not sure where to obtain the best insurance deal, you can arrange to see a broker. Insurance brokers work independently of insurance companies and, therefore, are able to give you unbiased advice.

What to do if you are in financial trouble

If you have financial problems, approach one of the following bodies.

Citizen's Advice Bureaux

Citizen's Advice Bureaux are an invaluable source of advice, and there is probably one in your area. They help to deal with people's financial problems, unemployment problems and debts. Staff are well trained and offer free, independent advice.

Department of Social Security

It is possible that you qualify for a loan from the Social Fund. To find out, you must contact your local Department of Social Security.

Regulation of financial services

The Financial Services Authority (FSA)

Financial institutions are regulated to make sure that they carry out their business properly and financial advisers must be qualified and authorised. The Financial Services Authority (FSA) regulates the industry and protects consumers who use financial services, such as banks and building societies. It also ensures that all consumers are aware of the fees and charges made by these financial businesses.

CASE STUDY – Anna's trouble

Anna left college when she was 18 years old and obtained a good job as sales assistant with a company that makes fitted kitchens. Anna started on a good salary and things looked well for her.

Two months before Christmas, Anna went shopping with her friends and noticed that every store she went to offered a charge card. They also offered incentives for customers to take advantage of these cards (e.g. discount vouchers or 10% off sales). Anna thought this was a great idea and she applied for four different store cards. She paid for all her Christmas presents with these cards and the total amount came to £546. Unfortunately, two weeks before Christmas, Anna was made redundant as the business was struggling to survive.

Initially, Anna did not panic. She thought she would soon be able to get another job. She managed to pay off three instalments at the minimum amount they suggested, but this was only enough to cover the interest. In the end the total outstanding balance on the statements was just getting higher and higher each month. Anna did not dare tell her parents about her troubles and so the money she owed kept building up and up.

By chance, Anna's mum found out about the money problems when she saw a statement in Anna's bedroom. She immediately contacted all the stores and explained the situation. The stores agreed to freeze the interest and, gradually, with her parents' help, Anna managed to pay off the full outstanding amount over the next 10 months.

Read the case study carefully and then answer the following questions:

1. Do you think it was a good idea for Anna to use the store cards to pay for her Christmas shopping? Give reasons for your answer.

2. What could Anna have done to stop her outstanding balance from building up?

3. Anna was fortunate in that her parents were prepared to help her. To whom could she have turned for help or advice if she did not have such understanding parents?

Looking after customers

You have learnt in Unit 1 that there are people who will affect and influence business activity (e.g. customers, employees, shareholders, and others). We have called these people 'stakeholders'. Customers are the most important people for any business organisation.

In this unit you will find out what different types of customers need and how business organisations try to meet these needs through customer service. Selling is an important part of customer service. You will take the part of a sales assistant either in work experience or in role play.

The topics you will learn about in this unit are:

- the importance of customer service
- types of customer
- customers' expectations
- types of customer service
- legal protection for customers
- selling.

The importance of customer service

Good customer service simply means a happy customer, and bad customer service simply means an unhappy customer. You have learnt in Unit 1 that improving customer service is one of the means a business uses to attract more customers and to compete with other businesses.

The benefits of having satisfied customers

You learnt in Units 1 and 2 that good customer service means a satisfied customer, and a satisfied customer means a successful business.

Retailers know that, by having a choice of quality goods, competitive prices, reliable guarantees, after-sales service, helpful, polite and knowledgeable staff, and pleasant surroundings, they can gain many benefits:

- They attract more customers.
- They increase their sales.
- They have a better reputation.
- They are more competitive.
- Staff who work for the business will benefit from working for a successful business.

The cost of having dissatisfied customers

A dissatisfied customer means:

- A future sale may be lost.
- Bad publicity.
- Bad business image and reputation.
- Inability to cope with the competition.

ACTIVITY

Ask your parents or your friends if they have ever made any of the following comments about a business's customer service. If they can remember, ask them what it was that caused them to make such a comment, and where the incident occurred.

- I asked if they stocked it and no one seemed to know.
- He was really rude. Said it wasn't his department.
- She said she'd have a word with the supervisor about it and I still haven't heard anything.
- I stood in a long queue for 15 minutes waiting to be served.
- She said to go and have a look on the shelf, and if you don't find it, it means we don't have it.

ACTIVITY

Say whether the following statements are true or false. Give reasons for your answers in each case.

1. Good customer service reduces the number of customers who purchase the product.
2. Good customer service increases the number of products sold.
3. Good customer service increases business's ability to compete..
4. Bad customer service reduces business efficiency.
5. Bad customer service reduces customer satisfaction.
6. Good customer service reduces business profits.

Types of customer

The people who buy a product are called *customers*. The people who use a product are called *consumers*. Not every customer is a consumer and not every consumer is a customer. If you asked your friend to buy you some crisps from the corner shop, your friend is the customer and you are the consumer (the person who *consumes* or *uses* the product).

Businesses must work out who their customers are and produce what their customers want. Who and where the customer is for a business depends on many factors. For example:

- Where the business is located.
- How well off the area is.

- The type of product the business is selling.

- The price of the product and how much people can afford to pay for it.

Not all customers are individual people. An entire business organisation may itself be a customer. For example, when Nestlé buy their coffee beans to process them into instant coffee, Nestlé is a customer.

Customer characteristics

Every individual person is different and every individual business is different. For example, look at yourself and the other students in your classroom. You are simply not all the same. You are different in terms of sex, ethnic origin, background (where you have come from), the area where you live, etc. Because we are different we spend our money in different ways. The crisp flavour I like is not necessarily the flavour you like or what your friend likes.

It is very important for any business to find out who its customers and consumers are (if you are unsure about the difference between customer and consumer, look back at the explanation given earlier in this unit). For example, for a toy manufacturer, the main *consumers* are children in certain age groups and, for a car dealer, the main *customers* and *consumers* are adults, aged over 18 years who have a reasonable income.

ACTIVITY

Match the following three means of transport with the people listed below:

- A small family car.
- Bus travel.
- A bicycle.

1 Joan is 16 years old. She lives 4 miles from school.
2 Simon is a single parent with one child.
3 Barakash is a doctor. He is married with two children.
4 Geoff Cox is a 75-year-old pensioner. He lives on his own.
5 Ahmed Amran's work is situated very close to his home. He likes to keep fit.

Paying for goods and services

When customers want to buy something, they usually have to pay for it. However, there are some types of goods and services we do *not* pay for – *merit goods*.

Merit goods are mostly provided by the government or the public sector. They include such things as health care, education and the emergency services. However, while it may seem such things are provided free of charge, in actual fact they are paid for. People pay taxes and council tax to enjoy services provided by the government and local councils.

ACTIVITY

Working in small groups of three or four, discuss the following statements. When you have finished discussing each one, makes notes about what each person has said. Did you all agree with each other, or were you split on some of these issues?

1 A shop or store should treat all customers the same – whether a customer is spending 50p or £5,000.
2 Big retailers such as supermarkets and chain stores don't need to bother about individual customer's needs and preferences. If someone cannot find what he or she

wants in a store, that person will have to go somewhere else. It won't affect the store – there are plenty of customers to go round!

3 People who pay for goods or services should be treated with more respect than people who receive goods or services free.

Customers' expectations

You have already learnt in Units 1 and 2 about customer rights and business responsibilities.

When you go out to buy goods or a service, there are certain things that you expect to happen and expect to receive. For example, if you go out to a restaurant, you would expect the meal to be tasty, of good quality, served in clean and pleasant surroundings, reasonably priced and good value for money. You would also expect good customer service. If these expectations were not met, the restaurant would lose your and other customers' business and would become less profitable.

Generally, customers have the following expectations when they buy goods or services.

Good-quality services and products

Customers (whether individuals or businesses) are looking for good-quality services and products. For example, the main secret behind the success of Marks & Spencer is the quality of its products. Customers who buy Marks & Spencer goods are fairly confident the products are of high quality.

A range of different products and services

These days, customers expect to have a variety of products to choose from. You will usually be able to buy what you want in more than one shop, but the range of goods and the help you can expect from the staff can make one shop much more attractive than the other. Large stores such as supermarkets do not sell just food, they also sell furniture, electrical goods, clothes, and some of them have restaurants and chemists. This range of products appeals to many different customers and saves them the time and effort of shopping in many different places.

Products are available at the right time

Customers buy goods or services to satisfy their needs and wants *now*. Therefore, customers expect to find products when they want them. For example, there is no point in buying a computer to do your coursework that is not going to be available for six months. Equally, for a business, if it orders stock or raw materials it is likely to want them as soon as possible. Delay means losses.

 # ACTIVITY

Can you remember a time when you wanted to buy something (e.g. a pair of jeans) from a particular shop but it was not in stock?

- What was your reaction?
- What did you decide to do?

Products are available at the right place

You have already learnt in Unit 2 that the location of a business is an important factor in its success. Any business must make sure that its customers can get to it easily, thus ensuring the products are within their reach. Businesses must also ensure that there are enough products reaching the people who want them.

Therefore, businesses employ people to organise how often deliveries are made to the right retailers at the right time.

Well-packaged products

You have already learnt in Unit 1 that the packaging and the design of a product are very important if the product is to catch the customer's eye. For example, if you go to buy coffee, tea or sugar, the packaging will enable you to identify the product immediately, and this will save you time looking for it.

Packaging also provides information about the product (e.g. the ingredients, the sell-by date, any precautions you must take when using the product, etc.). Packaging not only attracts customers to the product but it also protects the product from being damaged. Customers expect products to be well packaged and in good condition when they receive them.

Polite service

You learnt in Units 1 and 2 about customer service, which means keeping customers happy and satisfied. While we have already seen that customer service covers a wide range of issues, perhaps the most important and obvious part of customer service is the way customers are treated in the shop or at the checkout.

ACTIVITY

We can all tell stories of times we have felt unhappy about the service we have received in a shop. The sales assistant seemed too pushy, forcing us into buying something we were not sure we really wanted, or seemed utterly bored with us, as if he or she was simply waiting for the shop to close so he or she could go home, or treated us as if we knew nothing at all about the product we wanted to buy and so made us feel foolish and ignorant.

For this activity, you are going to assume two roles: that of the customer and that of the sales assistant. You are going to work in pairs and are going to swap these roles round between the two of you. First, decide who of your pair is going to be the customer and who is going to be the sales assistant. Then take the first situation below and role play being that person. Now swap roles and do the role play again.

Each time you finish role playing a situation, and *before* you go on to the next one, discuss with your partner what your feelings were:

- What was your attitude towards the person? Did you like him or her, find him or her annoying or did you simply want to thump that person?
- If the situation were real, would you ever go into that shop again?
- If you encountered someone like that on another occasion, would you treat that person differently this time around?

Situations

1 A shoe shop. *Sales assistant*: well trained, pleasant and efficient. Knows the stock of shoes in the shop well. *Customer*: has no

idea what he or she wants, if he or she wants anything at all – could just be passing time because it is raining outside.

2 A small computer shop. *Sales assistant*: young, Saturday worker, knows a lot about computers and likes to show this off. Very keen on quoting facts and figures. *Customer*: quite elderly, has never owned a computer before and knows very little about them. Rather timid – wants to be told simply and clearly what he or she should buy.

3 A fast-food restaurant. *Sales assistant*: bored, tired and ready to go home. Has had a long day. Nothing has gone right. Can't wait to clock off and get changed to go out to a party. *Customer*: does not speak English very well. Speaks quietly and hesitantly. Is frightened of making a fool of him or herself. Does not know what food to order.

Honest dealings

Customers expect an honest and fair deal from traders. Customers expect that any product sold is honestly and fairly priced. Customers should not be misled or cheated over the quality, the description or the price of a product.

Value for money

Value for money means a product is worth what we are paying for it. Customers do not like to feel the goods or services they are buying are over-priced. However, some customers do not mind paying a little bit extra to obtain what they are looking for (good quality, special service, etc.). For example, a customer might be quite happy to pay extra providing he or she feels he or she is getting value for the money in terms of quality and speed of service.

ACTIVITY

What would be your replies to the following statements? Give reasons for your answers.

1 I bought these shoes from that discount shop on the high street. They don't fit well and they don't match. I think they must be an odd pair. People shouldn't be allowed to sell shoes like that.

2 50p? I don't believe you! I pay 90p at my shop for a loaf of bread like this. There must be something wrong with it. No one can produce a loaf of bread like this for 50p.

3 You paid a pound for one pair of socks? I get mine in bundles of five for a pound. Someone must be ripping you off. I'd never pay that much for socks – they only last for a couple of months anyway.

4 You'd never see me in a shop like that. I don't care how cheap you say it is or how good you say their stuff is, it's not somewhere I would like to do my shopping. Besides, at prices like that there must be something wrong with what they sell.

Safe products

Acts of Parliament have been passed that make it an offence to sell goods that do not measure up to stipulated safety requirements. Toys, for example, must be made of flame-resistant materials, must have no sharp edges, must use lead-free paint and have no pieces that could be easily swallowed if the toy came apart.

Some of the other products for which there are very strict safety standards include electrical goods, paraffin heaters, cosmetics, night-wear clothes and cooking utensils.

Types of customer service

You learnt in Unit 1 that customer service comes under the province of a firm's sales and marketing department. In some large businesses, however, customer service may be a separate department that offers customers help, information and advice, and that deals with customer complaints and queries.

Customers expect different things of the organisations they deal with, and the efficient and successful organisation will do all in its power to deal with its customers' queries. Such organisations will train their staff to handle customer queries in the most appropriate and efficient manner possible.

Information and advice

Before a customer buys a product, he or she will usually want to know as much about the product as possible. The amount of information customers need will depend on the nature of the product (e.g. whether it is durable or non-durable, its cost and how suitable it is for the purpose the customer has in mind). For example, when customers want to purchase durable, expensive products (such as computers or washing machines), they will want detailed information and advice from the sales people before committing themselves to buying them. Good customer service should provide the information and advice customers need when and where they demand it. By law businesses must:

- Provide a correct description of the item or service on offer.

- Display a valid sales ticket.

- Ensure that the product is fit for the purpose for which it is intended.

ACTIVITY

What sort of information would a customer expect to be given before purchasing the following products or services?

- a washing machine
- a holiday in China
- a bottle of medicine
- a travel insurance policy?

Most large retailers and chain stores have a customer services department whose function is to deal with customers' enquiries while the customers are actually in the store.

Sales

Selling is the most important part of customer service. Selling, however, does not come naturally to most people. It is a skill that needs to be taught. Customers like to deal with a helpful, cheerful and patient salesman or saleswoman who can give them satisfaction and who can make them feel happy and comfortable in their purchasing decisions.

You will learn more about selling techniques later in this unit.

Delivery

Good customer service means the speedy delivery of goods and services customers have bought. Sometimes, however, it is difficult (especially with bulk products) to find space in a shop to store goods. Orders, therefore, have to be sent to the warehouse or stockroom. Because of the problems of holding large stocks of goods, some retailers offer customers free delivery of the products they have ordered or that are not stocked in the store.

Help-lines

Some businesses have set up free help-lines to give advice and help to their customers. For example, if you buy a new computer you will often be given a free-phone number to ring if you encounter problems. And you expect the person on the other end of the line to be courteous and helpful – even though he or she may be dealing with dozens of calls from confused customers such as yourself! Most organisations that set up free-phone help-lines train their staff to handle even the most difficult of customer enquiries.

After-sales service

Customer service does not end simply with selling the product. It extends to after-sales service. Customers are sometimes tempted to buy products – especially expensive ones – that afterwards they regret buying. Therefore, most businesses or shops have a refund and exchange policy.

Most of the goods or services we buy also have a guarantee, especially the more expensive ones. This means that, should something be wrong with the product, we can expect a full refund of our money or a replacement for the product or service we have bought.

Salespeople should deal with complaints without argument. Faulty goods should be exchanged for a cash refund, even if the fault does not appear until the item has been used for some time. Unwanted presents or items returned because the customer has a change of mind, should be exchanged for a credit note or other goods. However, we cannot expect to exchange goods (or be refunded for them) if we were clearly warned at the time of purchase that they were imperfect, seconds or second-hand.

Retailers are responsible for any faults in the goods they sell and the customer has the right to a refund or replacement should the goods be faulty. As long as the customer was not responsible for the damage, or the fault was not caused by misuse, the retailer must return the customer's money or supply a replacement. A retailer might offer a credit note to purchase another item from the same store, but customers do not have to accept these.

Some retailers extended the customers' right to a refund even if the goods are not faulty. If a customer buys something he or she does not need, stores such as Marks & Spencer and BHS may give a refund as long as the goods have not been used.

ACTIVITY

Choose two big retailers in your area and find out about the customer service they provide. For example, how are customer complaints and queries handled (e.g. the retailers' refund or the exchange policies)?

Compare the customer service offered by these retailers. Which one do you consider offers the best customer service?

Legal protection for customers

How many times have you bought something and realised afterwards it was damaged or something was wrong with it? Hence, customers need to be protected when they buy goods. For example:

- The goods are damaged, broken or unusable.

- The goods are not fit for the purpose for which they were sold.

- The seller described the goods inaccurately.

- The quantity of the goods is not what the customer paid for.

In such situations customers are protected by the following laws.

The Sale of Goods Act 1979 and 1995

This 1979 Act of Parliament (amended in 1995) covers all kinds of goods bought from all kinds of retail outlets and mail-order companies. It contains three rules that must be followed by traders:

1 *The goods must be of merchantable quality.* This means the goods must be reasonably fit for the purpose for which they were bought. An item must not be broken or damaged and must work correctly.

2 *The goods must be as described.* If you buy a punnet of 'freshly picked' strawberries, you expect the punnet to contain 'freshly picked' strawberries and not mouldy,

rotten strawberries. This clause in the Act covers the wording on the package, display signs and any statement the trader makes about the goods you are buying.

3 *The goods must be fit for the purpose intended.* If you buy a carpet to lay in your hallway and the retailer assures you the carpet is hard wearing, you do not expect it to wear out in six months!

The Trade Descriptions Act 1968 and 1972

The 1968 Act made it illegal to give a false description of goods for sale. This covers description in writing, in advertisements or in anything the seller says when discussing the goods with a customer. The Act also covers the way in which goods are priced. For example, the seller cannot charge a higher price than the one marked on the goods. It is also illegal to claim the price of a good has been reduced (for example, in a sale) unless the same good was previously offered at the higher price.

The 1972 Act makes it illegal to give the customer the impression the goods were made in the UK if they in fact were not.

The Weights and Measures Act 1985

This Act covers the weights and measures of goods sold and the labelling of quantities on packaging. It is an offence to sell short weights or measures. However, since 1980 a short-weight packet in itself is no longer an offence as *average* weight is now the system of control. This means that, if the average of a batch of goods falls below the level stated on the packaging, is it an offence to sell those goods at the weight stated on the packaging. This does not apply, however, to prepacked goods such as meat or beer and spirits sold in a pub.

The Food Safety Act 1990

This Act of Parliament makes it an offence to sell food that is unfit for human that consumption, or to treat food in such a way that it becomes a danger to health. This would be the case, for example, if too much fat was added to a beefburger or harmful colouring was added to children's sweets. It also covers the labelling of food with regards to its contents, any other ingredients and artificial colorants and preservatives.

These sections of the Act concern the ways people may be misled about the quality of food and about what has been put into the food. The Act also lays down strict hygiene regulations for retailers who handle food, e.g. ice-cream.

ACTIVITY

Which of the above Acts of Parliament have not been observed in the following situations? Give reasons for your answers.

1 A skin allergy developed as a result of using a suntan lotion that was claimed to be suitable for very sensitive skin.
2 A customer buys a 'diet' chocolate that actually contains as many calories as an ordinary bar of chocolate.
3 A retailer claimed a dishwasher had been reduced from £200 to £165. However, a few months after buying the dishwasher the customer discovers that the original price for the dishwasher was £165.
4 In a supermarket, bottles of an orange drink are on sale. On the label is written 'Refreshing Lemonade Drink'.
5 A mother bought a packet of sweets for her son. It was stated on the package the average weight of the sweets was 250 g. When the mother went home and weighed

CASE STUDY – Simon

Simon works for a car dealer as a sales assistant. What would you advise Simon to do in each of the following situations?

1 Simon's telephone rings when he is busy serving a customer.

2 A customer approaches Simon to ask about the price of one of the cars while he is busy with another customer.

3 A disabled woman complains to Simon that the customer whom he is serving has parked in the disabled car-park space.

4 A customer asks Simon if he can show him one of the cars outside the showroom. It is very wet and cold and Simon has a cold.

5 Simon sees a potential customer hanging around the showroom, looking at the cars.

For each answer you give, make sure you give your reasons for the action you recommend.

the packet, she found the actual weight was only 220 g.

6   A customer bought a pair of shoes the shop claimed were pure leather. He later discovered the uppers of the shoes were not leather.

Selling skills

By now you should be aware of all the skills a good salesperson should have: politeness, honesty, helpfulness and a good knowledge of the products for sale. A good salesperson should also be careful not to give customers wrong ideas about the products he or she sells.

ACTIVITY

You are going to play the role of a salesperson and you are going to try to sell a product to the rest of your group. To do this, you will have to use all your selling skills to make your customers want to buy your product and to feel happy and satisfied with what they have bought.

First, select a product you are very familiar with. This should be something you can readily get hold of and can easily bring into class. Make sure you also choose something a customer is likely to want advice about before buying. Suggestions for the kinds of products you might choose are listed below:

- a pair of shoes
- an electric drill
- a hairdryer
- a calculator
- a radio
- glue
- a mobile phone
- an iron
- a fountain pen
- a kettle
- a sports bag.

Think about the kinds of questions customers might ask you about the product you have chosen and make sure you have as much information as you can about the product you intend to sell. For example:

- The cost of the product if you bought it today.
- The features of the product you would like to bring to the attention of potential customers.
- The availability of the product in the shops.
- Payment methods (e.g. cash only, hire purchase, etc.).
- Guarantees.
- Any safety aspects the potential customers should know about.

You may also need to demonstrate how the product works and how to handle it safely.

Since you are going to assume the role of a salesperson, you should pay attention to what you wear, your personal appearance and your body language. Be prepared to answer any questions about your product that may arise from the rest of the group.

Take it in turns to try to sell your product to the rest of the group. Remember, although you are trying to *sell* this product you must also observe all the qualities a good salesperson should have (e.g. oral skills, friendly personality, knowledge of the product, good manners, initiative, etc.).

People are an important part of businesses. In this unit you will learn about:

- *what it is like to work in business*

- *the rewards people may get through pay and benefits*

- *the training and development people need in order to work in business*

- *the legal rights of both employers and employees with regard to pay, benefits, working arrangements and training.*

This unit will be assessed through an external assessment only. The grade you achieve in this assessment will be your grade for the unit.

Job roles

In any business there will be many different jobs. The jobs people do will vary, depending on:

- The *type* and *size* of the business (e.g. from the independent sole trader, such as a window cleaner, to the large, multinational organisation, such as McDonald's).

- The nature of the business's *activity* (e.g. whether it is in retailing, banking, manufacturing, insurance, etc.).

However, in most businesses, the jobs people do usually come under one of the following categories:

- managers

- supervisors

- operatives

- general members of the staff.

Each of these people has a role to play in a business, but the type of decisions they make and the responsibilities they are given will depend on their position within the organisation:

- *Managers* make the long-term decisions. They set the targets they hope the business will achieve, and make the important decisions about what they think the business should be doing in the future.

- *Supervisors* make sure that the targets set by the managers are met. It is the supervisors who usually come into day-to-day contact with those people who do the jobs that actually make the business's products or who sell to the customers – the operatives.

- The *operatives* make the products or are the people who sell the goods to the customers. In retailing and service industries (such as banks and travel agents), it is these people the customers come into contact with.

- Finally, *general members of staff* are all those people who do the jobs no company can do without but whose jobs *support* the company's main activities: secretaries, cleaners, technicians, receptionists, even the person who makes the tea!

If all this sounds a little complicated, let's look at a few examples of these various types of jobs.

CASE STUDY – Job roles

Read through each case study below and then answer the questions that follow each one.

Manager – Peter Churchill

Peter Churchill set up his own management consultancy business 15 years ago, offering companies tailor-made training programmes to help them improve their staff's performance. The programmes he devised became so well known and respected he was able to expand his business. From being a sole trader, he now employs five full-time staff and three part-timers. This is how he describes his job:

'The part of the job I really enjoy is running the training programmes themselves, but now most of my time is spent organising my staff and looking after the financial side of the business – budgeting, chasing outstanding invoices, keeping track of where the staff are and what they are doing. It's not that I don't trust the staff – I do, I picked them myself! – but I feel my company has a reputation for doing things in a certain way and I want to make sure we keep doing it in the way our customers expect.

'Another thing I miss is working alongside other people. I run the business from home, and so some days the only contact I have with other people is over the telephone or through emails (apart from my wife and children, of course! But they have strict orders not to come into the office when I'm working!). I really do miss that, but someone has to be here running the ship.

'I also feel very responsible for my staff. If our business was to fail, they would be out of a job. So I must make sure everything we do is of the highest standards. All the time I am keeping an eye on the day-to-day running of the business I have also got to keep another eye on the future! What will we be doing in one year's, two years' or even ten years' time? Will our customers still want our services? Are we going to have to offer different types of services? How can we improve ourselves so that we are always ahead of the competition?

'I work all hours, sometimes late into the night and over weekends. I don't know how many hours I work – I just work when I have to and when something has to be done. One thing I do know is, I don't just start at nine in the morning and clock off at five at night! The trouble is, I have no time now for my main interest – gardening. I have to leave most of that to my wife. We've got a large garden, and it takes some looking after. But I try to help when I can.

'This might all sound like very hard work – and it is! – but I enjoy it. I don't think I could ever go back to being an employee again. I'd miss all the personal challenges and triumphs and, I suppose, the failures. But it's the success that keeps me going!

'To sum up, I make the decisions, make sure we get our work done well and on time, and I organise my staff. I suppose I do anything that needs doing and that the staff can't do for themselves!'

- What do you think Peter would consider to be the most *important* part of his job role?

- What part of Peter's job do you think he enjoys the least?

- What sort of personal skills and qualities do you think it takes to run a business like this?

Remember to give reasons for your answers.

Supervisor – Tanya Williams

Tanya Williams works for a supermarket. This is how she describes her job:

'I am responsible for the checkouts operating efficiently and for the service we provide to our customers. I work under the store's general manager. It's my job to supervise the 12 checkout operatives we employ and the other staff who come into direct contact with our customers.

'Some of my main duties are as follows:

- I ensure that company policy is carried out correctly at the checkouts.

- I make sure that all our supermarket assistants receive the right training so that we can maintain a high standard of service to all our customers.

- I keep an eye on procedures to make sure that everything runs smoothly.

- I make sure that all dealings with refunds and customer complaints are carried out properly.

- I assess how much training any new staff might need.

'I suppose you could say I deal with everything and anything, really. Customer complaints, mainly.

I'm also responsible for training, motivating and supervising the checkout operatives. If one of the operatives has a problem with a till or has any other problem, I have to sort it out as soon as possible. I try to get everybody working together as a team. Working a till is a difficult job, and I appreciate the problems the operatives have – impatient customers, customers who haven't the money to pay for all their shopping. But if we all pull together as a team it makes things like this easier to deal with. You feel you have the support of your colleagues when you're handling something difficult and you don't think you have to tackle everything on your own. I worked my way up from being a checkout operative myself. Because I was eager to learn, the company sent me on training courses and I also went to classes at night school so that I could become a supervisor.

'My contract says I must work 39 hours a week but you'll probably have worked out by now I do in fact work much longer than that! You can't just put your coat on and go home leaving an irate shopper at the customer services desk! I work six days a week and sometimes have to work on Sundays, which I don't like because I think Sundays should be a day for families. Still, now we're open on Sundays there's not a lot I can do about that. Sunday is one of our busiest days of the week.

'All in all, I could sum up my job as making decisions, working to deadlines, motivating and organising staff, identifying problems and providing solutions! If this sounds difficult, it is! There are some perks to a job like this – the company has lots of facilities employees can take advantage of, like staff discounts, help with personal finance and so on – but it's the work I enjoy the most.'

- What sort of things does Tanya do that are similar to the things Peter Churchill does?

- Tanya says she tries to get the staff to work together as a team. What are the benefits of staff working as a team?

- Tanya also says she has to make sure company policy is carried out correctly at the checkouts. What do you think she means by this?

Remember to give reasons for your answers.

Operative – Sally Tye

Sally works for a food-processing company. The company buys in raw fruit and vegetables and washes, peels, chops, cooks, etc., these to make the ready-prepared salads and desserts we buy in the shops. This is what she says about her job:

'We work on a shift system – the factory keeps working round the clock and so sometimes I work from eight in the morning to five at night or from five at night to two in the morning. Sometimes you can work double shifts and then you get a day off work, but I don't like doing that because of my family.

'I work on a conveyor belt with five other women. We pack the salads. At the moment we're doing this sort of green salad. It's my job to put the spring onions in. These have been washed and trimmed before they get to me. I have to make sure they're exactly the right shape and size before I put them in the pack. We have to work fast. You soon get to tell if they're right or not. And you can't make mistakes. They take out samples to test all the time. We have to work as a team. You can't be sloppy in your work or you mess it up for the others. And that annoys everybody.

'Everything in the factory is spotlessly clean. We have a very strict drill for changing into our work clothes. Nothing can be dirty. We wear surgical gloves and breathing masks so we don't contaminate the food. This means we can't talk to each other much when we're working.

'The pay isn't too good and the hours can be a problem, but I like my job. So long as you do what you're told and do your job well, it's good, regular work. We only work on monthly contracts so that if there's a lull in trade they can lay you off. That tends to happen most to the more inexperienced workers. I've worked on most things we produce in this factory and so they keep people like me on so I can train new people when they have to take them on.

'I like some of the perks, too. If a batch goes wrong, they sell it off cheap to the staff. We're never short of a salad or pudding in our house! And me and the other girls often get together at night when we can to have a good night out!'

- What do you think are the good things and the bad things about doing a job like this?

- Sally says 'so long as you do what you're told'. What do you think she means by this?

- Sally does not say whether she finds the strict hygiene routine something that annoys her or something she is quite happy with. What do you think that is so?

Remember to give reasons for your answers.

General staff member – Lily Chang

Lily Chang is a receptionist for a large dental practice. This is what she says about her job:

'My main responsibility is to greet the patients when they come into the surgery and to check their appointments. I also have to find out how their treatment will be paid for and I get them to fill in the right forms. I also keep records of treatment on the computer and work out times for patients to make repeat appointments. Ours is a very big practice so most of the day I am at the reception desk – I don't have time to do much else. I start at nine and we close at five, but sometimes we have to stay on a bit longer if we're running behind with the appointments, but it's never much later than 5.30. I don't mind that, as long as it's not too late. I live at home with my parents and my mother has bad arthritis in her hands so I do most of the cooking and cleaning. My parents depend on me, so I like the regular working hours here.

Answering the telephone is another big part of my job. We often get calls from people who aren't our patients but who want urgent treatment. These people are very difficult to deal with. We don't have room for any new patients at the moment and I usually have to tell them to try another practice or to go to the hospital if it really is an emergency.

'Much of what I do, though, is very routine. There aren't many decisions I have to take on my own. If I'm not sure what to do, I refer it to the particular dentist involved.

'Before I worked here I was a receptionist with a local printing firm. Before that I was at college doing a secretarial course. We did not have a quarter of the visitors at the printers that we do here, so I used to do other jobs as well while I was at the reception desk, such as putting mailing shots into envelopes or even a little bit of proofreading. But I prefer my job at the dentists'. It's the contact with people I like. I also feel more as though I'm working as part of a team. We all seem to be rushing about all day getting things done. I don't know how we manage it sometimes!'

- Hundreds of different types of businesses and organisations employ receptionists. Do you think a receptionist's job is different, depending on the type of business or organisation the receptionist works for?

- Lily describes her work very clearly, but what do you think is the most important *role* or *function* of the job she does?

- How important do you think Lily is to the overall success and smooth running of the dental practice?

Remember to give your reasons.

Finally, there is one more job role we need to look at. We have just read about the role of the *owner* of a company – Peter Churchill – but in larger businesses there will be other managers apart from the owner or managing director. These are the people who manage a particular department within a company – for example, marketing and selling, finance or production. These managers are in overall charge of running their own departments but, at the same time, they are responsible to the company's top management (look back to Unit 1, Chapter 1, if you need to refresh you memory on organisational structures).

ACTIVITY

For this activity you need to work in small groups of three or four. We have looked at the job role of a supervisor in a supermarket and an operative in a food-processing firm. In what other businesses or organisations might you find supervisors and operatives?

Among you, decided on *three* different firms or organisations that will have supervisors and *three* that will have operatives. For each business or organisation, describe in as much detail as you can what sort of things the job role of the supervisor/operative will entail. The following are two examples to get you going:

Supervisor – chocolate factory

- Will make sure hygiene standards are met.

- Will make sure the employees are doing their job properly.

- Will keep an eye on time-keeping.

- Will make sure the correct clothing is worn.

Operative – fast-food restaurant

- Will make sure the customer gets what he or she ordered.

- Will make sure the customer is served quickly and politely.

- Will keep an eye on the quality of the food he or she is serving.

Did you find parts of these jobs were basically the same in the businesses or organisations you chose? Why do you think that is?

In the case study we also looked at an example of a general member of staff – the receptionist. There are many other types of jobs in businesses or organisations we could categorise as 'general' or 'support' jobs:

- secretaries

- technicians

- canteen staff

- caretakers.

Remember, we said earlier these people's jobs *support* the work of the other employees in a business or organisation. Without these support staff no business or organisation could function effectively.

ACTIVITY

Think carefully about **all** the staff who work in your school or college (not just the teaching staff – everyone you can think of). Make a list of all these jobs (you do not need to include people's names, and if more than one person does a particular job you need only list that job once – for example, 'teacher' or 'tutor'). How many of these jobs are general (or support) jobs? Put a star or asterisk next to these.

When you are sure you have identified all the *support* staff in you school or college, make a separate list of these. Now, next to each job, make a note of:

1 The *general* type of work each member of the support staff does.

2 Who in your school or college *benefits* from the support of each of these members of staff.

Working arrangements

Employees' working patterns have become much more flexible in recent years. New working arrangements have been introduced that enable organisations to meet customer needs while, at the same time, allowing employees to have the time to look after their families or to attend to other personal commitments. Working arrangements, therefore, depend on the business's needs and the employees' circumstances. Hence,

employees work in a variety of ways (e.g. part time or full time or on temporary or permanent contracts). For example, 70% of McDonald's crew members work part time with most of their hours being concentrated in the evenings and at weekends.

Contracts of employment

The type of employment will usually be stated in a *contract of employment* between employees and employers. A contract is an agreement between people or organisations. It will state the obligations and responsibilities agreed between both *parties* (the people who sign and agree to the contract). When a new employee is taken on, he or she must be given a written contract of employment within 13 weeks of starting work.

The Contract of Employment Act 1978 requires employers to give employees *particulars* (details) of their terms of employment.

- The job's title.

- Hours of work.

- Holiday arrangements.

- The rate of pay and how the employee will be paid (e.g. weekly or monthly, etc.).

- The period of notice to be given by either side (i.e. how many days or weeks one party must give the other if one party wants to end the employment).

- The person to contact in the event of a grievance or dispute.

- Any legal rights the employee has, such as the right to belong (or not to belong) to a trade union.

One of the most important terms in a contract of employment is the hours of work. This refers not only to the total number of hours to be worked but also to the times of the day or night the hours have to be worked.

Types of employment

The *type* of employment someone has (e.g. part time or full time or day work or night work) will depend on the nature of his or her employer's business. For example, someone who works for a shop will have to work the hours the shop is open (e.g. nine in the morning to six at night). Some types of employment might entail the employee working part time (e.g. a waitress in a restaurant or a cleaner who works a few hours only in the evening). Some work might entail working from home (e.g. sewing work or some simple assembly work, such as making Christmas crackers). Outdoor work, needless to say (such as farming or building work), can usually be done only during the daylight hours!

Part time

An employee might be on a part-time contract if he or she works less than the business's or organisation's standard working hours (e.g. a teacher who works only two days a week). Part-time jobs are becoming more common as employers try to reduce their costs (it is cheaper to employ part-time staff rather than full-time staff).

Full time

An employee will be on a full-time contract if he or she works the business's or organisation's standard working hours (e.g. a

teacher who works 5 days a week). In some cases, two part-time employees might 'job share' one full-time job (i.e. do the job between them).

Temporary employment

Temporary employment means an employee will be on either a short-term or long-term contract *for a specific period of time*. After the period of the contract is over, the employment will end (in some circumstances, however, both the employee and employer might agree to *renew* the contract for a further period).

Short-term contracts are used when an employee is needed for a specific short period of time only (e.g. 6 months or one year), perhaps to cover in someone's absence for one reason or another. *Long-term contracts* are issued when an employee works for a specified longer period of time (e.g. 3 or 5 years). In the case of both short-term and long-term contracts, the employment may be either part time or full time, as agreed by both parties to the contract.

Temporary workers, therefore, are often hired for a specific reason. Temporary work is very common in *seasonal* businesses (e.g. the holiday trade – hotels, holiday camps, etc., during the summer – or in shops around Christmas time).

Permanent employment

In this type of employment, no specific period of time is mentioned in the contract of employment. This means an employee should be able to work for the business or organisation for an indefinite period of time.

ACTIVITY

Interview twenty people (ten males and ten females, if possible) who are in employment (members of your family, friends, neighbours, and others). Ask them the following questions (make a note of *who* said *what*; you will need this information later!):

1 What sort of work do you do?

2 Are you in full-time or part-time employment?

3 Are you in temporary or permanent employment?

Use your results to answer the following questions:

* Are more people on part-time contracts than full-time contracts?

* What sort of work do people do who are in part-time work? Full-time work?

* Are more men employed in full-time work than women?

* What sort of work do people do who are in temporary employment? In permanent employment?

Try to give the *reasons* for your findings.

ACTIVITY

Look back at the case studies you read earlier in this unit. For each person, try to work out:

* Whether his or her employment is full time or part time.

* If the employment is temporary or permanent.

* What, if anything, in each person's working arrangements causes that person difficulties or problems (e.g. family commitments, spare time for leisure pursuits and hobbies, etc.).

Pay and benefits
Wages (or salaries)

Wages or salaries are the reward paid for people's labour. Not surprisingly, wages are considered to be the most important thing in life to most people: the amount of income we receive influences the type of house we can afford, the make and age of the car we run, where and for how long we can go on holiday, etc.

If an employee is paid on monthly basis, this is called a *salary*. An employee's salary is usually fixed at an annual rate of payment, that is paid monthly. Salaries are a common form of payment for workers in professional, managerial and scientific employment (e.g. doctors, managers and teachers).

If an employee is paid on a weekly basis, this is called a *wage*. Wages are a common method for paying workers in manual and semi-skilled employment (e.g. builders).

The factors that affect the actual wage or salary earned by a particular employee include the following:

* The type of job he or she does.

* The business he or she works in.

* The employee's position in the business's or organisation's structure (organisational charts were explained in Unit 1; look back if you need to refresh your memory about these). Obviously, the higher the level in an organisation an employee is, the higher the wage or salary he or she will earn.

There are, however, many other things *not* related to the nature of the job being done, the business or the employee's position within the organisation that will also affect the employee's wage of salary. Some of these are as follows:

- The power of trade unions to bargain for higher wages.

- How much profit the company has made.

- The payment system in operation (e.g. piece work, bonuses, commission, etc. – see below).

- The individual employee's experience (generally, more experienced workers are paid more than less experienced workers).

Payment basis

Wages are calculated in many ways and, sometimes, the wage someone is paid will combine several of these methods.

Flat rate

A flat rate of pay is a set payment received each week or month based on a standard number of hours an employee is expected to work each week or month. Many workers are paid in this way, but this system does not always provide employees with the incentive to put in extra time or effort. If you are going to be paid the same flat rate each week or each month, there is little incentive to work harder because you are not going to receive any more pay than if you worked as normal!

Time rate

Under this system, the worker is paid a set amount for each hour worked. A worker might be paid *overtime* at a higher rate of pay for any additional hours he or she works. (Overtime is when you put in more hours of work than you are normally expected to. For example, you may be asked to work overtime at the weekends in order that the business you work for gets an order finished on time or to clear any backlogs in work that might have been building up.)

Piece rate

This method of payment is not as common today as it was in the past. When paid on a piece work basis, a payment is made for each good-quality item a worker produces. For example, machinists in a factory producing jumpers might be paid for each jumper they knit to an acceptable standard. As long as the employee meets a minimum standard of output (i.e. how many jumpers he or she is expected to knit each day or each week), the amount of time this takes is of limited importance.

Under this payment system, workers are often paid a *bonus* (see below) once they produce more than a certain target level. Being paid for each piece of an acceptable quality you produce should encourage you to work harder and to put the maximum effort into your work.

Bonus

Bonuses are a share of any additional profits a business makes as a result of increased efforts or efficiency on the part of the employees. Bonuses are paid to employees as a reward for their good work.

Bonuses are very common in banks and building societies, when the staff have brought in extra business (perhaps in the form of new accounts, mortgages, personal pension plans, etc.) over and above the targets set by the management. Bonuses are often paid out around Christmas time. If employees know they may get a bonus at Christmas (at a time when we all need extra money), this may give them the incentive to work harder the rest of the year.

Commission

Commission is a payment made (in addition to the flat or time rate) as a percentage of the value of sales or services an employee achieves either on a weekly or monthly basis, etc. Therefore, the more you *sell* the more you will be paid. (Commission is not the same as a bonus. Commission is paid to each employee based on the amount of sales achieved by each employee; bonuses are worked out from the business's overall extra profits and are usually paid to all employees.)

Commission is a very common payment method among car dealers, insurance agents and double-glazing salespeople. For example, if the rate of commission is 10% of sales made, the salesperson gets 10% of the value of the sales he or she achieves. If that person sells a car to the value of £5,000, he or she will get £500 commission.

 **ACTIVITY**

Each payment basis described above has its advantages and disadvantages to employees. For example, one of the *advantages* of the flat rate system is that you know exactly how much money you will have coming in over the next few weeks or months. A *disadvantage* is that, unless you have the opportunity to work overtime, you cannot *increase* the amount of money you will have coming in in the next few weeks or months.

For each payment basis you have just read about, make a list of the advantages and disadvantages of each system to employees.

Payment methods

You learnt in Unit 1 that the wages section in the finance department is responsible for paying wages. Employees will receive their wages in different ways, depending on the jobs they do and the types of business they work in.

Cash

Payment by cash is not as common as it used to be as most people these days have bank accounts and are, therefore, paid by cheque or credit transfer instead (see below).

Cash payments are often made to people who work on a part-time basis. For example, if you have a Saturday job the chances are you will be paid in cash. Similarly, people who work only a few hours a day or week might be paid in cash (cleaners, workers in the catering trade – bar staff, waitresses and waiters, and others – part-time sales assistants in shops and so on).

Cash payments may also be made to people who work on a casual basis – for example, people employed to work on the land. These workers may be employed on a day-to-day basis only, depending on, for example, the amount of crops to be picked or even the weather conditions. They might be paid in cash at the end of each day as there may be no guarantee there will be

197

work for them the following morning. People who work in the construction industry, who work from home on a piece rate basis or who work in seasonal businesses (e.g. the holiday trade – see above) may also be paid in cash.

Cash payments may also be paid to people who do not have bank accounts and who therefore cannot be paid in any other way.

Cheques

Cheques are a safer way of making payments than cash because a cheque can be drawn by (paid to) only the person named on the cheque. Hence there is less chance of the wages being stolen or lost (cheques can be cancelled and replaced if they go astray).

Like cash, cheques are used to pay people who work on a temporary or part-time basis, and they are often used as a way of paying people who receive their wages through the post (e.g. home workers). They are a simple and convenient way of paying people who are paid only on irregular occasions and who may not be on the business's permanent pay roll (i.e. employees who do not receive a regular weekly or monthly wage from the organisation).

Cheques, however, can go missing in the post, and it will cost the business extra bank charges to cancel and replace them. Credit transfers (see below), therefore, are a much more popular way of paying wages these days than cheques, although to be paid by either cheque or credit transfer the employee must have a bank account.

Credit transfers

Credit transfers are a way of eliminating the need to pay employees by cash or cheque. Instead, the money is transferred out of the employer's bank account directly into the employee's account. This system has many advantages over cash and cheques:

- The wages are safe – the money is transferred electronically between the two accounts.

- The employee does not have to wait for a cheque to clear before he or she can draw on his or her wages.

- Unlike waiting for a cheque to turn up in the post, a full-time employee knows his or her wage will be paid on the same date each and every month. This enables employees to plan out their spending for the month (e.g. to arrange with their banks or building societies to have regular payments made out of their accounts, knowing their wages will have been paid well in time to cover these payments).

- It gives employees stability and security. If your bank or building society knows you are paid *regularly* each month, and how *much* you are paid each month, it will be more likely to let you have a loan or an overdraft for a short period of time as it knows money will be coming into your account with which you will be able to pay them back.

The credit transfer system can be used only by people who have bank or building society accounts and who are paid on a regular (e.g. monthly) basis. This system is, therefore, most commonly used for full-time or part-time workers who are on longer-term contracts.

Pay slips

Whether payment of your wages or salary is made by cash, cheque or credit transfer, you will usually receive a pay slip (or pay

CASE STUDY – Staff benefits at Marks & Spencer

Marks & Spencer provide a range of benefits to everyone employed by the company, such as:

- A profit-sharing scheme for all employees with at least two years' service.

- Generous help for employees who suffer hardship.

- An extensive range of other facilities, including catering, hairdressing and health promotion for all members of staff.

These benefits cost the business £2 million per year (over £50 per employee).

You will readily appreciate how the staff benefit from these perks, but how do you think Marks & Spencer itself benefits from offering its staff such facilities?

advice). This is a slip of paper filled in by the wages department (often by computer) so that you can see how much you have been paid and what *deductions* have been made from your wages.

A pay slip will usually contain the following information:

- The employee's name and work number.

- The employee's tax code and National Insurance number.

- Gross pay (i.e. pay *before* any deductions are made from the wages).

- Any bonuses, commission or overtime payment made on top of the flat rate payment.

- Deductions made (e.g. taxes, National Insurance, contributions to a pension scheme).

- Net pay (the amount left after all the deductions have been made).

Other benefits

In addition to the pay an employee receives, he or she may be entitled to other benefits provided by the business. These benefits are known as 'fringe benefits' or 'perks'.

You learnt in Unit 1 that the human resources department in a business or organisation is responsible for motivating staff by offering them extra benefits or perks. Benefits include the use of a subsidised staff canteen, a company car, luncheon vouchers, sports or recreation facilities and discounts when the staff purchase the firm's goods. Cheap medical insurance and opportunities to buy shares in the business at reduced prices are further examples of benefits or perks.

ACTIVITY

Look back at the case studies you read earlier in this unit. Do any of these people receive any benefits or perks? If so, what are these and why do you think the employer offers these to its staff?

Training and career development

Training is the process of teaching people new skills or improving their existing skills so they can do their jobs more effectively and may be able to advance in their careers as a result of acquiring these new or improved skills (see Unit 1). Training is an important function of the human resources department in a business or organisation, and businesses are often keen to train their workforce to increase production and efficiency.

Types of training

Training takes many forms (e.g. day-release or short courses, instruction manuals, instruction in the workplace, etc. Training is important to ensure that the workforce possesses the skills and knowledge necessary to undertake the work effectively.

There are various types of training, which we have already looked at in Unit 1, Chapter 2. For example:

Induction training. New members of staff are trained to do the jobs they will be expected to do during the course of their work (e.g. how to operate specialised machinery or equipment or how to use a particular program on a computer).

Skills upgrading. If the equipment someone uses is changed in some way (e.g. a piece of machinery is modified to make it work better, or new equipment is brought in that is more efficient than the old equipment), that person's skills will need upgrading (bringing up to date) so he or she can operate the modified or new equipment effectively and safely.

Retraining. Sometimes the job someone does becomes redundant – it is no longer needed because a piece of machinery can now do that job more efficiently, more quickly and more cheaply. This has happened recently in a great many businesses. In banking, for example, automated teller machines (the 'holes in the wall' where we can draw out and pay in our money) have largely replaced the need for banks to employ a great many counter staff to provide us with these services. While some job losses will inevitably occur as a result of these changes, many businesses will retrain their staff in new skills so they can continue to work for the company but doing other, more useful jobs (in the example of banks, these jobs might include selling customers personal financial services, such as pensions schemes or life assurance).

Methods of training

There are two basic methods of training – on-the-job training people and off-the-job training. Such businesses as supermarkets and banks offer a variety of training opportunities for new and old employees alike. If you started work with a bank, for the first six months you would follow a carefully structured training programme at the branch where you were employed (on-the-job training). If you completed this training satisfactorily, you might be eligible for promotion. Training in banking work is very practical and is supported by the largest interactive video-training scheme operating in Britain.

Off-the-job training, on the other hand, as its name suggests, takes place away from the workplace. For example, if an employer sends staff to a local college (perhaps on a day-release basis) to acquire training in computer, catering or construction skills, this is off-the-job training. The employer needs to send staff away to a company or organisation that can supply training not available in the workplace. Other examples of off-the-job training include:

- *Management training courses*, where the management team go away together (perhaps to a hotel in the country) to learn better leadership skills. Very often courses like this will involve some form of demanding outdoor activities, where each member of the team learns to co-operate with the others.

- *Language training courses.* These days most businesses appreciate the benefits of their employees speaking more than one language. Companies and education institutions, therefore, often offer intensive language training courses for such businesses.

- Some businesses or organisation might require some members of staff to have *highly specialised skills* that cannot be obtained from within the company or locally. For example, a business or organisation might need someone skilled in specialised computer programming techniques, or in the skills needed to operate a highly expensive new piece of equipment. Obviously, these people would need to be sent to a specialist training centre to acquire those skills. On their return, they might be expected to pass on their new skills to other employees so these can be shared throughout the business or organisation.

 **ACTIVITY**

Look back at the case studies earlier in this unit:

- What sort of training have any of these people received?

- Are any of these people involved in training other people?

- Do you think any of these people might benefit from further training?

Remember to give reasons for your answers.

Protecting the employee

Employers have obligations towards their employees to protect them and provide the best working environment.

There are two main ways in which employees are protected at work, and while they are looking for a job:

1. Acts and legislation which are imposed by government on businesses
2. Trade unions which ensure that employers enforce and comply with the law.

Acts and legislation

There are five important pieces of legislation which protect the employee in the workplace and while he or she is trying to find a job.

1 The Employment Rights Act 1996

This is the legislation which protects employees from unfair dismissal, and sets out their rights in case of redundancy and maternity.

Unfair dismissal
- In the case of gross misconduct, e.g. theft, employers have the right to dismiss employees instantly.

- Employees may also be dismissed for other reasons such as incompetence, or other forms of misconduct, e.g. a long

201

period of absence for no reason, or not working or doing the required job.

- If employers decide to dismiss someone, there is a disciplinary procedure which they have to follow. Employees must be informed of these procedures, e.g. one formal verbal warning for the first offence and two written warnings for further offences or misconduct.

To avoid dismissal employees must also be aware of the following rules. They must:

- arrive on time.

- have a very good reason for being late or away from work.

- maintain the health and safety guidelines.

Redundancy

Employees must have worked in the business for at least 2 years to be entitled to a redundancy payment.

If employers offer employees an alternative job they must take it if it is suitable for them.

Maternity

- Employees have the right not to be dismissed on the grounds of pregnancy.

- Employees don't have to be in a business for a minimum of 2 years to be entitled to the statutory 14 weeks maternity leave.

- Employees have to have been working for the business for at least 2 years to be entitled to 40 weeks maternity leave, and have the right to return after that to their original job.

The Sex Discrimination Act 1975

This piece of legislation rules that women and men should be treated equally and given the same opportunities to learn and be promoted.

ACTIVITY

Are any of the employers in the following situations breaking the Sex Discrimination Act? In your groups, think of some other situations in which people might be discriminated against on the grounds of their sex. How does this Act help protect people?

a A company refused to offer a job to a female candidate unless she has signed an agreement not to have children for 3 years.

b The canteen ladies at Harwood Soft Drinks PLC are paid less than production staff who have the same level of responsibility and qualifications.

3 The Race Relations Act 1976

This legislation protects people in employment or people who are looking for a job from being discriminated against because of their colour, religion or ethnic origin. Every employee should be treated fairly and equally.

Think about why there is a need for this piece of legislation and do the following activity.

ACTIVITY

Discuss each of the following situations in your groups. Find out if the situation breaks the Race Relations Act or not.

a A West Indian checkout operator in Asda was caught stealing some money. She was sacked.

b Amran Ahmed only managed to get a job when he changed his name on his CV to John Smith.

4   The Disability Discrimination Act 1995

This Act states that people should not be discriminated against because of a disability, both when they are applying for jobs and in employment. It also states that employers should try to employ a representative number of disabled people in the workplace.

5   The Health and Safety at Work Act (HASAWA) 1974

In Unit 2, you learned how the health and safety of employees is a major aspect of working conditions. According to the Health and Safety at Work Act, employers have to provide safe working conditions for all employees. The Act also sets out the duties of the employee relating to health and safety. Think of some examples of the employer's responsibility towards employees in the following workplaces: an office, a building site; a shop. What kinds of responsibilities does an employee who works in each of those three workplaces have according to this Act?

Trade unions and employee's organisations

You learnt about the role of employee's organisations and trade unions in protecting the employee in Unit 1 (see page 17). So you already know that trade unions are organisations which represent employees at work. You also know that employees have the right to either join or not join a trade union, under the Employment Act. These days most employers in business are aware of the need to build effective communication with employees to create a happier and friendlier working environment. The trade unions make sure that employers comply with all the acts and legislations which protect employees at work. They also try to improve working conditions and pay.

The human resources department negotiates with trade unions and their representatives. This may be in relation to:

- wages
- health and safety procedures
- training
- redundancies
- grievances.

The human resources manger of an organisation will liaise with local union officials at either branch or district level over issues which concern the union.

The environment and the customer

Our environment is affected by how we spend our money. However, the effects of our spending are not always easy to identify as many aspects of producing and transporting goods take place far away from where we buy them.

In this unit you will follow the 'supply chain' for a product you might buy, identifying each stage and location of its manufacture, distribution, consumption and disposal. This helps you to gain an understanding of how the choices made at each stage affect the social and natural environment.

You will learn:

* *that the environment is about more than just nature*

* *how to follow a supply chain by finding out where goods come from and how they are produced, distributed, consumed and disposed of*

* *about the environmental benefits and costs to be considered at different stages of the supply chain*

* *how public concern can influence the supply chain.*

You will also learn what is meant by environmental sustainability and will explore ways in which individuals, groups and government influence this.

This unit links with Foundation Unit 2 (Investigating Businesses) and Unit 5 (Looking After Customers). This unit is assessed through an external assessment. The grade you achieve on that assessment will be your grade for the unit.

What is the environment?

The environment is the place in which we live and work. It is everything that surrounds us. At the moment the environment you are in might be your classroom (or perhaps a room in your house if you are reading this at home). When you go outside into the street, your environment is that street and, on a larger scale, the town or city in which that street is situated. Your *town* or *city's* environment is the country in which it is located. And a *country's* environment is the entire world itself!

What this means is that the biggest environment of all – the entire world – is made up of smaller and ever smaller environments, and that anything that happens in a small environment will affect the overall environment of the earth itself. And of course this works the other way round. Changes in the 'big' environment of the entire world itself will cause changes in all the smaller environments.

We could therefore say that everything we do affects the environment. If you throw a piece of litter into a stream or river, you have *polluted* (damaged) that river. You have put something into it that does not belong to that river's *natural* environment. If we were all to throw things into that river it might become so polluted that all life in the river might die. This polluted river might flow into a bigger river and, hence, would pollute that bigger river. And the bigger river might flow into a sea or ocean and pollute that sea or ocean. And so it goes on.

You will readily appreciate, therefore, that *businesses* can affect the environment and are, in their turn, affected *by* the environment. Therefore, *environmental considerations* (i.e. asking questions about the impact a particular strategy or action will have on the environment) are an important part of making business decisions.

The environment consists of four interlinked parts:

1 The *natural* environment.
2 The *built* environment.
3 The *cultural* environment.
4 The *social* environment.

We will look at each of these interlinking parts below.

The natural environment

Raw materials and *energy resources* must be extracted from the environment so that products can be manufactured. Everything we buy or use, from pencils to aeroplanes, tins of tuna to computers, all rely on raw materials and energy resources (e.g. oil, water, wood, minerals extracted from the earth, etc.) for their manufacture. And the process of manufacturing these raw materials into a final product, and burning the energy resources to supply the power to do this, creates new substances (called *by-products* or *waste*) that are pumped out into the natural environment. The more we manufacture, the more resources we will use up and the more waste we will create.

Many people today, particularly young people, have become increasingly concerned about the effects on the natural environment of producing and consuming such large quantities of manufactured products. Businesses, therefore, have become more and more concerned that their products and the activities that go into manufacturing their products do not harm the environment. They also know that people might not buy their products if they know the manufacture of these products has damaged the natural environment unnecessarily or irresponsibly.

The better *management* and *efficient use* of energy and other natural resources, *waste control* and *recycling* are some of the means businesses can use to reduce their harmful impact on the natural environment.

We need to make a clear distinction here, however. We know that *efficiency* means doing something in such a way that we do not waste either time, money, or energy and materials. If you are doing the work you need to do to study for your Foundation Business course *efficiently*, you will not be wasting time doing unnecessary work or the wrong sort of work (or even no work at all!), and you will not be wasting materials by using up unnecessary amounts of paper or energy by doing far more work than you need to. Businesses similarly need to be efficient – they, too, do not want to waste time, money, or energy and materials. However, there are *two* ways they can be efficient: *economically* and in their use of *resources*. *Economic* efficiency means doing things in a way that reduces *costs* to a business. An economically efficient business does things in such a way as to reduce all unnecessary costs. *Resource* efficiency means using raw materials and energy resources in a way that does not *waste* raw materials and energy resources unnecessarily. It means getting as much as possible out of the raw materials and energy resources with the least possible wastage. An *economically* efficient business might not be *resource* efficient: to keep down costs it may waste resources in the manufacture of a product if these products are cheap and easily obtainable. It may consider spending money to use these resources more efficiently uneconomic.

In an ideal world, all businesses should aim to be both economically and resource efficient.

The built environment

This part of the environment comprises all the roads, bridges, houses, hospitals, etc. that we have built in our environment. In general, we need these things in order to live and in order that our society can function effectively.

For example, having good roads and motorways makes transport easier, causes fewer traffic jams and saves us time and money. However, some people are concerned about the effects of pollution from transport on the natural environment. Building more roads, with no investment in improving public transport, they say, will only generate more traffic, thus making matters even worse.

The cultural environment

Most businesses exist mainly to satisfy their customers' needs and wants (and, don't forget, to make a profit!). These needs and wants will vary from one customer to another, depending on the customer's values, beliefs, life styles, etc. It is these differences among customers that make up the *cultural* part of the environment.

Values and desires

Businesses must always be prepared to adapt their goods and services to their customers' values and desires. For example, food manufacturers may decide not to use genetically modified products or may decide to use environmentally friendly products to cater for their customers' values and desires.

Beliefs

Businesses also have to consider people's religious beliefs before making decisions about what to produce. For example, in Muslim countries, people do not eat pork, so there would be no point in setting up a business that makes pork sausages in Muslim countries.

Life styles

Businesses must respond to changes in people's life styles. As more and more women now work, this has led to an increase in the number of sales of household appliances and an increase in the manufacture of ready-made meals.

ACTIVITY

Can you think of any further examples of the following?

* A business has changed the *ingredients* in a

product to cater for its customers' changing values or desires.

- A business is offering different *products* because of changes in its customers' life styles.

- Products a business would not try to *sell* to certain people because of their religious beliefs.

If you can, try to give the *reasoning* behind these changes or decisions.

The social environment

The social part of the environment comprises all those things that go towards creating good standards of living for all.

- Good health and education.

- Safe employment that does not have a bad effect on our health.

- Communities to live in that are clean, free of harm (e.g. free of crime) and where people co-operate with each other.

A great many of these will depend on things beyond our control: how much money we have, where we choose to live (or *have* to live) and the work we do, if we have a job at all. However, having a *clean* environment is everyone's responsibility, including businesses, the local community and the local council.

Business ethics

The general public expect businesses to follow certain guidelines in their everyday operations. These values and principles are referred to as *business ethics*. These may be adopted by the firm as part of its overall business strategy or forced upon it by consumers or pressure groups. A poor environmental reputation, for example, may lead to a loss of customers, a reduction in shareholder confidence and a loss of sales.

Above all, however, all businesses have a responsibility for the health and safety of their employees, customers and neighbours.

The supply chain and the environment

As we have already seen, manufacturing is the process of turning raw materials into a finished product. From the first stage of the manufacturing process (the acquisition of the raw materials) right through to the final stages of marketing and distributing the product to the shops, there are three things a business needs to consider:

1. How well the product will do the job it was designed to do.

2. How much it will cost to produce the product.

3. The business's environmental responsibility (which includes the health and safety of its employees as well as its customers).

When planning the stages that will go into the manufacture of a product, a business will need to keep those three factors clearly in mind.

 **ACTIVITY**

For this activity it would be best if you worked in twos or threes. Together, think of a fairly simple product you all know and use. This should preferably be something quite small you can bring into the classroom.

For example:

- A can of fizzy drink.

- A snack food (a packet of crisps, a tub of yoghurt, a chocolate bar, etc.).

- An item of clothing (a jumper, a hat, a pair of gloves, etc.).

207

(If you know someone who works for a company that manufactures a product like these, perhaps you could use that product and try to enlist that person's help!)

Try not to choose something that is too complicated – a mobile phone, a CD or an item of make-up, etc. – you don't want to bog yourself down in too much technical detail! And try to choose something that was manufactured in the UK.

In your group, try to decide on all the stages that went into the production of the product you have chosen:

- The raw materials needed (and where these may have come from). You might find this information on the product's packaging. Don't forget to include the means of transport used to get the raw materials to the factory.

- The stages involved in manufacturing the product (you do not need to go into too much detail here). Can you also find out where exactly the product was made?

- How the product is packaged. It may be you no longer have the packaging. Can you remember how it was originally packed? If you can, make a list of all the raw materials that went into the manufacture of the packaging as well!

- How the product was distributed to the shop where you bought it.

- Finally, do not forget the energy that was used in its production. Energy includes the fuel used in transporting the raw goods as well as the energy used in the manufacturing process itself. This is a difficult area to work out, but try to be as specific as you can.

You may need to find out more information about your product or about the raw materials that went into its manufacture. The following sources may be of help:

- Your school or college library.

- The manufacturer themselves (manufacturer's addresses are usually printed on the packaging).

- The Internet. Most companies these days have web sites you can access.

When you have gathered as much information as you think you need, try to represent all the stages that went into the manufacture of your product as a diagram. Figure 7.1 suggests ways you could arrange your chart. You may find other, better ways than these to present your work, and you may need to add other stages to the process, depending on the product you have chosen.

- By the time you have finished this activity, you will probably be very surprised to learn just how much is involved in the manufacture of what seems a very simple product indeed!

Now we have a clearer idea of the stages involved in the manufacture of even a simple product, we need to look in more detail at how each stage of the production process can affect the environment.

The manufacturing processes

When a product is manufactured, many other businesses and people will be indirectly involved in its production. For example, food manufacturers rely on suppliers of such raw materials as milk, fruit and vegetables. Food manufacturers, therefore, must find out if their raw materials come from reputable or acceptable suppliers. For example, they may need to make sure the raw materials that are used in manufacturing their products have not been fed with chemically based fertilisers and pesticides that may prove harmful to the environment. Similarly, some consumers are increasingly avoiding genetically modified food and are

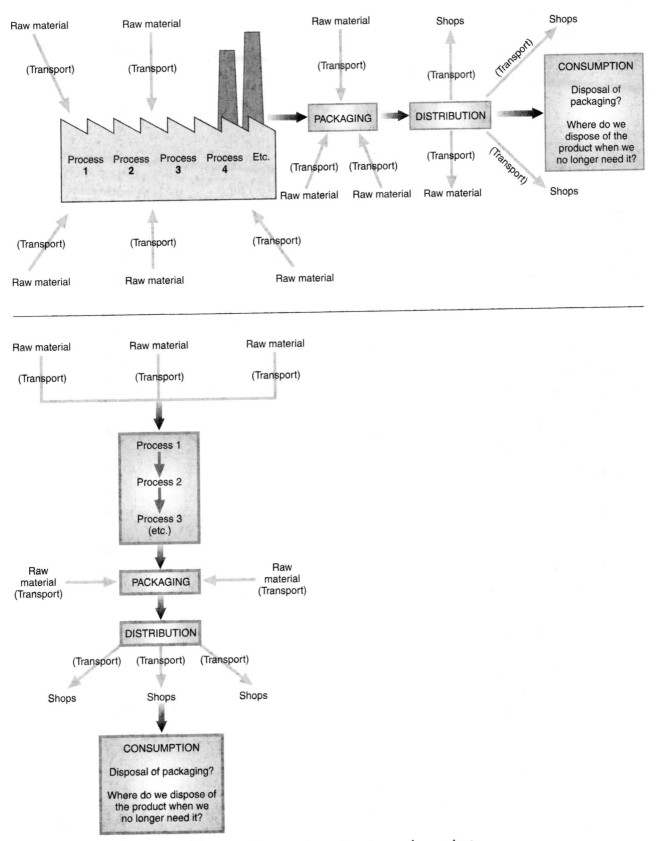

Figure 7.1 Different ways of showing the manufacturing stages of a product

more keen on eating produce that has been grown organically without the need for chemical fertilisers or pesticides.

Businesses should ensure that they manage their waste products effectively and safely, and that health and safety regulations are followed by everyone. However, it is not just pollution from waste that is of concern, but also the chemicals contained in the products we buy. For example, until quite recently aerosols and many other products contained gases called CFCs. In aerosols, these gases were used to help propel your hairspray or deodorant out of the can. It was then found that these CFC gases, after leaving the aerosol, went straight up into the atmosphere where they were beginning to destroy the ozone layer. It is this layer in the atmosphere that protects all life on earth from the most burning rays of the sun. If we were to continue to destroy the ozone layer, we would be threatening the survival of every living thing on the planet!

Packaging

Unnecessary packaging puts unnecessary pressures on the world's natural resources. Mining to extract the metals to make cans and tin foil, etc., and forestry to grow the timber from which we make paper and cardboard can destroy habitats that have taken centuries to develop. On top of this, most packaging is thrown away and buried in the holes called landfill sites. These sites can pollute the water supply.

Today, however, we tend to throw less and less packaging away. We take empty bottles to bottle banks, and put our aluminium cans in bins so that they can be *recycled* (used again). However, even the process of recycling demands that we consume energy and other resources in order to use that particular commodity again.

Transport methods

Businesses should be aware – as must all of us – of the harm motorised transport does to the air we breathe. Whatever method of motorised transport a business uses to deliver its products, it pollutes the environment unless very effective measures to prevent pollution are taken. Of the four main methods of transporting goods (road, rail, sea and air), road transport is by far the biggest polluter of the air.

? Did you know?

The excessive quantity of motorised traffic on our roads continues to threaten human health. It has been estimated recently that air pollution leads to the death of up to 24,000 people a year in this country and is the cause of another 24,000 hospital admissions and re-admissions.

Advertising

Before any product or service can be bought, people need to be aware of its existence. Manufacturers and service producers, therefore, must *advertise* their products and services. All advertising should be fair, honest, legal and decent, and advertising is sometimes used to promote environmentally friendly products. This may seem a valid role for advertising to play in preventing damage to the environment, but consider the following:

- The amount of junk mail we receive through our letter-boxes each week, trying to persuade us to buy products or services.

- The amount of money spent worldwide by companies advertising their products and the amount of money spent worldwide on measures to reduce pollution.

CASE STUDY — Road hauliers

Lorries consume 10.2 million tonnes of diesel every year and emit 32 million tonnes of carbon dioxide, the main cause, it has been suggested, of global warming (the process by which the earth's overall temperature might be increasing). Lorries are also significant contributors to urban smog and particularly the small particles that kill up to 9,000 people every year.

Environmentalists believe that the government should use some of the money raised through fuel duties to invest in 'piggy back' facilities. These facilities would be used to transfer lorries on to trains, on which they could cover the bulk of the distance they need to travel.

Others believe the government should not be persuaded into cutting duties on diesel as this would only encourage more companies to send their goods by road, causing more heavy lorries to thunder through the back streets and country lanes of Britain. If the government is worried about business costs, they argue, it should invest in better rail freight facilities rather than cutting fuel duties.

Read this case study carefully and then answer these questions. Remember to give reasons for your answers.

1 Explain how cutting the duty on diesel could increase pollution from road traffic.

2 Why do you think the government would be reluctant to *increase* duty on diesel?

3 What measures do you think the government should take to reduce the pollution that results from the traffic on our roads?

Energy

You learnt from the activity you did earlier in this unit that businesses use up energy in all stages of production: from the manufacturing process to the distribution of the goods themselves. Therefore, every business aims to save on energy costs. While individuals increasingly demand *green* energy (i.e. energy from *renewable* resources, such as wind and solar power), businesses are also increasingly demanding energy from such sources. Switching to green energy not only helps to save natural resources but it also saves having to dispose of the harmful by-products created when converting traditional fuels into energy (there are no harmful by-products from wind and solar power).

You will notice we used the word 'renewable' in the last paragraph. When applied to energy resources or raw materials, renewable means things that can be *replaced*. In the example of energy above, renewable was used to describe wind and solar power. There is an *endless* supply of wind and of light and heat from the sun, and so, no matter how much energy we create using these resources, there will always be more wind and sunlight to replace what we have used up. There is not, however, an endless supply of coal, oil and natural gas. When we use up these sources of energy, there will be none left. We will have used up all the world's reserves of these sources of energy.

NORTHUMBERLAND COLL OF ARTS & TECHNO LIBRARY

211

ACTIVITY

Can you think of any *raw materials* that are *not* renewable? Remember to give reasons for your answers.

Finally, we must not forget that most businesses operate to make a profit. When they make decisions about raw materials and energy, they may put profit first and the environment second. However, public opinion and government legislation have made it more difficult in recent years for businesses to ignore environmental considerations. Indeed, some businesses have found it *more* profitable to be 'environmentally aware': people are more prepared to buy their products in the knowledge that their production has not harmed the environment or has made use of *renewable* resources.

How consumer choice affects the supply chain

We have already seen how consumers' preferences and opinions can affect not only what a manufacturer produces but the way the manufacturer produces that product. And it can cost *more* for a company to be environmentally responsible and this extra cost, inevitably, is passed on to the customers. Ultimately, however, customers decide for themselves how much they are willing to pay for a product and, if they decide a product manufactured in a less environmentally friendly way is better value for money, they may decide to buy that product rather than a more expensive, environmentally friendly product.

However, consumers still have strong views about certain issues concerning the manufacture of products, and these views will affect their buying decisions. The following are a few examples of how consumer attitudes can affect manufacturers.

Food

Nowadays, people are increasingly concerned about the food they eat. Most of us like to make sure our food is safe and not chemically treated. Organic food (food produced from safe, sustainable farming systems and which has not been treated with chemicals) has become an increasingly popular alternative to more traditional mass-produced food. Similarly, people are worried about the risks of food that contains genetically modified (GM) substances. Genetic modification is where scientists alter the natural properties of plants and animals so that, for example, a particular crop is more resistant to attacks from pests than it would be naturally, or produces more or better-quality substances for use in food manufacture. Some people are concerned that we do not yet know the impact that these GM plants and animals will have on the environment and whether they could be dangerous to human health.

Recycling

As we have already seen, recycling means using a product again. In the UK, it is estimated that each household throws away over a tonne of waste every year (which comes to a total of around 26 million tonnes of waste). Many of these items could be recycled (e.g. glass, cans, paper and plastic).

Products are available in different sorts of packaging. For example, some food products are available in a choice of containers (you can buy orange juice in a glass bottle, a plastic bottle or in a carton). Hence, customers may have a choice in the way they buy their products and may choose to buy a product in a type of packaging that can be reused or recycled.

? Did you know?

Christmas wrapping paper costs 50,000 trees a year. Yet, despite this, almost no Christmas wrapping is made from recycled paper, and high - street stores are reluctant to stock recycled wrapping paper.

Why do you think this is so?

Non-renewable fuels

Motorised traffic causes pollution, which not only harms the environment but also people's health. It also uses up vast quantities of non-renewable fuel. People who are concerned about the environment try to reduce the amount of motorised traffic on the roads by taking the following measures:

- Minimising their use of private motorised transport by cutting out unnecessary journeys, sharing cars, using public transport and, if they can, by living nearer to work or working from home.

- Using bicycles as much as they can (e.g. for going to the local shops or going to work).

- Walking instead of using the car.

- Avoiding travelling by plane, which is by far the most polluting method of transport.

Animal welfare

People are increasingly concerned about the way animals are treated in the production of food and other products. For example, some people will not buy *anything* that contains animal products or will buy only

products they know have not caused any suffering (e.g. free-range eggs rather than battery eggs).

Manufacturers are well aware of this fact. They often put labels on their packaging to the effect 'No animal testing was involved in the manufacture of this product'. You often see this on cosmetics and shampoos – which were until very recently tested on animals to ensure they had no harmful side-effects.

Environmental sustainability

There are limits to the amount of raw materials and energy resources the environment can provide. There are also limits to the amount of waste the environment can absorb. So should businesses stop making products so that we do not run out of raw materials and energy resources? Of course not. Businesses cannot stop producing for the simple reason that the survival of a business means being able to produce products to sell at a profit. And if businesses did not operate we would have no work, no money, no goods in the shops . . . Society would come to a complete halt.

Businesses and governments have realised a way must be found out of this problem – a way whereby businesses can continue their activities with the minimum waste of natural resources and the least harm to the environment. However, not all businesses have co-operated in finding solutions to this problem so there have been increasing amounts of legislation on businesses to enforce environmental awareness and to help limit damaging effects on the environment.

Environmental sustainability is a term often used to describe this problem of balancing the needs we have now that with the needs we may have in the future. It is a complex idea. It means we must not use up resources at such a rate now, there will be none left in the future. We must continue to try to improve the lives of all the people in the world now but in doing so we must not threaten the quality of the lives of the people who will come after us. And all this while avoiding damaging the environment!

Trying to achieve environmental sustainability and protecting the environment is everyone responsibility – governments, businesses and individuals.

Different governments in the world have different environment policies. Some of these policies are more effective than others in protecting the environment.

In the UK, the government has policies that aim to protect different parts of the environment (e.g. recycling and transport policies).

The UK government's transport policy

In 1998 the British government launched a new transport policy that aims to improve public transport and to minimise the pollution that is caused by motorised traffic.

The objectives of the government's transport policy are as follows:

1 Promoting environmental objectives.

2 Promoting economic development across all parts of the country.

3 Enhancing the vital role of town centres.

4 Meeting the needs of rural areas.

5 Taking into account the needs of special groups of people (e.g. disabled people).

6 Ensuring a safe and secure travelling environment for all.

7 Raising public awareness of the need for transport to be environmentally friendly.

The UK's largest cycling organisation strongly welcomed the government's transport policy because it provides more road space for cycles and new funding to make cycling and walking safer.

However, people who are concerned about the environment criticised the policy because of its lack of clear targets for motorised traffic reduction. It is predicted that road traffic will grow by 30% over the next 20 years. This will lead to a 10% increase in carbon dioxide emissions (the gas produced when we use petrol and diesel as a fuel and that is the chief pollutant of the earth's atmosphere). Therefore, they argue, the government should have set clear and precise targets for reducing motorised traffic and air pollution in the future.

As we have already seen, there are groups of people who are keen to protect the environment. Friends of the Earth and Greenpeace are independent voluntary groups that were mainly set up to look after the environment. Their main aims are to:

- Influence government policy to take action to protect the environment.

- Raise people's awareness of environmental issues.

- Put pressure on businesses and government to reduce pollution and save wildlife.

- Raise awareness of the environmental benefits of recycling, animal welfare, green energy and other issues.

We do not have to wait for the government to protect our environment – the main responsibility lies with us. As we have seen in this unit, how we live and what we buy affect the environment in either negative or positive ways.

Preparing for employment is about choosing the right type of job, knowing where to look for this job and presenting yourself well.

In this unit you will learn about:

- *how to present personal information about yourself in a way that is acceptable to potential employers*

- *how to find out about suitable jobs and where to look for these*

- *the selection methods employers use to choose the best job applicants.*

It will help you to work out your strengths, skills and interests and how to use these to best effect when applying for jobs.

This unit will be assessed through your portfolio work. The grade awarded will be the grade for the unit.

Presenting personal information

When an employer has a job vacancy, it is more than likely that they have in mind the sort of person they would like to fill the post. Hence, when you apply for a job you need to give the potential employer as much useful information about yourself as you can, so that they can decide from what you have written if you might fit the bill. Employers like to know why you have applied for that particular job and what skills and interests you have that may be relevant to that job.

Employers also like to have certain personal information about you. For example:

- Personal details about you (e.g. your name and address, date of birth).

- The subjects you have studied and the qualifications you have gained (e.g. GCSEs, GNVQs and AVCEs).

- The name of the school and/or college where you obtained your qualifications.

- Any skills you might have (e.g. information communication technology, keyboard skills).

- Your personal qualities (e.g. your reliability, your punctuality, your organisation skills, etc.).

- Your personal experience and any achievements you have gained through work (whether paid or unpaid). You need to think very carefully about this. If you have had *paid* employment of any kind, include this with details of what you did – even if it is only a paper round. This sort of work shows you are reliable, punctual and can organise yourself to get up early in the morning! Babysitting falls into the same category. If someone trusts you enough to leave you in charge of their children, then you must be a trustworthy and dependable person. Similarly, think about the *unpaid* work you have done – looking after your younger brother or sister, or helping an elderly relative. If you care enough and are responsible enough to do this sort of unpaid work, it tells a potential employer a great deal about your character.

- Finally come your hobbies and interests (e.g. music, sport, reading, films, etc.).

 ACTIVITY

You are now going to supply some personal information about yourself. If you can, word process this information. If not, handwrite it neatly. Whichever method you use, make sure you arrange the information clearly and include everything you can about yourself. Use the headings we used above to organise this information. To remind you, these are:

- Personal details.

- Subjects studied and qualifications.

- Schools and/or college.

- Skills.

- Personal qualities.

- Personal experience and achievements.

- Hobbies and interests.

When an employer asks you to send in information about yourself, they might ask you to send in this information in a particular way. The four most common ways an employer might ask you to send in this information are as follows:

1 A *curriculum vitae* (or *CV* for short).

2 A *letter of application*.

3 A completed *application form*.

4 A *progress file* (or *portfolio* of your achievements so far).

We will look at each of these in turn below.

Curriculum vitae (CV)

A curriculum vitae is not as difficult as it sounds. All this means is 'an outline of your life so far' – and you produced a simple CV in the activity you have just done: personal details about yourself, the subjects you have studied and the qualifications you have achieved so far etc.! Just as you did in the activity, you need to *organise* your CV and arrange it in a logical order.

A CV is best prepared on a word processor so you can keep it on disk. That way you can update it when you need to and can send out an original (not a photocopy) each time you apply for a job.

Head it with the words 'Curriculum vitae' the divide it into sections, just like you did in the activity above. The following is a suggested outline you could use when setting out your CV:

Section 1: personal details
- Name, title (Mr, Miss, etc.) and address.
- Telephone number.
- Date of birth.

Section 2: educational details
- Schools attended (not your primary school) and the dates you started attending and the dates you left.
- GCSE results.
- Other awards at school and positions of responsibility held, etc. (e.g. prefect, sports captain).
- Further education details – college (dates attended and courses taken).
- Examinations awarded/taken or being taken and results (if known).
- Any other details (e.g. member of student union, member of school/college clubs or societies, etc.).
- Work experience details (which you undertook at school/college).

Section 3: employment details
- Details of any part-time or Saturday jobs you have done.
- Details of any other work experience and voluntary (*unpaid*) work you have done.

Section 4: other useful information
- Details of any hobbies/interests or sports.
- Details of any organisations to which you belong.
- Any useful skills you have.
- Other skills you have gained outside education and work that may be useful to an employer (e.g. helping in fund-raising events, etc.).

Section 5: referees
You need to name two referees. Referees are people a potential employer can approach to obtain a confidential report about you to see if you are suitable for the job you have applied for. These people are usually your two most recent employers, but if you have never had a job you could perhaps ask your school or college tutor to act as one of your referees. But don't worry about this at this stage. Most schools and colleges have systems in place to supply students with *references* (the reports on people referees supply to potential employers). However, whomever you decide to name as a referee, you must ask his or her permission first.

ACTIVITY

Create your own CV. Use the five section headings given above and fill in your own details. You may have to leave certain parts blank (such as the names of referees). This does not matter at this stage. Look back at the activity you did earlier in the unit where you recorded very similar information. Can you improve on it this time? Can you give more details? Is there anything you missed out?

Again, if you can, use a word processor and *keep a copy of your CV on a floppy disk*. This may save you a great deal of time later when you come to apply for jobs!

Letter of application

Sometimes an employer will ask you to send a letter of application. This is like any other letter you would send as a *business* letter, but should contain the following information.

1 An opening paragraph to say where you saw the job advertised (or how you found out about the job) and that you would like to apply for the post being advertised.

2 A second paragraph to give general background information about yourself (the school or college you attend and the courses you are studying). At this stage

you **could** refer to the fact you have enclosed a copy of your CV but **only if you have been asked to include your CV with the letter.** Do **not** send your CV with the letter if you have **not** been asked to do so! Although some job advertisements do not ask you to send the business your CV, it might be a good idea to get your CV up to date. You will then have it ready to send with your letter of application and application form if you need to.

3   A third paragraph giving the particular reasons you have for wanting either this job or to work for this particular organisation – or anything you can think of to make your application a little different and a little bit special.

4   A final paragraph to say you are available for interview at any time (or to say when you are not available for interview).

Points to note when writing a letter of application:

- It must be neat and tidy (no spelling, punctuation or grammatical mistakes).

- It must give a good impression about you.

- Do not use an over-friendly or 'chatty' style of writing. A letter of application should be written in a *formal* way, not in the way you would write to a friend or relative.

- It must state clearly which post you are applying for.

- It should help to *sell* you by stating your personal abilities and qualities that are relevant to the job.

- It should have the correct form of ending. Remember, if you write 'Dear

Sir/Madam', you must end the letter with 'Yours faithfully'. If you write 'Dear Mr Roberts', you must end the letter with 'Yours sincerely'.

- Finally, do not forget to sign it!

Application forms

Most businesses use application forms to recruit their staff and you will already have filled in many application forms of different sorts yourself – to apply for a place on a course, to join a club, etc. Filling in applications forms is not difficult if you prepare yourself well beforehand:

- Collect together all the information you need before you start to fill in the form, otherwise you will be stopping and starting each time you want to find your examination results, the date you started school or college, etc. The record of achievement you have been compiling at school or college will help, provided you have kept it up to date! You could also use the CV you have created to help you fill in the form.

- Photocopy the form before you write anything at all and practise on the photocopy to make sure you can display all the information neatly and in the best way.

- Ask someone to check your photocopy before you begin to transfer the information over to the real form – especially your spelling, punctuation and grammar.

- Keep a photocopy of the form so you can read it again before you attend for interview. If you have forgotten you said your leisure interests include visiting art galleries, the interviewer might be a bit surprised if you suddenly change your mind and say that you spend most of your spare time playing football! Remember, however, there is a difference between presenting yourself in the best possible light and telling downright lies!

When you are filling in the form, remember to:

- Use black ink as the forms are often photocopied.

- Answer every question.

- Look carefully at each question to work out why the employer has asked you that question.

- Send a covering letter with the application form when you send it back. Write this letter as you would any other formal business letter. It does not have to repeat what you have put on the form but should state you have enclosed the application form and that you look forward to hearing from them in due course.

 ## ACTIVITY

Most applications forms have a small section that says something like: 'Write a short paragraph in support of your application.' In this you really have to sell yourself – in other words, in three or four sentences say why the company should employ you.

Imagine you have applied for a job (make up a *realistic* job you could have applied for!) and have received an application form with such a space for you to complete. Write a short paragraph saying why you are an ideal candidate.

Progress file

While you are doing your GNVQ course, you will be keeping all the work you do towards your qualification, plus work experience evidence and details of activities you have done on work experience. You should also keep a record of any extra-curricular activities that you undertake. This and your Key Skills work will be useful for any employer so that they can see what progress you have made on your course. Usually all of this material is kept in a large portfolio file for easy access to individual pieces of material should you need it. Some students like to keep their work in chronological order which gives an idea of their progress throughout the course.

Finding out about suitable jobs

There are many places where you can find out about jobs and many people you can ask for advice.

Your careers adviser at school or college

Your careers adviser at school or college will be happy to help you and he or she will often have useful contacts in the local community. He or she will also be able to offer you help in choosing the right career, and may be able to put you in contact with someone who already works in your chosen career and who might be able to give you 'inside' information.

The career adviser at your local careers office or library

Career advisers have lots of information and many contacts and they should know about all the job opportunities available in your local area. The careers section of the library will also have a selection of useful books and pamphlets.

Your local job centre

Job vacancies are displayed on boards by job category or you could ask one of the job centre's staff to help you.

Careers fairs

Careers fairs are held in many towns and cities throughout the country. They are well worth going to, to pick up information and for the chance to meet local employers.

Work experience and talking to people in work

The work experience you do at school or college is a good opportunity for potential employers to get to know you. If you enjoy your work experience and feel this is the sort of work you would like to do, let the people you work with on your work experience know. You never know, you might just fit the bill if a job becomes vacant!

Also, talk to people you know who have jobs similar to the one you would like to have. Apart from the background information they can give you, they might know the names of useful contacts.

Finally, don't forget your family and friends. We often overlook the people we know well. Family and friends can be a mine of information and advice!

Computer programs and the Internet

Special computer programs are available that help you decide on the right career for your particular interests and abilities. Your school

or college library may have copies of these. There are also many sites on the Internet that could help (see later in this unit).

Looking for jobs

There are many different ways you can find out about the jobs available in your local area – and beyond!

Local and national newspapers

Local and national newspapers contain job adverts and, very often, articles on looking for jobs. The jobs pages of newspapers usually appear on a particular day of the week and you must respond to them promptly, certainly by the closing date.

Job centres and recruitment agencies

We have already looked at job centres. You can register with a job centre, who will take down your personal details and make notes of the type of work you are looking for. They will then contact you if they are informed of a vacancy that might be suitable for you. Remember, though, if you are told of a vacancy you will still have to go for an interview with the prospective employer.

Recruitment agencies work in a similar way but these are privately run. They often specialise in certain types of work (e.g. secretarial, nursing, ICT, etc.). Some recruitment agencies also specialise in looking for people who went to work on a part-time basis only (e.g. to cover for employees who are off work as a result of maternity leave or who may otherwise be away from work for a fairly lengthy period). Some people like to work on a part-time basis for the freedom and variety it gives them.

The Internet

If you have access to the Internet, there are many web sites you could explore. There are more than 13,000 web sites to do with careers and job hunting! For example:

- www.dfee.gov.uk/mapintro.htm (contains information on the 'Modern Apprenticeship' scheme).

- www.dfee.gov.uk/ntintro.htm (contains information on 'National Traineeships').

- www.ngfl.gov.uk (the 'National Grid for Learning' contains information and links to many useful web sites about learning, schools, colleges and careers).

- www.careersfot.gov.uk (this site has links to nearly 600 higher education institutions and over 200 professional organisations, plus other sites of interest when exploring jobs. It also has information on job seeking, including CVs, letters of application and interviews).

Other ways of looking for jobs

Other ways of finding jobs include the following:

- Specialist magazines and papers. You should be able to obtain these from your local library.

- Through part-time or voluntary work.

- Local radio and TV.

- Teletext's Job Finder service.

- Shop windows and supermarket noticeboards.

- Family and friends who know about vacancies at their workplace before they are advertised.

- Using your own initiative to write to businesses to apply for jobs. Some jobs are never advertised, as advertising costs businesses money.

ACTIVITY

Visit your school or college's careers library or your local library's careers section. The following are some books that go into more detail about job hunting:

Your First Job: Choosing, Getting and Keeping It. By Vivien Donald and Ray Gorse. Published 1997 by Kogan Page (ISBN: 0 7494 2150 9).

Developing your Employment Skills. By Helen Vandevelde. *The Express Skills Focus Series.* Published 1998 by Trotman (ISBN: 0 85660 308 2).

The Jobsearch Manual. By Linda Aspen. Published 2000 by Management Books (ISBN: 1 85252 229 1).

Once an employer has received all the completed application forms (or letters of application, etc.) sent in as a result of advertising a job vacancy, they will study these carefully. (Remember, any applications received after the closing date will usually be thrown away!) The employer will sort these out into such categories as:

- Totally unsuitable – wrong skills, wrong qualifications or a *badly presented application*.

- Possible – some of the right skills and qualifications. Well-prepared application. However, there are still some doubts.

- Very suitable – the right skills and qualifications, and the applicant has made a good case for him or herself. A very well-presented application.

221

Needless to say, those applications that come into the first category will be dismissed immediately. Those that fall under the last category will go to the top of the pile, and those in the middle category will be put to one side. Eventually, after a great deal of consideration, those applicants who are considered most suitable will be called for an interview.

An interview is a meeting between a job applicant and the potential employer. During this meeting, the applicant should be able to tell if the job is right or not for him or her and the employer should be able to tell if the applicant is the best person for the job vacancy they wish to fill.

The formal interview

In a formal interview you meet the employer, usually in a private office, and talk informally for a few minutes. This is to put you at your ease. The employer then turns to your written application and he or she might take you through this, asking you to add or clarify some points. This is the formal, *serious* part of the interview where nothing said or asked should be treated any other way but sensibly, honestly and seriously.

During this time the employer is appraising and assessing you, seeing how confident you are, how easily you can talk about certain topics and how interested you are in the job. You should listen carefully to the questions and answer them appropriately. If you do not understand a question, say so and ask your interviewer *politely* to repeat or explain the question.

Performing a task related to the job and assessment tasks

In this type of situation, the employer might ask you, at the end of a formal interview, to perform a task. Some employers are very keen to make sure you are not only good on paper but also capable of handling a practical task.

The task will be similar to the sort of thing you would do if you were offered the job. For example, if you apply for a secretarial post, the interviewer might ask you to write a formal letter using your word processing skills.

Some employers, especially banks and building societies, use assessment tests in interviews. There are hundreds of such tests, measuring everything from your ability to deal with figures and numbers, or words, to your personality and your reaction to certain situations.

Tour of the premises

Some employers organise a guided tour for candidates, usually before the interview. The main purpose of this tour is to give candidates the opportunity to see the premises, the workplace and, perhaps, to meet some people who work there. Remember, first impressions are important and so you must not appear over-friendly or over-enthusiastic: a tour is all part of the interview! An applicant should be able to make up his or her mind after this tour if he or she would still like to work in this place.

Preparation for the interview

To do your best in an interview you need to prepare yourself well in advance of attending the interview. Interviews are generally stressful situations, and so thorough preparation can take a great deal of the pressure off you and make you feel more relaxed.

If you are invited for an interview, you have to do some background research, perhaps through people you know who work for the organisation, through your tutor at a school or college, or perhaps through the Internet. Try to obtain as much background information about the business as you can before the interview. This is very important. Do not go to an interview without having read anything about the business or organisation. Also remember to:

- Reread the job description and your application form (remember, we said earlier to keep a photocopy of all application forms you send in).

- Find out the right address for the business and identify this on a map – there is nothing worse than getting lost before an interview!

- Read the local, national and specialist press for any new information you can find out about the organisation.

- *Confirm at the earliest opportunity that you will/will not be able to attend for the interview.*

Adopt a positive attitude before the interview. If you get all your preparation out of the way well before the interview, things will be fine. Make sure you know all you need to know and let things rest easily in your mind for a day or two. Be confident and believe in yourself and your ability.

The day of the interview

Punctuality

On the day of the interview, allow yourself plenty of time to get there. The worst thing is to arrive late – this gives the wrong impression about yourself.

A major part of your assessment for this unit will be an interview you will attend at your school or college. This interview will be carried out in as realistic a way as possible. You will probably not know the person who interviews you, although your tutor will be present. This interview will be designed to see how would tackle a *real* job interview. It may also be video-taped.

Therefore, do not treat this 'mock' interview lightly. Make sure you take note of all the following advice when you attend for your assessment job interview.

Dress

Most jobs have a *dress code* (a certain way all employees are expected to dress). While no one will expect you to dress perfectly for the job or to wear very expensive clothes, whatever you do, do not go to the interview wearing a pair of jeans and your hair coloured red or blue. Therefore:

- Dress smartly (e.g. for any sort of office job, men are expected to go to the interview in a jacket, tie and sober trousers, or a suit. Some organisations require women to wear skirts, smart suits or dresses. For a non-office job, still dress as smartly as possible).

- Dress in clean and tidy clothes and shoes.

Arriving for the interview

On arrival at the interview:

- Be pleasant and polite to the receptionist who greets you.

- Knock before going through a closed door into an office.

- Do *not* sit down until you are offered a chair.

223

Body language

Your body language is the way you communicate your feeling and thoughts through your body. This does not mean you must worry too much about the way you talk, move and walk. Your interviewer knows that you are naturally going to be nervous because you are in a stressful situation. However, you should be aware of what your body language is telling the interviewer about you.

Questions

As we have already seen, an interview is a two-way process. The interviewer will want to find out as much as possible about you. You will also want to find out as much as possible about the job.

Generally, interviewers ask you questions to find out more about your qualities, personality, attitudes, commitment and social skills. They like to make sure you are the right person for the job. Some of the questions they might ask are as follows:

- Why do you want this job?
- Why do you want to work here?
- Which subjects did you enjoy most at school or college?
- Which school or college activities did you join in?
- Are you prepared to work overtime?
- Do you enjoy working as part of a team?
- What do you do in your spare time?
- What kind of books do you read?
- Is there anything you would like to ask us?

At the end of the interview most interviewers will ask you if you have any questions to ask. You should think about

some questions you can ask your interviewer *before* the interview. Try to remember them, but there is no harm in writing them down on a piece of paper. Ask only questions that have not been answered in the interview. Some questions you might ask are as follows:

- When will I be able to start the job?
- What training opportunities do you offer?

Do *not* ask questions that are irrelevant, silly or that show you are 'only in it for the money':

- Could I bring my friend in to show them where I work?
- Could I leave early on Fridays to get ready for the weekend?
- How often do you give your employees pay rises?

 # ACTIVITY

Put a cross next to the following statements that are wrong and a tick next to those that are right. In an interview:

1 Feel free to smoke or chew.

2 Speak up, do not mutter or mumble. Try to act with modest confidence.

3 Be flippant and crack jokes.

4 Make sure you know the interviewer's name and use it if a natural opportunity occurs.

5 Always over-estimate your own qualities and abilities.

If you don't get the job

If you go to an interview but do not get the job, treat this as a learning experience. Try to remember what happened (e.g. the employer's questions, your attitude, your answers to questions, your body language and your appearance). Approach your careers tutor or careers adviser for advice. It is time to reflect and evaluate.

Health and safety

Health and safety issues are important wherever you work and whatever job you do. In many business organisations, such as shops, offices, health-care centres, schools and colleges, the premises need to be safe for members of the public as well as for employees.

In this unit you will find out about:

- *how the more usual risks and hazards in the workplace can be reduced*

- *the laws and regulations that will help to protect your health and safety in the workplace.*

This unit will help you to identify typical hazards, and the methods used to reduce the risks they pose to employees and the public. Accident and emergency procedures are introduced, together with the reasons why it is necessary to keep and maintain reports of these. You need to understand that laws exist to protect people in the workplace and that employers and employees need to work together to achieve a high standard of safety.

This unit will be assessed through your portfolio work. The grade awarded will be your grade for the unit.

Common hazards

There are many hazards or potential sources of danger in the workplace. The nature of the potential danger will depend on the following:

- The nature of the *workplace* (e.g. office, bank, hospital, school, factory, etc.).

- The nature of the *work* (e.g. manual work or office work).

- The *employees' and employer's attitudes* towards health and safety at work.

The most common potential dangers (or hazards) in the workplace are caused by some, but not all, of the following.

Unsafe working areas and accommodation

Working areas can be made unsafe for a variety of reasons. Some of these hazards or dangers are the result of the employees being careless in their work habits; others are the result of the employer not renewing or repairing worn-out equipment or failing to institute safe working practices. For example:

- Leaving the working area untidy and dirty.
- Leaving floors and stairs cluttered or slippery.
- Letting wires or cables trail across passageways.
- Frayed carpets or loose tiles.
- Too much equipment stacked on to tables or into cupboards.
- Too many plugs inserted into one electric socket.

Sometimes, poorly maintained or badly designed *accommodation* can result in potential health hazards. For example:

- Offices or other workplaces are too small and overcrowded so that the workers have little space between them.
- There are no blinds or curtains at windows to keep out direct sunlight.
- Rooms or work areas are poorly lit.
- The toilets are dirty with poor hand-washing facilities, and there are inadequate facilities for workers to eat their meals.
- The accommodation is poorly maintained, with a consequent risk of draughts, pest infestation (mice, rats, cockroaches, etc.), damp and so on.

Noisy equipment

Sounds and noises are an important part of everyday life. In moderation these are harmless but, if they are too loud, they can permanently damage our hearing. The danger depends on how loud the noise is and for how long you are exposed to it.

Some machines can be very noisy, which can lead to potential health hazards. For example, noisy printers or photocopiers should have special covers (known as acoustic hoods) to dampen down the noise, and people who work with very noisy equipment (tractors, road drills, etc.) must be given protective sound mufflers to cover their ears.

Noise at work not only causes hearing problems but also other problems as well, such as disturbing our concentration, interfering with our communications and, ultimately, causing us undue stress.

The wrong temperature

The wrong temperature and poor ventilation can cause serious health problems. The place where you work should not be too hot or too cold. The temperature, ideally, should be around 16°C.

If there are no windows in the place of work, adequate ventilation should be provided.

Hazardous substances and materials

Hazardous substances (i.e. substances that could harm us in some way) can be found in all sorts of work environments – factories, offices, quarries, mines, farms, shops, swimming pools, etc. These range from the obvious (such as petrol, paint thinners, welding gases and heating fuels) to the not so obvious (such as cleaning materials, packaging materials, dusts from woodworking and dusts from foodstuffs, such as flour and sugar).

Examples of bad practice with such hazardous substances are as follows:

- Leaving dangerous or flammable liquids and substances in open containers and/or not storing them in a safe place.

- Storing dangerous or flammable liquids and substances in a poorly ventilated place and/or in unlabelled containers.

Unsafe use of machinery and equipment

Some equipment and machinery (e.g. electrical equipment, machinery used for cutting or sawing and equipment used in cooking) can be very dangerous unless a great deal of care is taken when using it. Accidents may happen for the following reasons:

- Ignoring, or not following, the manufacturer's instructions before operating the equipment.

- Not checking for trailing leads, broken sockets and frayed wires.

- Allowing rings and other jewellery to become trapped in the machinery.

- Insufficient ventilation when using equipment that gives off dangerous fumes (e.g. drills and photocopiers).

- Leaving drawers and filing cabinets open.

Technology is not used safely

In some situations, exposure to, or the use of technology for a long period of time may pose potential health hazards. For example:

- Operating VDU (computer screen) equipment for long periods of time without a break.

- Not using sun blinds to eliminate the glare on VDU screens.

- Using working surfaces that are not at the correct height for writing or keying.

There may be other health risks for people who use computer input devices for long periods of time during the course of their work. Touch screens, joysticks and other tools are used by some people for long hours in both office and industrial settings, and this can lead to pain in the muscles, discomfort and medical disorders.

Similarly, people who look at VDUs all day long must take care they do not strain their eyes. There has also been some concern recently that VDUs may emit harmful radiation. While the amounts of radiation emitted by VDUs are extremely small, special screens are available that can be put over the VDU to reduce the amount of radiation given out. Some employers, especially in large businesses, arrange for their employees to have regular eye tests to ensure their safety.

Unsafe working practices

Unsafe working practices or habits cause a great many health problems and accidents. For example:

- Lifting heavy objects in the wrong way (carrying all the strain on your back instead of on your legs).

- Bending your back and not sitting straight for long periods of time when doing office work.

- Getting too close to the document or the paper you are writing on.

- Using a stool or chair to reach a high shelf or cupboard instead of a pair of steps.

- Taking 'short cuts': not wiring a plug properly, not making sure a ladder is firmly positioned against a wall, not wearing gloves or protective eye goggles when handling a dangerous substance, etc.

 **ACTIVITY**

Look round the classroom you are in. Can you see any health hazards? What should be done to overcome these? Make a list of the hazards and what should be done for each one.

Now look around again. Can you see any potential health hazards that *have* been noticed and for which precautions have been taken? Make a list of these as well, but this time note down *what was done* to overcome the hazard and *why*.

Possible risks

Most accidents at work can be avoided as many accidents are the result of carelessness. All the above potential sources of danger or hazards can have serious consequences. They can result in:

- Electric shocks.

- Cuts and grazes.

- Trips and falls.

- Damage to hearing (e.g. permanent ringing in the ears – called tinnitus).

- Disorders of skeleton and muscles (such as slipped discs, hernias and pulled muscles).

- Health problems (e.g. breathing, skin or eye problems caused by dangerous substances or poor working conditions).

- The spread of infectious diseases.

- Headaches and eye strain.

- Insect stings or bites.

- Asthma.

- Poisoning.

- Infection from bacteria.

 **ACTIVITY**

The following health problems have been reported at Speed Engineering Ltd. Below the list of health problems is a list of their possible causes. Match up the health problem to the possible cause (e.g. if you think the hazard that caused health problem 1 is e write 1e).

Health problems

1 A worker in the finance department (who sorts employees' wages) complains constantly about headaches and eye strain.

2 A driver who is in charge of delivery and distribution has hurt his back.

3 Six workers, all female, caught an infectious disease that caused them sickness and diarrhoea.

4 A man who has been working in the production department for the last six years has been complaining recently that he cannot hear properly. He keeps asking people to speak up and other people complain that he is shouting.

5 A cleaner in the company – who has been working there for ten years – has been complaining recently about a skin irritation on her hands.

Possible causes

a No protection for the ears when operating noisy equipment.

b Exposure to a dangerous substance over a long period of time.

c Operating computers for long periods of time without a break.

d Lifting objects that are heavy in the wrong way.

e Dirty toilets with poor hand-washing facilities.

Ways to reduce the risks posed by such hazards

Potential hazards need not necessarily result in accidents or damage to people's health. There are precautions employers and employees can take to prevent accidents and ill-health from occurring.

Education and training

It is important that organisations offer adequate training to their employees on issues related to health and safety. There is nothing worse than panicking in emergency situations and not knowing what to do. It is the employer's responsibility to offer training to all employees (especially new ones) in health and safety matters.

Training in the use of machinery and equipment

Training in the safe use of machinery and equipment will be needed by *all* staff, not just inexperienced staff, new starters or temporary staff – particularly if these people have to use powered machinery. For some high-risk work, such as driving fork-lift trucks, using chain saws or operating cranes, training is usually carried out by specialist instructors.

Similarly, the people who service and repair equipment should have been trained thoroughly in all aspects of safety.

First aid

Whenever someone suffers an injury or falls ill at work, whether caused by that person's work or not, the most important thing is that he or she receives immediate attention and that, in serious cases, an ambulance is called. First aid at work covers the arrangements an employer must make to ensure that this happens. First aid can save lives and can prevent minor injuries becoming major ones. Most businesses, therefore, have certain members of staff who are trained in first aid and who can be called upon in such emergencies.

A first-aider is someone who has undergone a training course in administering first aid and holds a current first-aid-at-work certificate. The training undertaken has to have been approved by the Health and Safety Executive (the government body with responsibility for health and safety in the workplace).

Some businesses, however, offer some form of voluntary first aid training to *all* their employees. The main reason for this is to equip them with the right training in life-and-death situations. Sometimes it can be a matter of seconds to save someone's life or to reduce the risk of damage to that person's health or well-being. It might take the business's first-aider a few minutes to arrive, so it is advisable that all workers are equipped with basic first aid training.

All businesses and organisations, no matter how small, must have at least one first aid box. However, there is no standard list of items that should be included in a first aid box – this will depend on what the needs of a particular business are. However, as a guide, and where there is no special, particular risk in the workplace, the minimum stock of first aid items should be:

- A leaflet giving general guidance on first aid.

- Individual, wrapped, sterile adhesive dressings.

- Sterile eye pads.

- Individually wrapped, triangular sterile bandages.

- Safety pins.

- Large, sterile, individually wrapped wound dressings.

- A pair of disposable gloves.

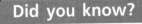

Did you know?

Drugs (for example, tablets and medicines) should never be kept in the first aid boxes and must *not* be offered to people who are feeling unwell.

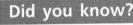

ACTIVITY

1 Find out who is the qualified first-aider in your school or college. Ask him or her what he or she must do in emergency situations.

2 Where is your nearest first aid box located?

Evacuation procedures in an emergency

If the building must be evacuated for some reason, *all* members of staff should be well trained in evacuation procedures and should know what to do. Every business, small or large, must make sure it has an effective, workable, practical and safe evacuation system or procedure. This procedure must ensure that:

- *Everyone on the premises* knows what to do.

- The premises are evacuated *in the shortest possible time*.

Did you know?

The McAlpine Stadium in Huddersfield was nominated the best-designed building in the UK in 1995. Although the stadium's total capacity is nearly 25,000 people, the building is designed in such a way that it can be evacuated in only 8 minutes.

Risk assessment

Employers are required by law to assess risks in the workplace. A risk assessment is nothing more than a careful examination of what, in the workplace, could cause harm to people. Risk assessment is undertaken so that the employer can take precautions to avoid accidents happening in the first place.

There are five steps in risk assessment:

1 Look for the hazards.

2 Decide who might be harmed and how.

3 Evaluate the risks and decide whether the existing precautions are adequate.

4 Record the findings.

5 Review the assessment and amend it, if necessary.

Co-operation between management, unions and the workforce

Although both the employer's and employees' rights and responsibilities are clearly stated in the Health and Safety at Work Act (you will learn more about this later in this unit), in reality, life can be quite different. Sometimes, employees might not be happy about a health and safety issue at work, which might cause problems or tensions between the employers and the workforce. On the other hand, when accidents happen, employers sometimes put the blame on employees for not following health and safety guidelines.

Therefore, a clear understanding of each other's rights and responsibilities, along with co-operation between employees and employers are vital to minimise hazards and to reduce potential risks at work.

You learnt in Unit 1 that one of the main responsibilities of a human resources department is to look after health and safety matters. If employees are unhappy with the way health and safety matters are handled, they might complain to their trade unions who will negotiate on their behalf with the management.

By law, employers must consult all their employees on health and safety matters. Consultation can be very important in maintaining a safe and healthy working environment. By consulting employees, an employer should motivate staff and make them aware of health and safety issues. Consultation includes such things as the following:

- Changes that may affect health and safety (e.g. in procedures, equipment or ways of working).
- The information employees must be given on the likely risks and dangers arising from their work.
- Planning for health and safety training.
- The consequences of introducing new technology (e.g. computers) on the health and safety of employees.

Accident and emergency procedures

In 1977 the government passed a piece of legislation called the Health and Safety at Work Act (HSWA for short). One of the main provisions of this Act was to make it the joint responsibility of both employers *and* employees to ensure safe working practices in the workplace. What this means is that *everyone* in the workplace – from a worker on the shop floor to the managing director – has joint responsibility for the health and safety of all the other people in the organisation (including visitors to that organisation).

For example, if you were to spill something on the floor and hence made the floor slippery and dangerous, it is *your* responsibility to ensure that you do not endanger anyone's safety. You must clean it up immediately or, at the very least, put out signs to say the floor is slippery and could be dangerous (you may have already seen such signs around your school or college or in other public places).

This Act also lays down certain accident and emergency procedures that all organisations must provide. It also specifies how such matters as first aid should be organised and how organisations should deal with emergencies and how emergencies should be reported. The following sections give examples of the things the Act requires all organisations to do or to provide.

First aid procedure

There are simple precautions that an employer can take to ensure that there is an adequate first aid system in the workplace:

- Make sure that there are adequate supplies of first aid equipment.
- Tell all employees about the first aid arrangements (e.g. by putting up notices to tell them who and where the first-aiders are and where the first aid box is).
- Provide treatment for minor injuries where medical treatment is not needed.

- Provide first aid and summon assistance when medical treatment is needed (e.g. ring for an ambulance).

Evacuation procedures

For an organisation to have effective evacuation procedures, all employees must be aware of the following:

- The layout of the building.

- The location of all entrances and exits (including emergency exits).

- The location of the alarms and how to operate them.

- The location and type of fire-fighting equipment (e.g. fire blankets, fire extinguishers, buckets of sand, etc.).

- The procedures for leaving the building in an emergency (e.g. closing doors and windows, leaving personal belongings behind, not using the lifts, etc.).

- The assembly point, where all employees and employers meet in cases of emergency.

- The methods for checking that all employees and visitors have left the building.

- Safety signs and signals (e.g. what the fire alarm sounds like).

All employees must practise these procedures regularly (this is often called 'fire drill'). Particular care must also be taken to ensure that new employees are made fully aware of these procedures.

 **ACTIVITY**

How well aware are you of the emergency evacuation procedures in your school or college? Using the above list, conduct a survey amongst your friends to see how much they know about the procedures.

What do your results tell you about people's attitudes to such emergency procedures?

Reporting accidents and emergencies

Apart from immediate first aid, employees should not deal with accidents themselves; these must be reported immediately to all or one of the following people:

- The supervisor on duty.

- The officer in charge of health and safety.

- The emergency services (e.g. the fire brigade, the ambulance service).

As we have already seen, large businesses usually have specific members of staff trained in first aid procedures and emergencies. However, if no such staff exist, in cases of major accidents and emergencies, the emergency services must be called in.

The recording of accidents and emergencies

Businesses are required to keep records of the accidents that happen in the workplace. Details of such accidents are usually recorded in an accident book. Some organisations also insist on the people involved in the accident completing an accident report form. This form is then kept safely as it may be needed in the future if the injured person makes a claim against the company for the injuries he or she sustained.

Unit 10 Working as part of a team

Almost all jobs involve working as part of a team. This unit will help you to develop teamwork skills. It is important that you can work well as a team member because you are likely, in your future employment, to do at least part of your work as a member of a team. In this unit you will learn about:

- *choosing a team activity and identifying the aims of the activity*

- *planning a team activity and identifying the roles and responsibilities of team members*

- *carrying out an activity*

- *reviewing an activity to find out if the team worked well together.*

You may be able to achieve this unit at the same time as completing another vocational unit. This unit can help you to produce evidence for the Key Skill unit 'Working with others'.

This unit will be assessed through your portfolio work only. The grade awarded will be your grade for the unit.

Before embarking on any work for this unit, it would be as well to read the entire unit first, particularly the note about log books on page 235.

Most people at some times in their working lives will have to work as part of a team. For example, this might be something as fairly straightforward as planning the staff Christmas party or as complex as devising a new training programme for the induction of new staff.

Every member of the team, no matter what its purpose, will have different skills. Some people are good at organising; some at writing up lists of what has happened and who will do what; yet others have an eye for detail.

While the make-up of one particular team will be different from all other teams, there are some qualities and skills that all team members must possess. The ability to:

- Communicate easily with other team members.

- Inform others in the team about new ideas.

- Start new activities.

- Discuss ideas.

- Listen to others carefully.

- Respect each other's ideas and views.

- Collect and organise information.

- Help others in the group.

To complete this unit, you will work with your fellow students to carry out a team activity. The activity you decide to undertake must be agreed with your tutor, and will depend on the facilities you have and the people who are available to help you. To help you with this activity, we will follow here the story of Anil, Patsy, Cleo, Kim, Winston and Suzy – six students who have decided to set up a fashion show to raise money for school funds as part of their GNVQ course. First, however, we must look at the stages these students went through before they arrived at their final idea.

Choosing an activity and identifying the aims

Note: Before undertaking *any* work for your activity, make sure every member of the team keeps a log or diary in which he or she records details of every team meeting, of things that happened between meetings, of things he or she did as part of his or her role in the team. This is very important. You will need this log when you come to evaluate your activity.

Choosing an activity is not as easy as it sounds: when you first get together as a team you may find people come up with lots of ideas, or with lots of *good* ideas, with lots of *silly* ideas or with *no* ideas at all! Somehow you have to sort all these ideas out – if you have any ideas to sort out in the first place!

Someone in your group must write down *all* the ideas that are suggested, even if at the time an idea seems impossible or slightly ridiculous. You never know; *inside* that idea might be another brilliant idea just waiting to get out! Give yourself a time limit for idea gathering and then stop. You now need to look at *all* the ideas that have been suggested.

Take each idea in turn and discuss the good things and bad things about each one (e.g. will it cost too much? Will it take too long to set up? Will we enjoy it? And so on).

By the time you have gone through each idea like this, you should all be forming an opinion about which ideas would work best and which you should reject. So reduce the ideas down to about the three most likely ones. And go through the whole process again, listing the good things and the bad things. If you can, try to come to an agreement at this stage as to which is the best idea. If you can't come to an agreement, it might be best to close the meeting and arrange to meet again at another time – to give people the opportunity to think about the ideas on their own.

Just to make the whole process of choosing your activity even more difficult, the following are some of the things you *must* bear in mind when sorting out your ideas:

- Will it involve other people? If so, will we be able to depend on their help?

- Will they be available at the times we need them? Will we need their help throughout the entire activity or just at certain stages?

- What do we hope to *achieve* by this activity? Who will benefit from it? Is it worth while doing it?

- Are all members of the team clear about what we aim to do? Are we all thinking in the same way?

- Finally, is everyone committed to the idea we have chosen? Some might have their reservations about the idea initially, but are they willing to give it a go?

Planning the activity

Having gone through stages similar to the ones outlined above, our six students have decided on the fashion show with a mixture of apprehension and excitement. Both feelings are understandable, but the apprehension can be reduced and the chances of success increased if you plan your activity carefully right from the start.

Our students have quickly realised that *they* are the workforce responsible for the success of the show. And to make the most of the time they have available, they must decide who is going to be responsible for what. If they are going to run a show and sell tickets, they need to make sure that what they are selling is worth buying. To ensure this, they must use all the skills and talents they have among themselves to organise and run the show.

For example, they decided that Cleo, who is very well organised, should arrange all the team meetings, provide the agendas and write up the minutes afterwards. Kim is very artistic. If posters have to be made, Kim would be the person to do these,

along with any other advertising material. Patsy is very clever with figures and numbers. Therefore, they decided she should be in charge of financial matters (e.g. hiring the stage, buying costumes and making records of tickets sold). Suzy is the only one who has a car. Therefore, they decide that she will be in charge of buying and delivering things. Winston is very confident and has a great ability to communicate with people. They decided he is going to be in charge of making contact with clothes retailers and manufacture as well as selling tickets. Anil says he would like to look after the technical side of the show: the sound system, the lighting and so on. He has helped run his brother's disco, so he says he knows something about all this!

You may not be so lucky in deciding who will do what. Sometimes people are a little reluctant to come forward about things they are good at. You may also find people volunteer to do things they are not really capable of doing. This is a very difficult stage in the planning process. It is therefore at this stage that people must be *honest* about themselves. When planning who should do what, it is as well to ask yourselves the following questions and to be *truthful* in your replies:

- Am I always up to date with my work?

- Do I get on well with other people?

- Do I cope well under stress, and not give in easily when the going gets tough?

- Do I like to work with people?

- Do I like to work on my own?

Your *honest* answers to these questions will show how organised you are, how sociable you are, whether or not you mind working under pressure, and whether you are a loner or someone who likes to work as part of a team. When deciding who should do what, bear in mind what a particular task involves (e.g. meeting lots of other people, long hours working on your own, or patience and persistence in getting a task done). Therefore do not take on (or let someone else take on) a task that does not suit your (his or her) personality or preferred way of working. If you do, it will only lead to trouble later.

Our six students seem to have worked out the tasks that need to be done to achieve their activity. You, too, must make a careful list of all the things you will need to do and, bearing in mind what we have learnt above about suiting jobs to people, delegate or give these jobs to the most appropriate members of your team.

In the planning stage you will also need to make careful notes of the following:

- Any *resources* you will need (money, the help of other people, materials, equipment, information, etc.).

- The *timings* of each stage of the activity (e.g. the dates when certain tasks must be finished). You must agree the *deadlines* by which certain things must be done. If, in the course of events, certain tasks take longer than expected or delays occur that you could not foresee, you may have to adjust your deadlines. However, unless something very major happens that throws your entire planning schedule out, try not to let one or two missed deadlines upset your overall time plan.

In planning their time, this is how our six students worked out how much time they had available for their activity:

1 First they looked at their college timetable.

2 They then assessed their commitments at home, including homework.

3 They also worked out how many lessons they would have available to them if they were to use these to organise the show.

4 Finally, they worked out how much time outside normal college hours they might need to spend on the fashion show.

When it came to working out resources, our students realised that they would need somewhere to work from when organising and running the fashion show. They would also need a place to practise or rehearse in, and somewhere to store clothes. Other resources included make-up, paper and equipment to print the posters and programmes, tickets, a video camera (they decided to record the event), a good sound system for the music, lighting, tea and coffee for the models — their list seemed almost endless!

At one stage the obstacles to their fashion show seemed so enormous they contemplated giving it up! However, with patience and a great deal of help from people throughout the entire college as well as their family and friends, they managed to acquire all they needed and, after many set-backs and quite a few arguments, the fashion show went ahead.

Carrying out the activity

Carrying out the activity does not mean just the event itself — it also means all the stages that go into the planning and creation of the activity. Throughout the entire process you will need to work as a *team*.

The following are just a few of the skills you will need to develop when working as part of a team:

Listening skills

- Understanding what the purpose of a discussion is and what the outcomes are.

- Concentrating on what other members of the team say.

- Valuing other group members' contributions.

- Listening for the main points and linking them to other main points of the discussion.

- Paying attention to other members of the group when someone is trying to make a suggestion or to say something.

Speaking skills

- Knowing what you are talking about.

- Expressing your ideas logically.

- Justifying your viewpoint (i.e. backing up what you say with evidence or proof).

- Speaking fluently and interestingly.

Interactional skills

- Speaking and responding politely to other members of the team (e.g. 'please' and 'thank you').

- Encouraging reluctant speakers to take part in the discussion (e.g. what do *you* think?).

- Clarifying ideas or suggestions. Putting forward arguments for other members of the team, where necessary.

- Repeating (for the benefit of other members of the group) any points that are particularly important and relevant to the discussion.

Apart from these skills, you must also:

- Understand and work towards the team's goals.

- Support other team members, when necessary.

- Know when you must call in expert advice, and where to get this advice from.

- Make sure that all members of the team are kept up to date with developments.

- Finally, and perhaps most importantly, fulfil your role in the team to the best of your ability and with least disruption to other team members.

Reviewing the activity

Once your activity is over, it is important that you look back and decide what went well, what went badly and *why*. If your activity went well, you might decide to use the same methods and techniques again. If something went wrong, you can learn from this and improve your performance next time. To sum up, you need to be able to identify:

- What went well.

- What did *not* go well.

- How well you carried out your *own* role.

- How well your team members worked together as a team.

- How you and your team could have worked *even better* together.

- How teamwork helped you to achieve your goal.

This is where you need your log book. Look back carefully at all the entries you have made. With hindsight, what could you have done better? Did you plan your time well? Was anything you did a waste of time? Could you have organised or run your team meetings better than you did?

In the planning stages you cannot be expected to foresee all the problems that might arise. No one can, no matter what their experience in teamwork or in organising activities like this. What you can do, however, when looking back at your log, is to judge whether you think you overcame the problems you encountered well, or whether you tended to shirk them off or try to ignore them.

Finally, you are going to have to present a report of your activity to your tutor. This report will include your evaluations of each stage of the activity. You must be honest about how well you think things went, and must, wherever possible, include the reasons why you think things went well or not so well.

To support your evaluation, you must include all relevant documentation (your log book, copies of minutes of meetings, copies of any letters sent, etc.). You might also like to include photographs of the activity itself or, as was the case with out six students, even a video tape of the event!

Good luck!

Index

A

accounts 22
acknowledgement of order 117
administration 7
administration department 23, 29
administration function 22
advertisements 47
advertising 35, 38, 210
advertising media 35, 38
after-sales service 39, 183
agenda 25, 29
animal welfare 213
annual report 47
application forms 218
articles of association 62, 72

B

bank statement 5, 169
banking services 77
banks 165, 174
beliefs 205
benefit payments 159
board of directors 3–4, 6, 62
bonus 196
brand 38
brokers 174
budget 110–111
building insurance 172
building societies 165, 174
built environment 205
bulk-decreasing industry 83, 85
bulk-increasing industry 83, 85
business activities 74–80
business ethics 206
business letter 47, 51–52
business location 82–85

C

capital goods 75
career adviser 219
career development 200
careers fairs 220
careers office 219
cash 111, 141, 197
cash flow 111
cash flow problems 21
cashbook 111
Certificate of Incorporation 62, 72
chairman/chairperson 3–4, 6
charge cards 141
charity activities 78, 81
cheque 112–113, 122–124, 145, 170, 198
cheque guarantee 123, 146
circulars 47
Citizen's Advice Bureaux 174
cleaning the work place 26
commission 197
common hazards 226
communication 46, 80, 84
community programs 220
company 61
competition 38, 72, 108
competitors 92
compulsory deductions 21
computer-on line 167
consumer 29, 38, 72, 81, 108, 177
consumer co-operatives 67
consumer goods 75
contract of employment 193
Co-operative Development Agency (CDA) 67
co-operatives 66
cost of premises 83
costs 82–83, 102, 108
credit cards 142, 171
credit notes 133, 183
credit transfers 198
credit unions 166
cultural environment 206–207
current accounts 168

D

debit cards 142, 145, 170
deductions 199
deed of partnership 72
delivery 183
delivery note 113, 117–118, 145
demand 34, 38
Department of Social Security 174
desk research 32, 38
direct mail 37
directors 3
dismissal 13, 18
dividends 102
drawee 122, 145
drawer 122, 145
drawings 111

E

economic efficiency 206
education and training 230
e-mails 47
employees 29, 62, 90
employees' organisation 7, 17
employers 11, 13, 15, 93
energy 211
environment 204
environmental consideration 205
environmental sustainability 213
evacuation procedure 231, 233
exhibitions 36
external communication 46
external recruitment 11, 18

curriculum vitae (CV) 216–217
customer 38, 92, 177
customer expectations 179
customer services 7, 39, 41–45, 87, 176, 182
CV 216-217

F

face-to-face communication 46
factors of production 29
field research 32, 38
filing information 26
finance department 19–21
finance function 19
financial advice 173
financial institutions 156, 165
financial records 19
financial services 77, 156, 161, 168, 200
financial protection 173
First Aid 230
fixed costs 104, 108
flat rate 196
flex-time system 17
flow of money 102
food 211
Food Act 185
formal interview 222
franchise 70, 72
franchisee 70, 72
franchiser 70
fringe benefits 199
full-time employment 194

G

goods 70, 72, 81
government 82, 90
government transport policy 214
green energy 211
gross pay 22

H

hand-written receipts 131
hazardous substances 227
health and safety 7, 13, 15, 84, 226
Health and Safety Act 15, 18, 26, 29, 231
health and safety policy 15
health care services 77
help lines 183
hire purchase 122, 145, 171
honest dealings 181
human resources 7, 29, 39

I

income protection 173
income tax 21–22
induction 15, 18, 200
Industrial Common ownership Movement (ICOM) 67
industrial trends 82
information and advice 182
Inland Revenue 159
instant electronic payments 143
insurance 77, 172
insurance brokers 166
insurance companies 166, 174
interest 162
internal communication 46
internal recruitment 11, 18
Internet 221
interview 222
invoice 109, 113, 118–122, 145

J

job advertisements 8
job centre 220
job description 9, 18
job enlargement 17
job enrichment 16
job rotation 16

K

keeping records 25

L

labour 29
land costs 83
language training courses 201
legal protection 184
leisure and sport 78
letter of application 217–218
letters 47, 51–52
limited companies 62, 73
limited liability 62, 73
life assurance scheme 170, 172, 200
life insurance 173
loan companies 167
loans 77, 161, 171
local community 93

location 82–85
logos 35, 38
long-term capital 77
long-term loans 172

M

management 91
managers 4–5, 187
managing director 3–4, 6
manufacturer 77
manufacturing process 208
market research 31, 38
marketing 7, 38
  department 41
  function 30, 39
meeting 46
memorandum 47
Memorandum of Association 62, 73
memos 53, 115
merit goods 178
methods of communication 46
methods of competition 86
mixed economy 58, 86, 73
mortgage 77, 161, 163, 172
motivation 18
motor insurance 172

N

National Insurance 21–22, 160
natural environment 205
natural resources 29
net pay 22
noisy equipment 227
non-renewable fuels 213

O

objectives 2, 73
off-the-job training 200
on-the-job training 200
operations 27
operatives 187, 188
oral communication 46
organisational chart 2, 5–6
organising meetings 24
overdraft 77, 110–111

over-the-counter service 167
overtime 196

P
packaging 210
partnership 58, 73
Partnership Act 58
part-time employment 194
pay 22
pay and benefits 195
pay slips 198
payee 122, 145
payment system 22
pension schemes 170, 200
pensions 159
perks and benefits 12, 18, 199
permanent employment 194
person specification 10, 18
personal appearance 36
personal budget 156, 161
personal finance 157
personal income 160
personnel 18
petty cash 136, 145
petty cash vouchers 113, 136–137, 145
piece rate 196
place 31, 89
polite service 180
post office 165, 167
premises 83
price 31, 38, 88
price list 114
pricing promotions 37
primary data 32, 38
primary sector 74–75, 81
printed receipts 131
private limited company 58, 62, 73
private sector ownership 58, 86
product 31
product development 86, 89
production 7, 29, 81
    cost 30
    function 27
    operatives 5
profit 30, 72, 102–103, 108

progress file 219
promotion 31, 33, 38
promotional materials 34
protecting employees 201
public corporation 70, 73
public limited company 58, 62, 73
public sector ownership 58, 70, 73, 86
public services 73
purchase order 113–114, 145
purchasing function 29

R
receipts 113, 131, 145
recruitment 7, 18
recycling 212, 214
redundancy 13, 18
regional advantages 84
Registrar of Companies 73
remittance advice 113, 130, 145
replacement insurance 173
resource efficiency 205
retailers 76, 81
retained profit 102
retention 7
retraining 200
revenue 102, 105, 109
risk 73, 108
risk assessment 231
running costs 104, 108

S
safe products 181
safety see health and safety
salary 21–22, 195
Sale of Goods Act 184
sales
    department 37
    function 30, 37, 182
    income 73, 108
    promotion 35, 38, 73
sampling 36
savings account 169
scale 71, 72–73
secondary data 32, 38
secondary sector 74–75, 81
security 26

service sector 27, 29
services 70
sex discrimination 18
shareholders 3, 6, 23, 29, 61–62, 90, 102
shift work 17
short-term loans 77, 171
skills upgrading 200
slogans 36
social environment 205, 207
sole trader 58, 73
sources of income 159
special offers 36
sponsorship 37
staff appraisal interviews 16–17
staff development and promotion 16
staff records 7, 17
staff welfare 12
stakeholders 23, 29, 90
standing orders 145, 171
start-up costs 104, 108
statement of account 113, 128, 145
stock control 29
Stock Exchange 52, 73
store charge cards 142, 145, 171
strike 18
supermarkets 167
supervisors 4–5, 187-188
suppliers 23
supply chain 207
support staff 5
survey 38

T
tax 22, 160
team members 4
telecommunication 80
telephone banking 167
telephone conversations 46
temporary employment 194
tertiary sector 74–77, 81
time rate 196
Trade Descriptions Act 184
trade unions 17–18, 232
trademark 38

training 7, 15, 18, 200
transport activities 78
transport cost 83
transport methods 209
travel insurance 173
turnover 108
types of employment 194

U
unemployment 18
unfair dismissal 18
unions 7
unlimited liability 59, 61, 73

unsafe use of machinery 228
unsafe working areas 227
unsafe working practice 227

V
value for money 181
values and desires 206
variable cost 104, 108
VAT (Value Added Tax) 20, 109, 119, 145
VDU screen 228
voluntary deductions 21

W
wages 21–22, 195
waste disposal 84
Weights and Measures Acts 184
wholesale activities 76
wholesaler 76, 81
worker co-operatives 66
working arrangements 193
working conditions 18
written communication 47
wrong temperature 227

Ready to move on?

This is exactly what you need for the GNVQ Intermediate Business award

. . . .

Choose from two student books

The *Student Book without Options* covers all of the compulsory units, making it ideal for a Part One GNVQ.

The *Student Book with Options* covers the compulsory units and four Edexcel option units: Individuals and the Organisation; Retailing; Consumer Protection; and Administrative Systems. It's ideal if you are taking the full award.

Learn about real businesses

'Snapshots' show you how real organisations apply the theory of business. Activities and case studies give you the opportunity to apply your knowledge to business situations.

Use the books easily

Chapters and sub-sections in the book match the headings in the GNVQ award specification, so it's easy to find your way around the text.

There's an easy way to find out all the latest information about GNVQs. Just visit *www.heinemann.co.uk/gnvq*

Heinemann GNVQ Intermediate Business without options - ideal for Part One GNVQs

ISBN: 0 435 45299 1

Heinemann GNVQ Intermediate Business with four Edexcel options

ISBN: 0 435 45602 4

Order from your local bookshop or call
(01865) 888068.

E683